英语专业系列教材

A COURSEBOOK ON C-E TRANSLATION
OF DIPLOMATIC TEXTS

外交文本汉英笔译教程

主编 刘晓晖 周小琴 霍跃红

清华大学出版社
北京

内 容 简 介

本教材共分为七章,分别探讨七类外交文本的翻译问题,包括外交讲话翻译、外交署名文章翻译、外交新闻翻译、外交公报翻译、外交宣言翻译、白皮书翻译以及外交条约翻译。

本教材根据文本特征讲授不同汉英翻译问题和处理方法,同时兼顾相关外交知识与背景,强化学生对中国特色表达的基本认识与深刻理解,牢固掌握外交领域相关概念,在此基础上,探索外交文本翻译的最佳方式,力求帮助学生提升翻译能力与外交素养。

版权所有,侵权必究。举报:010-62782989,beiqinquan@tup.tsinghua.edu.cn。

图书在版编目(CIP)数据

外交文本汉英笔译教程 / 刘晓晖,周小琴,霍跃红主编. —北京:清华大学出版社,2022.12

(英语专业系列教材)

ISBN 978-7-302-59793-3

Ⅰ. ①外… Ⅱ. ①刘… ②周… ③霍… Ⅲ. ①英语—翻译—高等学校—教材 Ⅳ. ①H315.9

中国版本图书馆CIP数据核字(2022)第001522号

责任编辑:钱屹芝
封面设计:子 一
责任校对:王凤芝
责任印制:刘海龙

出版发行:清华大学出版社
    网　　址:http://www.tup.com.cn,http://www.wqbook.com
    地　　址:北京清华大学学研大厦A座　邮　编:100084
    社 总 机:010-83470000　邮　购:010-62786544
    投稿与读者服务:010-62776969,c-service@tup.tsinghua.edu.cn
    质量反馈:010-62772015,zhiliang@tup.tsinghua.edu.cn
印 装 者:北京嘉实印刷有限公司
经　　销:全国新华书店
开　　本:170mm×230mm　印　张:17　字　数:301千字
版　　次:2022年12月第1版　印　次:2022年12月第1次印刷
定　　价:68.00元

产品编号:088251-01

前 言

　　翻译是国与国之间深化友谊、交流合作、互联互通的重要桥梁，是一个国家在外交活动及国际交往中表达思想理念、明确政策立场、建构国家形象等的重要媒介。近年来，中国外交在提升我国的国际地位，展现负责任的大国形象，推进对外开放，促进国际合作，维护国家主权、安全、发展利益，发挥在国际事务中的积极作用等方面的成就举世瞩目，翻译在此过程中发挥的作用举足轻重。随着中国综合国力的不断增强，中国的国际影响力日益扩大，培养一批熟知我国外交政策与理念、具备坚定的政治立场、熟悉各类外交文本语言表述、掌握各类外交文本翻译技巧的高水平外交翻译人才对中国外交事业的发展至关重要。

　　从以上外交人才培养目标出发，结合多年汉英翻译教学实践经验，基于丰富而典型的外交文本翻译案例，历经多轮论证与反复修改，本教材编写组倾力完成了《外交文本汉英笔译教程》的编写工作。本教材共分七章，围绕七类外交文本展开翻译探究与实践，包括外交讲话翻译、外交署名文章翻译、外交新闻翻译、外交公报翻译、外交宣言翻译、白皮书翻译以及外交条约翻译。所选文本皆源自官方媒体，讲究规范性、准确性、权威性和时效性。每章设计七个板块，包括各类外交文本的概念及其特点、汉英对照举隅、翻译原则与难点、英译技巧、中国关键词加油站、翻译练习，聚焦外交文本英译的核心和重点问题，彰显内容的丰富性，文本的代表性以及练习的多样性，做到翻译讲解融会贯通，知识背景与时俱进，关键表达实用为先。除此之外，本教材特别注重课堂教学与思政教育的有机结合，将思政元素系统融入教学内容，突出中西文化及思维比较，增强学生对中国特色话语的高度认识，深刻理解外交相关概念，从而掌握讲好中国故事、译好中国话语的有效路径，实现国家情怀与国际素养，翻译能力与外交素质的多重提升。本教材可广泛用于翻译方向、翻译专业、MTI 等本硕翻译教学之中。

《外交文本汉英笔译教程》的主编皆为翻译方向博士，是所在高校翻译教学或研究的骨干力量，从事翻译教学多年，科研项目、学术成果、翻译实践等积累丰富。团队成员通力合作，针对选题多次探讨，在质量上精益求精。与此同时，《外交文本汉英笔译教程》的顺利完稿也离不开诸多学生的大力协助，在此特别感谢硕士研究生郭兴莉、周宏玮、方宏哲、陈亚明、周秋伶、郭开来、李铤、黄洪、王歆翰、周莹，在编写过程中协助完成了部分材料的搜集与整理任务，同时也是本教材的首批读者，为教材质量的完善提供了宝贵反馈。由于编写时间有限，书中仍存不当之处，在此恳请专家学者及广大读者多多指正。

刘晓晖

2022 年 6 月于大连

目 录

第一章　外交讲话翻译　　1
一、外交讲话的概念及文体特点　　2
二、外交讲话汉英对照举隅　　3
三、外交讲话的翻译原则与难点　　23
四、外交讲话的英译技巧　　24
五、中国关键词加油站　　36
六、外交讲话翻译练习　　40

第二章　外交署名文章翻译　　43
一、外交署名文章的概念及文体特点　　44
二、外交署名文章汉英对照举隅　　45
三、外交署名文章的翻译原则与难点　　53
四、外交署名文章的英译技巧　　54
五、中国关键词加油站　　73
六、外交署名文章翻译练习　　76

第三章　外交新闻翻译　　79
一、外交新闻的概念及文体特点　　80
二、外交新闻汉英对照举隅　　81
三、外交新闻的翻译原则与难点　　91
四、外交新闻的英译技巧　　92
五、中国关键词加油站　　105

六、外交新闻翻译练习 110

第四章　外交公报翻译 **113**

一、外交公报的概念及文体特点 114
二、外交公报汉英对照举隅 115
三、外交公报的翻译原则与难点 127
四、外交公报英译技巧 128
五、中国关键词加油站 135
六、外交公报翻译练习 139

第五章　外交宣言翻译 **141**

一、外交宣言的概念及其文体特点 142
二、外交宣言汉英对照举隅 143
三、外交宣言的翻译原则与难点 156
四、外交宣言的英译技巧 157
五、中国关键词加油站 167
六、外交宣言翻译练习 172

第六章　白皮书翻译 **175**

一、白皮书的概念及其文体特点 176
二、白皮书汉英对照举隅 177
三、白皮书的翻译原则与难点 207
四、白皮书的英译技巧 208
五、中国关键词加油站 215
六、白皮书翻译练习 220

第七章　外交条约翻译 **223**

一、外交条约的概念及文体特点 224
二、外交条约汉英对照举隅 225
三、外交条约的翻译原则与难点 242
四、外交条约的英译技巧 243
五、中国关键词加油站 258
六、外交条约翻译练习 263

第一章 外交讲话翻译

一、外交讲话的概念及文体特点

外交讲话是指国家领导人或高级外交官在各类对外活动或重要场合为维护国家利益、传达对外政策、发展对外关系、表达外交立场及政治态度等发表的讲话。外交讲话是重要的外交文件，通常用口语呈现，以书面语传播，属于官方发布的正式文体。很多外交讲话具有重大政治、历史价值，已成为重要的国际性文件。

外交讲话是中国外交话语体系中的重要构成，是影响外交事件发展、改善双边或多边关系、引导对象国民众舆论的重要因素。中华民族伟大复兴离不开与世界各国的交流与合作，良好的外交话语体系的构建能为这一目标的实现创造有利条件。自党的十八大以来，以习近平同志为核心的党中央领导审时度势、运筹帷幄、创新思维、高屋建瓴地建构了中国外交话语体系，制定了一系列符合国家发展、具有中国特色的外交战略，为妥善处理中国与世界各国以及国际组织的关系奠定了坚实基础。在国际各类场合及重大事件中，领导人发表的讲话不但传达中国的立场、主张、原则、政策等，而且有利于树立国家形象、争取国际支持、加深彼此了解、扩大影响力度、传播中国文化。由此可见，外交讲话的作用和效果在很大程度上超出其他政治外宣形式，是外交活动成功与否的重要因素。

外交讲话使用正式的外交语言。外交语言是一种高级政治语言，具有典型的政论文体特征，体现领导人所代表国家的立场和身份、原则和主张等，具有政治性、政策性、严肃性和严谨性的特点。一般而言，外交讲话语体选词简洁凝练，生动准确，表达讲究分寸，新旧术语使用频繁，句式上长短句交错，以陈述句为主。与此同时，中国外交讲话中大量使用修辞手段，包括比喻、排比、反复、对偶等，起到增强感染力，提升影响效果的作用。除此之外，语言材料的使用也比较多样，时常可见俚语、谚语、歇后语和名言警句等。最后，尽管外交讲话具有普遍性特征，但也体现鲜明的个性风格，在表达上体现不同的特色。

二 外交讲话汉英对照举隅

共担时代责任　共促全球发展
——在世界经济论坛 2017 年年会开幕式上的主旨演讲
（2017 年 1 月 17 日，达沃斯）
中华人民共和国主席　习近平

Jointly Shoulder Responsibility of Our Times, Promote Global Growth
—Keynote Speech by Chinese President Xi Jinping at the Opening Session of the World Economic Forum Annual Meeting 2017
Davos, 17 January, 2017

尊敬的洛伊特哈德主席和豪森先生，

尊敬的各国元首、政府首脑、副元首和夫人，

尊敬的国际组织负责人，

尊敬的施瓦布主席和夫人，

女士们，先生们，朋友们：

很高兴来到美丽的达沃斯。达沃斯虽然只是阿尔卑斯山上的一个小镇，却是一个观察世界经济的重要窗口。大家从四面八方会聚这里，各种思想碰撞出智慧的火花，以较少的投入获得了很高的产出。我看这个现象可以称作"施瓦布经济学"。

"这是最好的时代，也是

President Doris Leuthard and Mr. Roland Hausin,

Heads of State and Government, Deputy Heads of State and Your Spouses,

Heads of International Organizations,

Dr. Klaus Schwab and Mrs. Hilde Schwab,

Ladies and Gentlemen,

Dear Friends,

I'm delighted to come to beautiful Davos. Though just a small town in the Alps, Davos is an important window for taking the pulse of the global economy. People from around the world come here to exchange ideas and insights, which broaden their vision. This makes the WEF annual meeting a cost-effective brainstorming event, which I would call "Schwab economics".

"It was the best of times, it was the worst of

最坏的时代",英国文学家狄更斯曾这样描述工业革命发生后的世界。今天,我们也生活在一个矛盾的世界之中。一方面,物质财富不断积累,科技进步日新月异,人类文明发展到历史最高水平。另一方面,地区冲突频繁发生,恐怖主义、难民潮等全球性挑战此起彼伏,贫困、失业、收入差距拉大,世界面临的不确定性上升。

对此,许多人感到困惑,世界到底怎么了?

要解决这个困惑,首先要找准问题的根源。有一种观点把世界乱象归咎于经济全球化。经济全球化曾经被人们视为阿里巴巴的山洞,现在又被不少人看作潘多拉的盒子。国际社会围绕经济全球化问题展开了广泛讨论。

今天,我想从经济全球化问题切入,谈谈我对世界经济的看法。

我想说的是,困扰世界的很多问题,并不是经济全球化造成的。比如,过去几年来,源自中东、北非的难民潮牵动全球,数以百万计的民众颠沛流离,甚至不少年幼的孩子在路途中葬身大海,让我们痛心

times." These are the words used by the English writer Charles Dickens to describe the world after the Industrial Revolution. Today, we also live in a world of contradictions. On the one hand, with growing material wealth and advances in science and technology, human civilization has developed as never before. On the other hand, frequent regional conflicts, global challenges like terrorism and refugees, as well as poverty, unemployment and widening income gap have all added to the uncertainties of the world.

Many people feel bewildered and wonder: What has gone wrong with the world?

To answer this question, one must first track the source of the problem. Some blame economic globalization for the chaos in the world. Economic globalization was once viewed as the treasure cave found by Ali Baba in *The Arabian Nights*, but it has now become the Pandora's box in the eyes of many. The international community finds itself in a heated debate on economic globalization.

Today, I wish to address the global economy in the context of economic globalization.

The point I want to make is that many of the problems troubling the world are not caused by economic globalization. For instance, the refugee waves from the Middle East and North Africa in recent years have become a global concern. Several million people have been displaced, and some small children lost their lives while crossing

疾首。导致这一问题的原因，是战乱、冲突、地区动荡。解决这一问题的出路，是谋求和平、推动和解、恢复稳定。再比如，国际金融危机也不是经济全球化发展的必然产物，而是金融资本过度逐利、金融监管严重缺失的结果。把困扰世界的问题简单归咎于经济全球化，既不符合事实，也无助于问题解决。

历史地看，经济全球化是社会生产力发展的客观要求和科技进步的必然结果，不是哪些人、哪些国家人为造出来的。经济全球化为世界经济增长提供了强劲动力，促进了商品和资本流动、科技和文明进步、各国人民交往。

当然，我们也要承认，经济全球化是一把"双刃剑"。当世界经济处于下行期的时候，全球经济"蛋糕"不容易做大，甚至变小了，增长和分配、资本和劳动、效率和公平的矛盾就会更加突出，发达国家和发展中国家都会感受到压力和冲击。反全球化的呼声，反映了经济全球化进程的不

the rough sea. This is indeed heartbreaking. It is war, conflict and regional turbulence that have created this problem, and its solution lies in making peace, promoting reconciliation and restoring stability. The international financial crisis is another example. It is not an inevitable outcome of economic globalization; rather, it is the consequence of excessive chase of profit by financial capital and grave failure of financial regulation. Just blaming economic globalization for the world's problems is inconsistent with reality, and it will not help solve the problems.

From the historical perspective, economic globalization resulted from growing social productivity, and is a natural outcome of scientific and technological progress, not something created by any individuals or any countries. Economic globalization has powered global growth and facilitated movement of goods and capital, advances in science, technology and civilization, and interactions among peoples.

But we should also recognize that economic globalization is a double-edged sword. When the global economy is under downward pressure, it is hard to make the cake of global economy bigger. It may even shrink, which will strain the relations between growth and distribution, between capital and labor, and between efficiency and equity. Both developed and developing countries have felt the punch. Voices against globalization have laid bare pitfalls in the process of economic globalization

足，值得我们重视和深思。

"甘瓜抱苦蒂，美枣生荆棘。"从哲学上说，世界上没有十全十美的事物，因为事物存在优点就把它看得完美无缺是不全面的，因为事物存在缺点就把它看得一无是处也是不全面的。经济全球化确实带来了新问题，但我们不能就此把经济全球化一棍子打死，而是要适应和引导好经济全球化，消解经济全球化的负面影响，让它更好惠及每个国家、每个民族。

当年，中国对经济全球化也有过疑虑，对加入世界贸易组织也有过忐忑。但是，我们认为，融入世界经济是历史大方向，中国经济要发展，就要敢于到世界市场的汪洋大海中去游泳，如果永远不敢到大海中去经风雨、见世面，总有一天会在大海中溺水而亡。所以，中国勇敢迈向了世界市场。在这个过程中，我们呛过水，遇到过漩涡，遇到过风浪，但我们在游泳中学会了游泳。这是正确的战略抉择。

世界经济的大海，你要还是不要，都在那儿，是回避不

that we need to take seriously.

As a line in an old Chinese poem goes, "Honey melons hang on bitter vines; sweet dates grow on thistles and thorns." In a philosophical sense, nothing is perfect in the world. One would fail to see the full picture if he claims something is perfect because of its merits, or if he views something as useless just because of its defects. It is true that economic globalization has created new problems, but this is no justification to write economic globalization off completely. Rather, we should adapt to and guide economic globalization, cushion its negative impact, and deliver its benefits to all countries and all nations.

There was a time when China also had doubts about economic globalization, and was not sure whether it should join the World Trade Organization. But we came to the conclusion that integration into the global economy is a historical trend. To grow its economy, China must have the courage to swim in the vast ocean of the global market. If one is always afraid of bracing the storm and exploring the new world, he will sooner or later get drowned in the ocean. Therefore, China took a brave step to embrace the global market. We have had our fair share of choking in the water and encountered whirlpools and choppy waves, but we have learned how to swim in this process. It has proved to be a right strategic choice.

Whether you like it or not, the global economy is the big ocean that you cannot escape

了的。想人为切断各国经济的资金流、技术流、产品流、产业流、人员流，让世界经济的大海退回到一个一个孤立的小湖泊、小河流，是不可能的，也是不符合历史潮流的。

人类历史告诉我们，有问题不可怕，可怕的是不敢直面问题，找不到解决问题的思路。面对经济全球化带来的机遇和挑战，正确的选择是，充分利用一切机遇，合作应对一切挑战，引导好经济全球化走向。

去年年底，我在亚太经合组织领导人非正式会议上提出，要让经济全球化进程更有活力、更加包容、更可持续。我们要主动作为、适度管理，让经济全球化的正面效应更多释放出来，实现经济全球化进程再平衡；我们要顺应大势、结合国情，正确选择融入经济全球化的路径和节奏；我们要讲求效率、注重公平，让不同国家、不同阶层、不同人群共享经济全球化的好处。这是我们这个时代的领导者应有的担当，更是各国人民对我们的期待。

from. Any attempt to cut off the flow of capital, technologies, products, industries and people between economies, and channel the waters in the ocean back into isolated lakes and creeks is simply not possible. Indeed, it runs counter to the historical trend.

The history of mankind tells us that problems are not to be feared. What should concern us is refusing to face up to problems and not knowing what to do about them. In the face of both opportunities and challenges of economic globalization, the right thing to do is to seize every opportunity, jointly meet challenges and chart the right course for economic globalization.

At the APEC Economic Leaders' Meeting in late 2016, I spoke about the necessity to make the process of economic globalization more invigorated, more inclusive and more sustainable. We should act proactively and manage economic globalization appropriately, so as to release its positive impact and rebalance the process of economic globalization. We should follow the general trend, proceed from our respective national conditions and embark on the right pathway of integrating into economic globalization with the right pace. We should strike a balance between efficiency and equity to ensure that different countries, different social strata and different groups of people all share in the benefits of economic globalization. The people of all countries expect nothing less from us, and this is

女士们、先生们、朋友们！

当前，最迫切的任务是引领世界经济走出困境。世界经济长期低迷，贫富差距、南北差距问题更加突出。究其根源，是经济领域三大突出矛盾没有得到有效解决。

一是全球增长动能不足，难以支撑世界经济持续稳定增长。世界经济增速处于7年来最低水平，全球贸易增速继续低于经济增速。短期性政策刺激效果不佳，深层次结构性改革尚在推进。世界经济正处在动能转换的换挡期，传统增长引擎对经济的拉动作用减弱，人工智能、3D打印等新技术虽然不断涌现，但新的经济增长点尚未形成。世界经济仍然未能开辟出一条新路。

二是全球经济治理滞后，难以适应世界经济新变化。前不久，拉加德女士告诉我，新兴市场国家和发展中国家对全球经济增长的贡献率已经达到

our unshirkable responsibility as leaders of our times.

Ladies and Gentlemen, Dear Friends,

At present, the most pressing task before us is to steer the global economy out of difficulty. The global economy has remained sluggish for quite some time. The gap between the poor and the rich and between the South and the North is widening. The root cause is that the three critical issues in the economic sphere have not been effectively addressed.

First, lack of robust driving forces for global growth makes it difficult to sustain the steady growth of the global economy. The growth of the global economy is now at its slowest pace in seven years. Growth of global trade has been slower than global GDP growth. Short-term policy stimuli are ineffective. Fundamental structural reform is just unfolding. The global economy is now in a period of moving toward new growth drivers, and the role of traditional engines to drive growth has weakened. Despite the emergence of new technologies such as artificial intelligence and 3D printing, new sources of growth are yet to emerge. A new path for the global economy remains elusive.

Second, inadequate global economic governance makes it difficult to adapt to new developments in the global economy. Madame Christine Lagarde recently told me that emerging markets and developing countries already

80%。过去数十年,国际经济力量对比深刻演变,而全球治理体系未能反映新格局,代表性和包容性很不够。全球产业布局在不断调整,新的产业链、价值链、供应链日益形成,而贸易和投资规则未能跟上新形势,机制封闭化、规则碎片化十分突出。全球金融市场需要增强抗风险能力,而全球金融治理机制未能适应新需求,难以有效化解国际金融市场频繁动荡、资产泡沫积聚等问题。

三是全球发展失衡,难以满足人们对美好生活的期待。施瓦布先生在《第四次工业革命》一书中写道,第四次工业革命将产生极其广泛而深远的影响,包括会加剧不平等,特别是有可能扩大资本回报和劳动力回报的差距。全球最富有的1%人口拥有的财富量超过其余99%人口财富的总和,收入分配不平等、发展空间不平衡令人担忧。全球仍然有7亿

contribute to 80% of the growth of the global economy. The global economic landscape has changed profoundly in the past few decades. However, the global governance system has not embraced those new changes and is therefore inadequate in terms of representation and inclusiveness. The global industrial landscape is changing and new industrial chains, value chains and supply chains are taking shape. However, trade and investment rules have not kept pace with these developments, resulting in acute problems such as closed mechanisms and fragmentation of rules. The global financial market needs to be more resilient against risks, but the global financial governance mechanism fails to meet the new requirement and is thus unable to effectively resolve problems such as frequent international financial market volatility and the build-up of asset bubbles.

Third, uneven global development makes it difficult to meet people's expectations for better lives. Dr. Schwab has observed in his book *The Fourth Industrial Revolution* that this round of industrial revolution will produce extensive and far-reaching impacts such as growing inequality, particularly the possible widening gap between return on capital and return on labor. The richest one percent of the world's population own more wealth than the remaining 99 percent. Inequality in income distribution and uneven development space are worrying. Over 700 million people in

多人口生活在极端贫困之中。对很多家庭而言，拥有温暖住房、充足食物、稳定工作还是一种奢望。这是当今世界面临的最大挑战，也是一些国家社会动荡的重要原因。

这些问题反映出，当今世界经济增长、治理、发展模式存在必须解决的问题。国际红十字会创始人杜楠说过："真正的敌人不是我们的邻国，而是饥饿、贫穷、无知、迷信和偏见。"我们既要有分析问题的智慧，更要有采取行动的勇气。

第一，坚持创新驱动，打造富有活力的增长模式。世界经济面临的根本问题是增长动力不足。创新是引领发展的第一动力。与以往历次工业革命相比，第四次工业革命是以指数级而非线性速度展开。我们必须在创新中寻找出路。只有敢于创新、勇于变革，才能突破世界经济增长和发展的瓶颈。

二十国集团领导人在杭州峰会上达成重要共识，要以创新为重要抓手，挖掘各国和世界经济增长新动力。我们要创

the world are still living in extreme poverty. For many families, to have warm houses, enough food and secure jobs is still a distant dream. This is the biggest challenge facing the world today. It is also what is behind the social turmoil in some countries.

All this shows that there are indeed problems with world economic growth, governance and development models, and they must be resolved. The founder of the Red Cross Henry Dunant once said, "Our real enemy is not the neighboring country; it is hunger, poverty, ignorance, superstition and prejudice." We need to have the vision to dissect these problems; more importantly, we need to have the courage to take actions to address them.

First, we should develop a dynamic, innovation-driven growth model. The fundamental issue plaguing the global economy is the lack of driving force for growth. Innovation is the primary force guiding development. Unlike the previous industrial revolutions, the fourth industrial revolution is unfolding at an exponential rather than linear pace. We need to relentlessly pursue innovation. Only with the courage to innovate and reform can we remove bottlenecks blocking global growth and development.

With this in mind, G20 leaders reached an important consensus at the Hangzhou Summit, which is to take innovation as a key driver and foster new driving force of growth for both

新发展理念,超越财政刺激多一点还是货币宽松多一点的争论,树立标本兼治、综合施策的思路。我们要创新政策手段,推进结构性改革,为增长创造空间、增加后劲。我们要创新增长方式,把握好新一轮产业革命、数字经济等带来的机遇,既应对好气候变化、人口老龄化等带来的挑战,也化解掉信息化、自动化等给就业带来的冲击,在培育新产业新业态新模式过程中注意创造新的就业机会,让各国人民重拾信心和希望。

第二,坚持协同联动,打造开放共赢的合作模式。人类已经成为你中有我、我中有你的命运共同体,利益高度融合,彼此相互依存。每个国家都有发展权利,同时都应该在更加广阔的层面考虑自身利益,不能以损害其他国家利益为代价。

我们要坚定不移发展开放型世界经济,在开放中分享机

individual countries and the global economy. We should develop a new development philosophy and rise above the debate about whether there should be more fiscal stimulus or more monetary easing. We should adopt a multipronged approach to address both the symptoms and the underlying problems. We should adopt new policy instruments and advance structural reform to create more space for growth and sustain its momentum. We should develop new growth models and seize opportunities presented by the new round of industrial revolution and digital economy. We should meet the challenges of climate change and aging population. We should address the negative impact of IT application and automation on jobs. When cultivating new industries and new forms models of business models, we should create new jobs and restore confidence and hope to our peoples.

Second, we should pursue a well-coordinated and inter-connected approach to develop a model of open and win-win cooperation. Today, mankind has become a close-knit community of shared future. Countries have extensive converging interests and are mutually dependent. All countries enjoy the right to development. At the same time, they should view their own interests in a broader context and refrain from pursuing them at the expense of others.

We should commit ourselves to growing an open global economy to share opportunities

会和利益、实现互利共赢。不能一遇到风浪就退回到港湾中去，那是永远不能到达彼岸的。我们要下大气力发展全球互联互通，让世界各国实现联动增长，走向共同繁荣。我们要坚定不移发展全球自由贸易和投资，在开放中推动贸易和投资自由化便利化，旗帜鲜明反对保护主义。搞保护主义如同把自己关进黑屋子，看似躲过了风吹雨打，但也隔绝了阳光和空气。打贸易战的结果只能是两败俱伤。

第三，坚持与时俱进，打造公正合理的治理模式。小智治事，大智治制。全球经济治理体系变革紧迫性越来越突出，国际社会呼声越来越高。全球治理体系只有适应国际经济格局新要求，才能为全球经济提供有力保障。

国家不分大小、强弱、贫富，都是国际社会平等成员，理应平等参与决策、享受权利、履行义务。要赋予新兴市

and interests through opening-up and achieve win-win outcomes. One should not just retreat to the harbor when encountering a storm, for this will never get us to the other shore of the ocean. We must redouble efforts to develop global connectivity to enable all countries to achieve inter-connected growth and share prosperity. We must remain committed to developing global free trade and investment, promote trade and investment liberalization and facilitation through opening-up and say no to protectionism. Pursuing protectionism is like locking oneself in a dark room. While wind and rain may be kept outside, that dark room will also block light and air. No one will emerge as a winner in a trade war.

Third, we should develop a model of fair and equitable governance in keeping with the trend of the times. As the Chinese saying goes, people with petty shrewdness attend to trivial matters, while people with vision attend to governance of institutions. There is a growing call from the international community for reforming the global economic governance system, which is a pressing task for us. Only when it adapts to new dynamics in the international economic architecture can the global governance system sustain global growth.

Countries, big or small, strong or weak, rich or poor, are all equal members of the international community. As such, they are entitled to participate in decision-making, enjoy rights and

场国家和发展中国家更多代表性和发言权。2010年国际货币基金组织份额改革方案已经生效,这一势头应该保持下去。要坚持多边主义,维护多边体制权威性和有效性。要践行承诺、遵守规则,不能按照自己的意愿取舍或选择。《巴黎协定》符合全球发展大方向,成果来之不易,应该共同坚守,不能轻言放弃。这是我们对子孙后代必须担负的责任!

第四,坚持公平包容,打造平衡普惠的发展模式。"大道之行也,天下为公。"发展的目的是造福人民。要让发展更加平衡,让发展机会更加均等、发展成果人人共享,就要完善发展理念和模式,提升发展公平性、有效性、协同性。

我们要倡导勤劳俭朴、努力奋进的社会风气,让所有人的劳动成果得到尊重。要着力解决贫困、失业、收入差距拉大等问题,照顾好弱势人群的关切,促进社会公平正义。要

fulfill obligations on an equal basis. Emerging markets and developing countries deserve greater representation and voice. The 2010 IMF quota reform has entered into force, and its momentum should be sustained. We should adhere to multilateralism to uphold the authority and efficacy of multilateral institutions. We should honor promises and abide by rules. One should not select or bend rules as he sees fit. The Paris Agreement is a hard-won achievement which is in keeping with the underlying trend of global development. All signatories should stick to it instead of walking away from it as this is a responsibility we must assume for future generations.

Fourth, we should develop a balanced, equitable and inclusive development model. As the Chinese saying goes, "A just cause should be pursued for common good." Development is ultimately for the people. To achieve more balanced development and ensure that the people have equal access to opportunities and share in the benefits of development, it is crucial to have a sound development philosophy and model and make development equitable, effective and balanced.

We should foster a culture that values diligence, frugality and enterprise and respects the fruits of hard work of all. Priority should be given to addressing poverty, unemployment, the widening income gap and the concerns of the disadvantaged to promote social equity and

保护好生态环境，推动经济、社会、环境协调发展，实现人与自然、人与社会和谐。要落实联合国2030年可持续发展议程，实现全球范围平衡发展。

"积力之所举，则无不胜也；众智之所为，则无不成也。"只要我们牢固树立人类命运共同体意识，携手努力、共同担当、同舟共济、共渡难关，就一定能够让世界更美好、让人民更幸福。

女士们、先生们、朋友们！

经过38年改革开放，中国已经成为世界第二大经济体。道路决定命运。中国的发展，关键在于中国人民在中国共产党领导下，走出了一条适合中国国情的发展道路。

这是一条从本国国情出发确立的道路。中国立足自身国情和实践，从中华文明中汲取智慧，博采东西方各家之长，坚守但不僵化，借鉴但不照搬，在不断探索中形成了自己的发展道路。条条大路通罗马。谁都不应该把自己的发展道路定为一尊，更不应该把自

justice. It is important to protect the environment while pursuing economic and social progress so as to achieve harmony between man and nature and between man and society. The 2030 Agenda for Sustainable Development should be implemented to realize balanced development across the world.

A Chinese adage reads, "Victory is ensured when people pool their strength; success is secured when people put their heads together." As long as we keep to the goal of building a community of shared future for mankind and work hand in hand to fulfill our responsibilities and overcome difficulties, we will be able to create a better world and deliver better lives for our peoples.

Ladies and Gentlemen, Dear Friends,

China has become the world's second largest economy thanks to 38 years of reform and opening-up. A right path leads to a bright future. China has come this far because the Chinese people have, under the leadership of the Communist Party of China, blazed a development path that suits China's actual conditions.

This is a path based on China's realities. China has in the past years succeeded in embarking on a development path that suits itself by drawing on both the wisdom of its civilization and the practices of other countries in both East and West. In exploring this path, China refuses to stay insensitive to the changing times or to blindly follow in others' footsteps. All roads lead to Rome. No country should view its own

己的发展道路强加于人。

这是一条把人民利益放在首位的道路。中国秉持以人民为中心的发展思想，把改善人民生活、增进人民福祉作为出发点和落脚点，在人民中寻找发展动力、依靠人民推动发展、使发展造福人民。中国坚持共同富裕的目标，大力推进减贫事业，让7亿多人口摆脱贫困，正在向着全面建成小康社会目标快步前进。

这是一条改革创新的道路。中国坚持通过改革破解前进中遇到的困难和挑战，敢于啃硬骨头、涉险滩，勇于破除妨碍发展的体制机制障碍，不断解放和发展社会生产力，不断解放和增强社会活力。近4年来，我们在之前30多年不断改革的基础上，又推出了1200多项改革举措，为中国发展注入了强大动力。

这是一条在开放中谋求共同发展的道路。中国坚持对外开放基本国策，奉行互利共赢的开放战略，不断提升发展的内外联动性，在实现自身发展

development path as the only viable one, still less should it impose its own development path on others.

This is a path that puts people's interests first. China follows a people-oriented development philosophy and is committed to bettering the lives of its people. Development is of the people, by the people and for the people. China pursues the goal of common prosperity. We have taken major steps to alleviate poverty and lifted over 700 million people out of poverty, and good progress is being made in our efforts to finish building a society of initial prosperity in all respects.

This is a path of pursuing reform and innovation. China has tackled difficulties and met challenges on its way forward through reform. China has demonstrated its courage to take on difficult issues, navigate treacherous rapids and remove institutional hurdles standing in the way of development. These efforts have enabled us to unleash productivity and social vitality. Building on progress of 30-odd years of reform, we have introduced more than 1,200 reform measures over the past four years, injecting powerful impetus into China's development.

This is a path of pursuing common development through opening-up. China is committed to a fundamental policy of opening-up and pursues a win-win opening-up strategy. China's development is both domestic and external oriented; while

的同时更多惠及其他国家和人民。

中国发展取得了巨大成就，中国人民生活得到了极大改善，这对中国好，对世界也好。中国的发展成就，是中国人民几十年含辛茹苦、流血流汗干出来的。千百年来，中华民族素以吃苦耐劳闻名于世。中国人民深知，世界上没有免费的午餐，中国是一个有着13亿多人口的大国，想发展就要靠自己苦干实干，不能寄托于别人的恩赐，世界上也没有谁有这样的能力。观察中国发展，要看中国人民得到了什么收获，更要看中国人民付出了什么辛劳；要看中国取得了什么成就，更要看中国为世界作出了什么贡献。这才是全面的看法。

1950年至2016年，中国在自身长期发展水平和人民生活水平不高的情况下，累计对外提供援款4000多亿元人民币，实施各类援外项目5000多个，其中成套项目近3000个，举办11000多期培训班，

developing itself, China also shares more of its development outcomes with other countries and peoples.

China's outstanding development achievements and the vastly improved living standards of the Chinese people are a blessing to both China and the world. Such achievements in development over the past decades owe themselves to the hard work and perseverance of the Chinese people, a quality that has defined the Chinese nation for several thousand years. We Chinese know only too well that there is no such thing as a free lunch in the world. For a big country with over 1.3 billion people, development can be achieved only with the dedication and tireless efforts of its own people. We cannot expect others to deliver development to China, and no one is in a position to do so. When assessing China's development, one should not only see what benefits the Chinese people have gained, but also how much hard effort they have put in, not just what achievements China has made, but also what contribution China has made to the world. Then one will reach a balanced conclusion about China's development.

Between 1950 and 2016, despite its modest level of development and living standard, China provided more than 400 billion yuan of foreign assistance, undertook over 5,000 foreign assistance projects, including nearly 3,000 complete projects, and held over 11,000 training workshops in China for over 260,000 personnel from other

为发展中国家在华培训各类人员26万多名。改革开放以来,中国累计吸引外资超过1.7万亿美元,累计对外直接投资超过1.2万亿美元,为世界经济发展作出了巨大贡献。国际金融危机爆发以来,中国经济增长对世界经济增长的贡献率年均在30%以上。这些数字,在世界上都是名列前茅的。

从这些数字可以看出,中国的发展是世界的机遇,中国是经济全球化的受益者,更是贡献者。中国经济快速增长,为全球经济稳定和增长提供了持续强大的推动。中国同一大批国家的联动发展,使全球经济发展更加平衡。中国减贫事业的巨大成就,使全球经济增长更加包容。中国改革开放持续推进,为开放型世界经济发展提供了重要动力。

中国人民深知实现国家繁荣富强的艰辛,对各国人民取得的发展成就都点赞,都为他们祝福,都希望他们的日子越过越好,不会犯"红眼病",不会抱怨他人从中国发展中得到了巨大机遇和丰厚回报。中

developing countries. Since it launched reform and opening-up, China has attracted over 1.7 trillion US dollars of foreign investment and made over 1.2 trillion US dollars of direct outbound investment, making huge contribution to global economic development.In the years following the outbreak of the international financial crisis, China contributed to over 30% of global growth every year on average. All these figures are among the highest in the world.

The figures speak for themselves. China's development is an opportunity for the world; China has not only benefited from economic globalization but also contributed to it. Rapid growth in China has been a sustained, powerful engine for global economic stability and expansion. The inter-connected development of China and a large number of other countries has made the world economy more balanced. China's remarkable achievement in poverty reduction has contributed to more inclusive global growth. And China's continuous progress in reform and opening-up has lent much momentum to an open world economy.

We Chinese know only too well what it takes to achieve prosperity, so we applaud the achievements made by others and wish them a better future. We are not jealous of others' success; and we will not complain about others who have benefited so much from the great opportunities presented by China's development.

国人民张开双臂欢迎各国人民搭乘中国发展的"快车""便车"。

女士们、先生们、朋友们！

很多人都在关注中国经济发展趋势。中国经济发展进入了新常态，经济增速、经济发展方式、经济结构、经济发展动力都正在发生重大变化。但中国经济长期向好的基本面没有改变。

2016年，在世界经济疲弱的背景下，中国经济预计增长6.7%，依然处于世界前列。现在，中国经济的体量已不能同过去同日而语，集聚的动能是过去两位数的增长都达不到的。中国居民消费和服务业成为经济增长的主要动力，2016年前三季度第三产业增加值占国内生产总值的比重为52.8%，国内消费对经济增长的贡献率达71%。居民收入和就业实现稳定增长，单位国内生产总值能耗持续下降，绿色发展初见成效。

当前，中国经济面临一定的下行压力和不少困难，如产能过剩和需求结构升级矛盾突

We will open our arms to the people of other countries and welcome them aboard the express train of China's development.

Ladies and Gentlemen, Dear Friends,

I know you are all closely following China's economic development, and let me give you an update on the state of China's economy. China's economy has entered what we call a new normal, in which major changes are taking place in terms of growth rate, development model, economic structure and drivers of growth. But the economic fundamentals sustaining sound development remain unchanged.

Despite a sluggish global economy, China's economy is expected to grow by 6.7% in 2016, still one of the highest in the world. China's economy is far bigger in size than in the past, and it now generates more output than it did with double-digit growth in the past. Household consumption and the services sector have become the main drivers of growth. In the first three quarters of 2016, added value of the tertiary industry took up 52.8% of the GDP and domestic consumption contributed to 71% of economic growth. Household income and employment have steadily risen, while per unit GDP energy consumption continues to drop. Our efforts to pursue green development are paying off.

The Chinese economy faces downward pressure and many difficulties, including acute mismatch between excess capacity and an

出，经济增长内生动力不足，金融风险有所积聚，部分地区困难增多。我们认为，这些都是前进中必然出现的阶段性现象，对这些问题和矛盾，我们正在着力加以解决，并不断取得积极成效。我们坚定向前发展的决心不会动摇。中国仍然是世界上最大的发展中国家，中国有13亿多人口，人民生活水平还不高，但这也意味着巨大的发展潜力和空间。我们将在创新、协调、绿色、开放、共享的发展理念指引下，不断适应、把握、引领中国经济发展新常态，统筹抓好稳增长、促改革、调结构、惠民生、防风险工作，推动中国经济保持中高速增长、迈向中高端水平。

——中国将着力提升经济增长质量和效益，围绕供给侧结构性改革这条主线，转变经济发展方式，优化经济结构，积极推进去产能、去库存、去杠杆、降成本、补短板，培育增长新动能，发展先进制造业，实现实体经济升级，深入实施"互联网+"行动计划，扩大有效需求，更好满足人们

upgrading demand structure, lack of internal driving force for growth, accumulation of financial risks, and growing challenges in certain regions. We see these as temporary hardships that occur on the way forward. And the measures we have taken to address these problems are producing good results. We are firm in our resolve to forge ahead. China is the world's largest developing country with over 1.3 billion people, and their living standards are not yet high. But this reality also means China has enormous potential and space for development. Guided by the vision of innovative, coordinated, green, open and shared development, we will adapt to the new normal, stay ahead of the curve, and make coordinated efforts to maintain steady growth, accelerate reform, adjust economic structure, improve people's living standards and fend off risks. With these efforts, we aim to achieve medium-high rate of growth and upgrade the economy to higher end of the value chain.

— China will strive to enhance the performance of economic growth. We will pursue supply-side structural reform as the general goal, shift the growth model and upgrade the economic structure. We will continue to cut overcapacity, reduce inventory, deleverage financing, reduce cost and strengthen weak links. We will foster new drivers of growth, develop an advanced manufacturing sector and upgrade the real economy. We will implement the Internet Plus

个性化、多样化的需求，更好保护生态环境。

——中国将不断激发增长动力和市场活力，加大重要领域和关键环节改革力度，让市场在资源配置中起决定性作用，牵住创新这个"牛鼻子"，推进创新驱动发展战略，推动战略性新兴产业发展，注重用新技术新业态改造提升传统产业，促进新动能发展壮大、传统动能焕发生机。

——中国将积极营造宽松有序的投资环境，放宽外商投资准入，建设高标准自由贸易试验区，加强产权保护，促进公平竞争，让中国市场更加透明、更加规范。预计未来5年，中国将进口8万亿美元的商品、吸收6000亿美元的外来投资，对外投资总额将达到7500亿美元，出境旅游将达到7亿人次。这将为世界各国提供更广阔市场、更充足资本、更丰富产品、更宝贵合作契机。对各国工商界而言，中国发展仍然是大家的机遇。中国的大门

action plan to boost effective demand and better meet the individualized and diverse needs of consumers. And we will do more to protect the ecosystem.

— China will boost market vitality to add new impetus to growth. We will intensify reform efforts in priority areas and key links, and enable the market to play a decisive role in resources allocation. Innovation will continue to feature prominently on our growth agenda. In pursuing the strategy of innovation-driven development, we will bolster the strategic emerging industries, apply new technologies and foster new business models to upgrade traditional industries; and we will boost new drivers of growth and revitalize traditional ones.

— China will foster an enabling and orderly environment for investment. We will expand market access for foreign investors, build high-standard pilot free trade zones, strengthen protection of property rights, and level the playing field to make China's market more transparent and better regulated. In the coming five years, China is expected to import eight trillion US dollars of goods, attract 600 billion US dollars of foreign investment and make 750 billion US dollars of outbound investment. Chinese tourists will make 700 million overseas visits. All this will create a bigger market, more capital, more products and more business opportunities for other countries. China's development will continue to offer opportunities to business communities in

对世界始终是打开的，不会关上。开着门，世界能够进入中国，中国也才能走向世界。我们希望，各国的大门也对中国投资者公平敞开。

——中国将大力建设共同发展的对外开放格局，推进亚太自由贸易区建设和区域全面经济伙伴关系协定谈判，构建面向全球的自由贸易区网络。中国一贯主张建设开放透明、互利共赢的区域自由贸易安排，而不是搞排他性、碎片化的小圈子。中国无意通过人民币贬值提升贸易竞争力，更不会主动打货币战。

3年多前，我提出了"一带一路"倡议。3年多来，已经有100多个国家和国际组织积极响应支持，40多个国家和国际组织同中国签署合作协议，"一带一路"的"朋友圈"正在不断扩大。中国企业对沿线国家投资达到500多亿美元，一系列重大项目落地开花，带动了各国经济发展，创造了大量就业机会。可以说，"一带

other countries. China will keep its door wide open and not close it. An open door allows both other countries to access the Chinese market and China itself to integrate with the world. And we hope that other countries will also keep their door open to Chinese investors and keep the playing field level for us.

— China will vigorously foster an external environment of opening-up for common development. We will advance the building of the Free Trade Area of the Asia Pacific and negotiations of the Regional Comprehensive Economic Partnership to form a global network of free trade arrangements. China stands for concluding open, transparent and win-win regional free trade arrangements and opposes forming exclusive groups that are fragmented in nature. China has no intention to boost its trade competitiveness by devaluing the RMB, still less will it launch a currency war.

Over three years ago, I put forward the Belt and Road Initiative. Since then, over 100 countries and international organizations have given warm responses and support to the initiative. More than 40 countries and international organizations have signed cooperation agreements with China, and our circle of friends along the Belt and Road is growing bigger. Chinese companies have made over 50 billion US dollars of investment and launched a number of major projects in the countries along the routes, spurring the economic

一路"倡议来自中国，但成效惠及世界。

今年5月，中国将在北京主办"一带一路"国际合作高峰论坛，共商合作大计，共建合作平台，共享合作成果，为解决当前世界和区域经济面临的问题寻找方案，为实现联动式发展注入新能量，让"一带一路"建设更好造福各国人民。

女士们、先生们、朋友们！

世界历史发展告诉我们，人类文明进步历程从来没有平坦的大道可走，人类就是在同困难的斗争中前进的。再大的困难，都不可能阻挡人类前行的步伐。遇到了困难，不要埋怨自己，不要指责他人，不要放弃信心，不要逃避责任，而是要一起来战胜困难。历史是勇敢者创造的。让我们拿出信心、采取行动，携手向着未来前进！

谢谢大家。

development of these countries and creating many local jobs. The Belt and Road Initiative originated in China, but it has delivered benefits well beyond its borders.

In May this year, China will host in Beijing the Belt and Road Forum for International Cooperation, which aims to discuss ways to boost cooperation, build cooperation platforms and share cooperation outcomes. The forum will also explore ways to address problems facing global and regional economy, create fresh energy for pursuing inter-connected development and make the Belt and Road Initiative deliver greater benefits to people of countries involved.

Ladies and Gentlemen, Dear Friends,

World history shows that the road of human civilization has never been a smooth one, and that mankind has made progress by surmounting difficulties. No difficulty, however daunting, will stop mankind from advancing. When encountering difficulties, we should not complain about ourselves, blame others, lose confidence or run away from responsibilities. We should join hands and rise to the challenge. History is created by the brave. Let us boost confidence, take actions and march arm-in-arm toward a bright future.

Thank you!

三　外交讲话的翻译原则与难点

在翻译外交讲话过程中，译员必须有高度的政治觉悟和使命担当，熟练掌握国家政策，对讲话内容做到字字了然于胸，深刻领会内涵，不容一丝马虎。此外，在注重政治性、严谨性的同时，译员也要注重传播效果，考虑目标受众的期待。在保证信息准确的情况下，把握翻译的灵活变通，尤其在处理文化空缺现象时，更应具备高超的语言驾驭能力。因此，外交讲话的翻译必须认真遵守原则，采取相应的有效策略，确保译文的忠实度、流畅性和可读性。

第一，外交讲话翻译要遵循精确无误的原则。翻译的基本要求是忠于原文，外交讲话翻译更是如此。外交语言是捍卫国家利益的有力工具，要想做到高度忠实，需要译者吃透原文，字斟句酌，掌握分寸，慎重措辞，在不违背目标语表达习惯和影响受众理解的情况下，可采取直译的方法，以保留原文的形式和内容。

第二，外交讲话翻译要遵循通俗易懂的原则。外交讲话大都在正式场合发表，但在翻译时，尽量使用通俗易懂的语言进行翻译，在确保译文忠实性的同时，提升译文的流畅度，以利于受众接受。因此，对于汉语原文中的长句，尤其是逻辑复杂的句子，译者要厘清逻辑关系，采用变序、重组、拆分等方法，化繁为简，提高可理解度。除逻辑清晰外，措辞的言简意赅也很重要。词句的选择不宜过大过繁，尽量使用清晰明了、易于理解的词语，避免过于华丽、夸张、生僻的语言，这样才能创造良好的受众接受条件。

第三，外交讲话翻译要遵循灵活变通的原则。在处理中国特色表达时，译者需要发挥主体性，通过灵活变通的方式准确传达原文信息。如上所述，外交讲话涵盖很多政治新词和词组。这些用语是中国政治、经济和社会发展的产物，是中国发展进程的见证。同样，外交讲话含有大量的谚语俗语、名人名言、修辞手段等，这些表达都是中国文化的典型代表。在翻译上述特色表达时，要根据目标语国家的国情、文化或语言习惯选择最佳翻译策略。对于容易让受众产生误解或理解障碍的表达，在不能采取异化策略传达中国文化特色的情况下，可以运用增译、重构、替换等技巧达到神似效果，或者弃形留意，通过意译方法达到意义上的准确再现。

最后，外交讲话翻译要遵循标准化、统一化的原则。在外交讲话翻译过程中，对于像"人类命运共同体""一带一路""中国梦"等已经被国际公认的政治术语或是专有名词，需要遵循标准化、统一化的原则，确保与中国官方公布的译文一致，以免造成概念混淆，引发错误理解。

四 外交讲话的英译技巧

1 外交讲话中格言谚语的翻译处理

格言谚语是中国几千年文化智慧的结晶,领导人外交讲话中经常援引或利用其中蕴含的丰富哲理,传播中国思想和全球治理理念,传播中国的处世之道和价值信念,建构相互理解的桥梁,拉近与其他国家的距离,从而实现传达中国声音和提升软实力的目的。在翻译这些格言谚语时,必须首先弄清其中的深意及领导人讲话的上下文语境,选择恰当的翻译策略和方法来达到交流目的。如能按照目的语习惯直接移植源语文化精髓最好,这样的异化策略既能满足传播中国文化思想的目的,又能满足目标受众期待,达到良好的传播效果。当然,由于汉英语言的巨大差异,为便于目标受众的理解和接受,在很多情况下需要译者灵活处理,采用意译或者增删等方法或技巧传播格言谚语承载的思想内涵。

原文 "甘瓜抱苦蒂,美枣生荆棘。"从哲学上说,世界上没有十全十美的事物,因为事物存在优点就把它看成完美无缺是不全面的,因为事物存在缺点就把它看成一无是处也是不全面的。

译文 As a line in an old Chinese poem goes, "Honey melons hang on bitter vines; sweet dates grow on thistles and thorns." In a philosophical sense, nothing is perfect in the world. One would fail to see the full picture if he claims something is perfect because of its merits, or if he views something as useless just because of its defects.

"甘瓜抱苦蒂,美枣生荆棘"出自汉代一首五言诗,收录于《古诗源》卷四之中,意思是:甘甜的瓜都长于苦蒂;美味的枣都生于荆棘。也有学者认为"甘瓜抱苦蒂,美枣生荆棘"最早应出自《墨子》。唐李商隐《上李太尉状》云:"甘瓜苦蒂,必兴叹于墨子。"这句诗看似平常质朴,但内蕴丰富,流传久远,千载之后,仍让人受益匪浅。"甘瓜苦蒂"现已成为一则俗语,用瓜甜蒂苦的道理,说明世上任何事物都不会完美无缺。在瑞士达沃斯,谈到如何看待经济全球化时,习近平主席引用这句诗,并从哲学的维度加以解释,强调看事物要全面,不能出现缺点就否定优点,也不能看到优点就忽略缺点。因此,尽管经济全球化带来新问题,但不能一下子完全否定其积极影响。

第一章 外交讲话翻译

在翻译"甘瓜抱苦蒂，美枣生荆棘"时，译者采用了两种处理方式，一是通过增译"As a line in an old Chinese poem goes"，点明这句引文出自中国古诗，让目标受众明晰大体出处；二是对诗句进行直译，译为"Honey melons hang on bitter vines; sweet dates grow on thistles and thorns"，即解释上文提及的诗文意蕴，阐明诗句的表层意思：甘甜的瓜都长于苦蒂；美味的枣都生于荆棘。译者未再深入解释诗句的深层内涵，因为习近平主席在接下来的讲话中已从哲学角度点明深意所在。译者进而同样采用直译法，将诗句的引申意义准确译出，创造翻译等值效果。

原文 <u>小智治事，大智治制</u>。全球经济治理体系变革紧迫性越来越突出，国际社会呼声越来越高。全球治理体系只有适应国际经济格局新要求，才能为全球经济提供有力保障。

译文 <u>As the Chinese saying goes, people with petty shrewdness attend to trivial matters, while people with vision attend to governance of institutions.</u> There is a growing call from the international community for reforming the global economic governance system, which is a pressing task for us. Only when it adapts to new dynamics in the international economic architecture can the global governance system sustain global growth.

"小智治事，大智治制"，源自古谚，也有学者认为出自墨子，其完整表述是"大智治制，中智治人，小智治事"。在《共担时代责任 共促全球发展》的主旨演讲中，习近平主席用"小智治事，大智治制"引出"小智""大智"辩证法，以中国智慧解题、以中国道理说事，为全球经济治理提供中国大智慧，旨在强调全球经济治理过程中，解决一个个问题的"小智"固然重要，但观气取势、确定格局、择其大端的"大智"更为关键。

"小智治事，大智治制"的意思是"小智慧者善于处理具体事务，通过处理好一件事获取利益；大智慧者则会建立健全制度达到目的，从而让所有人遵循制度行事，突显制度建设的重要性"。追求"大智"是中国治世之策，注重你中有我、我中有你，强调总体思维和辩证思考，杜绝零和博弈，表现对眼界、胸襟和境界的高度要求。译文首先用"As the Chinese saying goes"点明"小智治事，大智治制"源自古代佳句，而"people with petty shrewdness attend to trivial matters, while people with vision attend to governance of institutions"则是根据习近平主席的讲话内容，对"小智治事，大智治制"进行具体阐发，强调治理的大智慧。译文既考虑了原文语境，强调了中国文化蕴含的中国智慧，同时兼顾准确性、清晰度和可读性，为目标文本的传播与接收奠定基础。总体而言，译文形神并重，力求再现原文意蕴与风貌。下例也可视为译文形神效果兼顾的典型：

> **原文** "积力之所举，则无不胜也；众智之所为，则无不成也。"只要我们牢固树立人类命运共同体意识，携手努力、共同担当，同舟共济、共渡难关，就一定能够让世界更美好、让人民更幸福。

> **译文** A Chinese adage reads, "Victory is ensured when people pool their strength; success is secured when people put their heads together." As long as we keep to the goal of building a community of shared future for mankind and work hand in hand to fulfill our responsibilities and overcome difficulties, we will be able to create a better world and deliver better lives for our peoples.

"积力之所举，则无不胜也；众智之所为，则无不成也"意思为"将众人的智慧与力量集结起来就会所向披靡，百战百胜"，源自春秋战国时期哲学家、思想家、教育家文子所撰《文子》（又称《通玄真书》）。通过援引这句话，习近平主席强调了群体力量和群体智慧对人类命运兴衰的重要性，任何国家和个人都不应独善其身，也不能独立应对所有问题，所谓"众擎易举，独力难成"，只有"集众力，集众智"，同甘共苦、携手并进才能确保世界人民的幸福生活。

译文开头"A Chinese adage reads"同样用增译法指明引文源自中国格言。"Victory is ensured when people pool their strength; success is secured when people put their heads together"对照原文"积力之所举，则无不胜也；众智之所为，则无不成也"，译者尽量保留原文的形与神，译文跟原文一样分为前后两部分，且结构平行，工整对称，保留了原文的形式之美。就忠实原意而言，"积力之所举"译为"when people pool their strength"和"众智之所为"译为"when people put their heads together"都直接传达了原意，准确到位。更为突出的是，"则无不胜也"译为"victory is ensured"与"则无不成"译为"success is secured"属于意思相同、表达相异的结构，译文实现了双重效果，既准确传达了原意，又再现了语言的多样性。由于翻译主体的选择比较灵活，也会根据上下文语境采用意译的处理方式，如下例：

> **原文** "大道之行也，天下为公。"发展的目的是造福人民。要让发展更加平衡，让发展机会更加均等、发展成果人人共享，就要完善发展理念和模式，提升发展公平性、有效性、协同性。

> **译文** As the Chinese saying goes, "A just cause should be pursued for common good." Development is ultimately for the people. To achieve more balanced development and ensure that the people have equal access to opportunities and share in the benefits of development, it is crucial to have a sound development philosophy and model and make development equitable, effective and balanced.

党的十八大以来，习近平主席在国内外重大场合多次谈及"大道之行也，天下为公"。"大道之行也，天下为公"意指"大道实行的时代，天下人共同享有天下"，源自西汉戴圣编撰的儒家经典文献《礼记·礼运》，是孔子为人类描绘的最理想、最美好的社会愿景，亦即远大而崇高的"大同"理想。"大道"古指治理社会的最高准则，至高目标是国泰民安，今解比较多样，常指普遍道理或真理。"天下为公"包含所有人在内的人类整体，强调只有人类共享天下，才能实现社会的和谐美满。习近平主席通过援引孔子"大道之行也，天下为公"的思想，传达中国胸怀世界的崇高理想、道德情怀及价值信仰，从而将孔子思想提升到全球发展的高度，强调"造福人民"、公平发展和成果共享的重要性。

译文"As the Chinese saying goes, 'A just cause should be pursued for common good.'"虽然没有明确出处，但指明是中国名言。通过对比原文可见，译者并未采取直译法，按照原文形式译出"大道之行也，天下为公"的内涵，而是根据习近平主席讲话内容，专注核心，突出重点，用 a just cause 和 common good 强调事业发展的公正性及造福天下的愿景，点明"大同"理想的精髓。译文是基于上下文语境的阐发，以习近平主席讲话的思想目的为导向，未将原文的历史文化背景细致显化，便于听众直接理解和领会。

2 外交讲话中比喻修辞的处理方法

修辞在领导人外交讲话中使用频繁，其中以比喻最为常见。比喻形象生动、浅显易懂、易于接受、感染力强，主要包括明喻、暗喻、借喻三种形式。恰当使用比喻，能够拉近与观众之间的距离，收获更佳的传播效果，增强对讲话的理解度和接受度。但是，就翻译而言，因为涉及文化差异或空缺问题，译者在翻译比喻修辞时，经常会面临不可译或者不易译的难题。与此同时，译者的主体需求及原文的语境特征，也会给翻译带来一定困难。因此，在注重保留原有风格和内涵的基础上，译者也会发挥主体的主观能动性、变通性或创造性传达原文修辞的蕴意。下面以本章范例的相关修辞翻译为例，探讨比喻手法的几种处理方式，提供可借鉴性参考。

原文 经济全球化确实带来了新问题，但我们不能就此把经济全球化<u>一棍子打死</u>，而是要适应和引导好经济全球化，消解经济全球化的负面影响，让它更好惠及每个国家、每个民族。

译文 It is true that economic globalization has created new problems, but this is no justification to <u>write economic globalization off completely</u>. Rather, we should adapt to and guide economic globalization, cushion its negative impact, and deliver its benefits to all countries and all nations.

"一棍子打死"是借喻，常用来比喻对人或事不加分析就认为毫无用处，进而全盘否定，源自毛泽东主席的《在中国共产党全国宣传工作会议上的讲话》："收，就是不许人家说不同的意见，不许人家发表错误的意见，发表了就'一棍子打死'。这不是解决矛盾的办法，而是扩大矛盾的办法。"在习近平主席的讲话中，"一棍子打死"主要强调在应对经济全球化问题时，要全面权衡利弊，争取趋利避害，采取最有利的策略，不能看到问题就对经济全球化全盘否定。"一棍子打死"形象生动，通俗易懂，是中国老百姓耳熟能详的表达。然而，就目标受众而言，这种富有中国文化内涵的表达比较陌生，直译会造成误解或者曲解。因此，译者舍形取义，采用意译方法将原文译成 write economic globalization off completely，词组 write something off 的意思是摒弃或者放弃某物，译文根据上下文将"一棍子打死"的深层内涵译出，即"全盘否定经济全球化"，清晰明了，满足受众期待，准确传达领导人思想和主张。再看以下几个典型例子：

原文 中国人民深知实现国家繁荣富强的艰辛，对各国人民取得的发展成就都点赞，都为他们祝福，都希望他们的日子越过越好，<u>不会犯"红眼病"</u>，不会抱怨他人从中国发展中得到了巨大机遇和丰厚回报。中国人民张开双臂欢迎各国人民<u>搭乘中国发展的"快车""便车"</u>。

译文 We Chinese know only too well what it takes to achieve prosperity, so we applaud the achievements made by others and wish them a better future. <u>We are not jealous of others' success</u>; and we will not complain about others who have benefited so much from the great opportunities presented by China's development. We will open our arms to the people of other countries and welcome them <u>aboard the express train of China's development</u>.

犯"红眼病"指对别人的成功或者强大而产生嫉妒，表达不满，严重时甚至采取不正当手段。犯"红眼病"采用意译法翻译为 be jealous of others' success。事实上，中西方表达"红眼病"存在文化差异，西方用"绿眼"（green-eyed）表达嫉妒，源自莎士比亚《奥赛罗》第三幕第三场：

> Iago: O, beware, my lord, of jealousy,
>
> It is the green-eyed monster which doth mock
>
> The meat it feeds on（Act III, Scene iii）[1]

伊阿古（Iago）提醒主帅当心嫉妒，并将嫉妒比作"绿眼妖魔"。因此，此处不能简单直译，容易造成文化误读，如不采用替换法将嫉妒译成 green-eyed，意译是一种比较好的选择。

"搭乘……'快车''便车'"也是借喻，是政论文体中常用的表达方式。原文"搭乘中国发展的'快车''便车'"比喻世界各国从中国发展或快速发展中获得便利或者好处。因为"快车""便车"的深层喻意，译文"have benefited so much from the great opportunities presented by China's development"以传达原文内涵为旨归，放弃原文借喻的喻体，选择弃形留意。

原文 中国将不断激发增长动力和市场活力，加大重要领域和关键环节改革力度，让市场在资源配置中起决定性作用，<u>牵住创新这个"牛鼻子"</u>，推进创新驱动发展战略，推动战略性新兴产业发展，注重用新技术新业态改造提升传统产业，促进新动能发展壮大、传统动能焕发生机。

译文 China will boost market vitality to add new impetus to growth. We will intensify reform efforts in priority areas and key links and enable the market to play a decisive role in resources allocation. <u>Innovation will continue to feature prominently on our growth agenda.</u> In pursuing the strategy of innovation-driven development, we will bolster the strategic emerging industries, apply new technologies and foster new business models to upgrade traditional industries; and we will boost new drivers of growth and revitalize traditional ones.

---

1 Shakespeare, W. 2017. *Othello*. Charleston, South Carolina: CreateSpace Independent Publishing Platform.

牛鼻子是牛身上最弱的部位，在牛鼻子上穿入铁环，牵住牛鼻子就可让其驯服。汉语口语中常用"牵牛要牵牛鼻子"强调做事情要懂得抓住关键或者要害。在本例中，"牵住创新这个'牛鼻子'"，意指创新是推动中国经济发展的关键。译文同样放弃中国语言特色，采用意译方法译成"Innovation will continue to feature prominently on our growth agenda"。

原文是典型的汉语竹节式结构，比较松散，主语"中国"后面连续引出八个谓语结构。如果按照这种散式结构逐一对译，会影响译文的地道性和可读性。为避免这个问题，译者根据行文意思将原文长句切分成四个句子译出，使译文更加清晰明了。"牵住创新这个'牛鼻子'"是切分后的四句话之一，译文将原文结构重组，把innovation设为主语，整体上同样选择弃形留意，译成"Innovation will continue to feature prominently on our growth agenda."。

原文 二十国集团领导人在杭州峰会上达成重要共识，<u>要以创新为重要抓手</u>，挖掘各国和世界经济增长新动力。

译文 With this in mind, G20 leaders reached an important consensus at the Hangzhou Summit, which is to <u>take innovation as a key driver</u> and foster new driving force of growth for both individual countries and the global economy.

"抓手"近几年在政治文本中出现频次较高，常见于领导人讲话、新闻报刊中，源自汉语方言，原指"拉手、把手"，亦即"手可抓握的部位"。日常生活中，物品如有了"抓手"就等于有了凭借，便于使用或操控。在政治文本中，"抓手"意义的涵盖面比较广泛，可用来表示"方法、契机、手段、载体"等，也可指"重点工作、中心任务、重点举措"或是"切入点、突破口"等。常用的表达结构包括"以××为重要抓手""把××作为××的抓手""××是××的重要抓手"等。

在上例中，"以创新为重要抓手"通过暗喻形象传达了创新在经济增长中的重要地位，译文为 take innovation as a key driver。"抓手"译为 key driver, key 表示"重要的", driver 除了"司机"之意，也可指"驱动程序"。众所周知，驱动程序素有"硬件的主宰"之称，计算机操作系统只有通过驱动程序才能控制硬件设备的运行。就本文语境而言，driver 可指 one that provides impulse or motivation，即"促发动能、动力或动机之物"。译者采用替换法，将原有的中国特色暗喻表达转为目标受众易于理解的方式。替换法能够保留原文修辞的形象性，同时能使受众产生意义上的共鸣，便于受众理解和接受。

由此可见，在翻译比喻修辞时，译者应首先判断原文的比喻修辞能否让目标受众产生共鸣，如能达到普遍接受的效果，可采用修辞保留的方式直接移植，如果会对目标受众造成理解障碍，则要采用其他方式变通处理，以准确传达信息为主要目的。再举直接移植的例子：

> **原文** 中国的大门对世界始终是打开的，不会关上。开着门，世界能够进入中国，中国也才能走向世界。我们希望，各国的大门也对中国投资者公平敞开。

> **译文** China will keep its door wide open and not close it. An open door allows both other countries to access the Chinese market and China itself to integrate with the world. And we hope that other countries will also keep their door open to Chinese investors and keep the playing field level for us.

整句话用"大门"或者"门"的借喻手法表达"欢迎"或者"开放"的态度。强调中国与世界各国互相开放、互惠互利的倡议和希望。由于"大门"或者"门"的喻意具有普遍通识性，不会引发受众的理解障碍，本句采用异化直译方式处理。"对……是打开的"及"对……敞开"，统一采用 keep one's door wide open 传达原意。"开着门"根据英语表达需要，采用词性转换法将原有动词结构变为名词结构，译为 an open door，充当第二句主语。修辞在政论文体中使用比较频繁，有时会接连出现两个或几个比喻的情况，翻译时需以过硬的语言功底进行灵活变通处理。

> **原文** 世界经济的大海，你要还是不要，都在那儿，是回避不了的。想人为切断各国经济的资金流、技术流、产品流、产业流、人员流，让世界经济的大海退回到一个一个孤立的小湖泊、小河流，是不可能的，也是不符合历史潮流的。

> **译文** Whether you like it or not, the global economy is the big ocean that you cannot escape from. Any attempt to cut off the flow of capital, technologies, products, industries and people between economies, and channel the waters in the ocean back into isolated lakes and creeks is simply not possible. Indeed, it runs counter to the historical trend.

在此例中，比喻修辞出现了两次：前者为暗喻，将"世界经济"比作大海；后者为借喻，"孤立的小湖泊、小河流"指"脱离世界存在的个体经济体"。因"大海""小湖泊"和"小河流"是世界共知的普遍存在，其自身属性也广为周知，因而直接移植不会产生理解障碍。译者翻译第一处比喻时，采用异化策略，保留原有喻体形象，只有一点稍有不同——将偏正短语结构转换为句子，译为 the global economy is the big ocean；而在翻译第二处比喻时做了部分变通调整，将"世界经济的大海"去修辞化，译为 the waters in the ocean，保证英语表达的流畅性和可读性。就结构而言，原有的偏正结构得以保留，但为使译文更加地道，将原有的前置定语后置化。"孤立的小湖泊、小河流"借喻部分未做改变，仍采用异化手法直译，再现原有的修辞效果。事实上，即便两个平行比喻结构，也会产生迥然不同的翻译选择，如下例：

| 原文 | 中国坚持通过改革破解前进中遇到的困难和挑战，敢于<u>啃硬骨头、涉险滩</u>，勇于破除妨碍发展的体制机制障碍，不断解放和发展社会生产力，不断解放和增强社会活力。 |

| 译文 | China has tackled difficulties and met challenges on its way forward through reform. China has demonstrated its courage to <u>take on difficult issues</u>, <u>navigate treacherous rapids</u> and remove institutional hurdles standing in the way of development. These efforts have enabled us to unleash productivity and social vitality. |

"啃硬骨头、涉险滩"都是借喻，根据上下文语境，前者指勇挑艰巨任务，体现坚韧不拔的精神；后者中的"险滩"通指河流中水流湍急、布满礁石、航道弯窄，导致航行危险或是困难之处，因而"涉险滩"常用来比喻不畏艰险，在险境中开辟出路，体现迎难而上的精神。对比而言，"涉险滩"更易理解，直译成 navigate treacherous rapids 既保留原文修辞，也能传达原文意思；但如果采用异化策略直译"啃硬骨头"则易产生误解，其中蕴含的思想内涵不易被目标受众领会，因此意译成 take on difficult issues。由此可见，译者将受众放在了重要位置，以传达领导人思想精神为主要目标，如果不能原汁原味再现源语修辞效果，则会选择归化策略，以传递原文深蕴为目的。受文化差异所限，归化改写的途径很多，用替换法将原有比喻替换成目标受众熟悉的形式，也是再现源语修辞效果的常用方式。当然，在翻译过程中，由于行文效果需要，也有将比喻修辞省去不译的情况。

| 原文 | 我们要坚定不移发展全球自由贸易和投资，在开放中推动贸易和投资自由化便利化，<u>旗帜鲜明反对保护主义</u>。搞保护主义如同把自己关进黑屋子，看似躲过了风吹雨打，但也隔绝了阳光和空气。 |

| 译文 | We must remain committed to developing global free trade and investment, promote trade and investment liberalization and facilitation through |

opening-up and say no to protectionism. Pursuing protectionism is like locking oneself in a dark room. While wind and rain may be kept outside, that dark room will also block light and air.

"旗帜鲜明"，原指军旗耀眼，军容整齐，出自《三国演义》第二十五回："曹操指山下颜良排的阵势，旗帜鲜明，枪刀森布，严整有威。"现在是政论文体中的常用成语，比喻政治立场、观点、态度等十分明确。研究译文可见，译者采用了删减法将"旗帜鲜明"删去未译，一是因为"旗帜鲜明"是中国特色话语，直译容易增加目标受众的接受难度；二是因为本句主语+must引出三个动词结构，say no to protectionism是其中之一，must已经表达了坚定态度，如果再译"旗帜鲜明"体现明确的立场，就会显得啰唆冗余，不译反而利于行文的简明流畅。至于"搞保护主义如同把自己关进黑屋子，看似躲过了风吹雨打，但也隔绝了阳光和空气"，由于意思易于受众理解和接受，译者采用了直译法处理，译为"Pursuing protectionism is like locking oneself in a dark room. While wind and rain may be kept outside, that dark room will also block light and air."，大体还原了明喻的风貌，同时把原句一分为二，用两句话译出，避免繁复，对于领导人讲话的受众而言，接受起来更为轻松容易。

3 外交讲话中数据表述的处理方法

数据表达在领导人外访讲话中比较常用，常用于分享中国经济发展情况、回顾两国贸易往来成果或展望未来合作可能等，对加强对中国经济的认知、夯实经贸合作关系、拓展更多合作空间等起到重要作用。下面就本章范例中的译文详细解释数据表达的常用翻译方法。

原文 全球最富有的1%人口拥有的财富量超过其余99%人口财富的总和，收入分配不平等、发展空间不平衡令人担忧。

译文 The richest one percent of the world's population owns more wealth than the remaining 99 percent. Inequality in income distribution and uneven development space are worrying.

第一句例文比较简单，只涉及人口占比的数据。这句话总体上直译，有两处做了变通处理。第一处是采用拆分法将原句分成两部分，遵循了言简意赅的原则。另一处采用删减法，将"总和"略去不易，只译出涉及的百分比。"总和"通常译成词组in total，或用动词total、add up to、amount to等。根据译文可见，"总和"省去不译并未影响原文意思的传达，译文准确清晰。在数据描述中常用的"超过"直译成more...than...的形式，owns more wealth than...的表达方式符合英语表达习惯，行文更为简洁易懂。

| 原文 | 1950年至2016年，中国在自身长期发展水平和人民生活水平不高的情况下，<u>累计对外提供援款4000多亿元人民币</u>，实施各类援外项目5000多个，其中成套项目近3000个，举办11000多期培训班，为发展中国家在华培训各类人员26万多名。改革开放以来，<u>中国累计吸引外资超过1.7万亿美元，累计对外直接投资超过1.2万亿美元</u>，为世界经济发展作出了巨大贡献。国际金融危机爆发以来，<u>中国经济增长对世界经济增长的贡献率年均在30%以上</u>。|

| 译文 | Between 1950 and 2016, despite its modest level of development and living standard, <u>China provided more than 400 billion yuan of foreign assistance</u>, undertook over 5,000 foreign assistance projects, including nearly 3,000 complete projects, and held over 11,000 training workshops in China for over 260,000 personnel from other developing countries. Since it launched reform and opening-up, <u>China has attracted over 1.7 trillion US dollars of foreign investment and made over 1.2 trillion US dollars of direct outbound investment</u>, making huge contribution to global economic development. In the years following the outbreak of the international financial crisis, <u>China contributed to over 30% of global growth every year on average</u>. |

在此例当中，尽管涉及较多数据，但就翻译难点而言，涉及画线的三部分，其中前两个是有关"累计"数量的表述。根据译文可见，译者对三个"累计"都省去未译，直接译出了对外援款、吸引外资和直接投资的数据，总体上没有影响理解，未损原意的传达。当然，如果选择更加忠于原文，"累计"也可译出。比如，2017年6月，李克强总理在柏林出席中德论坛时发表的《做创新合作的"黄金搭档"》中有这样一句话："中国企业对德投资方兴未艾，累计直接投资超过百亿美元"，译为：Investment by Chinese companies in Germany has been fast expanding, exceeding 10 billion U.S. dollars in accumulative terms，"累计"在此译为in accumulative terms。再如，"累计"作定语修饰语时可译作cumulative，如"中方累计对吉尔吉斯斯坦的投资"译为cumulative Chinese investment in Kyrgyzstan。第三个画线部分"中国经济增长对世界经济增长的贡献率年均在30%以上"涉及占比的翻译，译文为"China contributed to over 30% of global growth every year on average"。"贡献率"采用词性转化进行翻译，通过用动词词组 contribute to 恰好引出比率，同时表达做出贡献的内涵。对于比例的相关表达有多种处理方法，再如下一例：

原文 按汇率法计算，这些国家的经济总量<u>占世界的比重接近 40%</u>。保持现在的发展速度，10 年后将<u>接近世界总量一半</u>。

译文 Based on exchange rate calculation, these countries <u>account for nearly 40 percent of</u> the global economic output. Growing at their current rates, these countries will see their economic output <u>approach half of the global total</u> in a decade.

第一个画线部分中的 account for（也可用 take up）也是表示占比的常用表达。此外，两处画线部分都用"接近"来引出占比数值，第一处因译文谓语用 account for 表示所占比重，故"接近"用副词 nearly 译出；第二处直接用动词 approach 表达所占比重和"接近"之意，准确传达原文信息，同时实现了语言的多样化，符合英语的表达习惯。

原文 2016 年，在世界经济疲弱的背景下，<u>中国经济预计增长 6.7%</u>，依然处于世界前列。现在，<u>中国经济的体量已不能同过去同日而语，集聚的动能是过去两位数的增长都达不到的</u>。中国居民消费和服务业成为经济增长的主要动力，<u>2016 年前三季度第三产业增加值占国内生产总值的比重为 52.8%，国内消费对经济增长的贡献率达 71%</u>。<u>居民收入和就业实现稳定增长，单位国内生产总值能耗持续下降</u>，绿色发展初见成效。

译文 Despite a sluggish global economy, <u>China's economy is expected to grow by 6.7% in 2016</u>, still one of the highest in the world. <u>China's economy is far bigger in size than in the past, and it now generates more output than it did with double-digit growth in the past.</u> Household consumption and the services sector have become the main drivers of growth. <u>In the first three quarters of 2016, added value of the tertiary industry took up 52.8% of the GDP and domestic consumption contributed to 71% of economic growth.</u> <u>Household income and employment have steadily risen, while per unit GDP energy consumption continues to drop.</u> Our efforts to pursue green development are paying off.

本例数据除涉及占比表达外，如将"占国内生产总值的比重为 52.8%"译为 took up 52.8% of the GDP，"对经济增长的贡献率达 71%"译为 contributed to 71% of economic growth，翻译处理方式与上文所述相同，此例还可见"增长"与"下降"的表达方式，这两种表达在数据表述中都是不可或缺的。总体而言，相关翻译皆需根据行文需求进行直译或者灵活调整，达到准确、明了、流畅的翻译效果。由四处画线部分可见，第一处"增长"是谓语动词部分，故"增长 6.7%"译为 grow by 6.7%，第二处"两位数的增长"是偏正结构，"增长"是名词，故译为 with double-digit growth。第四处"稳定增长"和"持续下降"皆可用动词表达"增长"和"下降"，故译文为 have steadily risen 和 continues to drop。当然，在确保信息准确、表达流畅的情况下，译者也可根据行文或者个人需要，通过词性转换或成分转换方式变通翻译。比如李克强总理 2018 年 5 月在中国－印尼工商峰会上的主旨演讲中有这样一句话："中国连续 7 年成为印尼第一大贸易伙伴，两国贸易平衡持续改善，今年一季度双边贸易额同比又增长 28%"，译为"China has been Indonesia's biggest trading partner for seven years. Two-way trade registered a year-on-year growth of 28 percent in the first quarter of this year, and has been moving toward greater balance."。"同比又增长 28%"译为"registered a year-on-year growth of 28 percent"，译者没有直接用动词词组 grow by 或者 increase by 翻译"增长"，而是选择 register a…growth of 结构，用 grow 的名词形式，便于使用定语成分 year-on-year。当然，这里也可译成 grow by 28% on a year-on-year basis。事实上，有关增降的相关表达很多，以"增长"相关表达为例，包括 grow/growth, increase (*n.*), increase to/by, grow by/to, rise by/to, up by/about, jump (*v.* & *n.*, a 50% jump, jump 50%) 等。

五 中国关键词加油站

1 习近平外交思想 Xi Jinping thought on foreign affairs

2018 年 6 月，中央外事工作会议在北京召开，这次会议最重要的成果是确立了习近平外交思想的指导地位。这一思想概括起来主要有以下 10 个方面：坚持以维护党中央权威为统领加强党对对外工作的集中统一领导，坚持以实现中华民族伟大复兴为使命推进中国特色大国外交，坚持以维护世界和平、促进共同发展为宗旨推动构建人类命运共同体，坚持以中国特色社会主义为根本增强战略自信，坚持以共商共建共享为原则推动"一带一路"建设，坚持以相互尊重、合作共赢为基础走和平发展道路，坚持以深化外交布局为依托打造全球伙伴关系，坚持以公平正义为理念引领全球治理体系改革，坚持以国家核心利益为底线维护国家主权、安全、发展利益，坚持以对外工作优良传统和时代特征相结合为方向塑造中国外交独特风范。这一思想是习近平新时代中国特色社会主义思想的重要组成部分，是以习近平同志为核心的党中央治国理政思想在外交领域的重大理论成果，是新时代我国对外工作的根本遵循和行动指南。

2 维护国家核心利益 safeguarding the core interests of China

中国走和平发展道路、倡导合作共赢是以坚决维护国家核心利益为底线的。中国的核心利益包括：国家主权，国家安全，领土完整，国家统一，中国宪法确立的国家政治制度和社会大局稳定，经济社会可持续发展的基本保障。习近平总书记指出："我们要坚持走和平发展道路，但决不能放弃我们的正当权益，决不能牺牲国家核心利益。任何外国不要指望我们会拿自己的核心利益做交易，不要指望我们会吞下损害中国主权、安全、发展利益的苦果。"

3 新型国际关系 a new model of international relations

2015年9月28日，在世界反法西斯战争胜利和联合国成立70周年之际，中国国家主席习近平首次登上联合国讲台，向世界清晰阐述了以合作共赢为核心的新型国际关系理念。他提出，"我们要继承和弘扬联合国宪章的宗旨和原则，构建以合作共赢为核心的新型国际关系，打造人类命运共同体。"建立平等相待、互商互谅的伙伴关系，营造公道正义、共建共享的安全格局，谋求开放创新、包容互惠的发展前景，促进和而不同、兼收并蓄的文明交流，构筑尊崇自然、绿色发展的生态体系，上述"五位一体"，构成了新型国际关系的主要体系。构建新型国际关系，是中国领导人对攸关人类前途命运的诸如和平与发展等关键问题给出的中国答案。以合作共赢为核心，蕴含着对实现世界和平、发展、公平、正义、民主、自由等全人类共同价值的关怀，亦是对联合国崇高目标的深刻思考。

4 总体国家安全观 a holistic view of national security

2019年10月，中国共产党十九届四中全会《决定》提出，坚持总体国家安全观，以人民安全为宗旨，以政治安全为根本，以经济安全为基础，以军事、科技、文化、社会安全为保障，健全国家安全体系，增强国家安全能力。总体国家安全观要求：既重视外部安全，又重视内部安全，对内求发展、求变革、求稳定、建设平安中国，对外求和平、求合作、求共赢、建设和谐世界；既重视国土安全，又重视国民安全，坚持以民为本、以人为本，坚持国家安全一切为了人民、一切依靠人民，真正夯实国家安全的群众基础；既重视传统安全，又重视非传统安全，构建集政治安全、国土安全、军事安全、经济安全、文化安全、社会安全、科技安全、信息安全、生态安全、资源安全、核安全等于一体的国家安全体系；既重视发展问题，又重视安全问题，发展是安全的基础，安全是发展的条件；既重视自身安全，又重视共同安全，打造命运共同体，推动各方朝着互惠互利、共同安全的目标相向而行。

5 中国的国际责任和义务 China's international responsibilities and obligations

作为一个发展中大国，中国在国际事务中有自己的责任和担当。随着经济体量的增大，中国在国际上发挥的作用也会相应增大。中国愿意更多参与国际治理，尽可能提供国际公共产品；与其他发展中国家分享减贫经验，提供力所能及的帮助；为全球经济强劲、可持续、平衡增长分担应有的责任。当然，中国依然是一个发展中国家。中国实现现代化还有漫长的、艰辛的路要走，中国承担的国际责任和义务只能与自己的发展水平相适应。

6 维护和发展开放型世界经济 maintaining and developing an open world economy

中国倡导维护和发展开放型世界经济，主张各国应进一步扩大相互开放，旗帜鲜明地反对各种形式的贸易保护主义，齐心协力做大世界经济这块大蛋糕。为此，各国应维护自由、开放、非歧视的多边贸易体制，不搞排他性贸易标准、规则、体系，避免造成全球市场分割和贸易体系分化。要探讨完善全球投资规则，引导全球发展资本合理流动，更加有效地配置发展资源。

7 正确的义利观 the greater good and self-interest

中国主张，在国际关系中，要妥善处理义和利的关系。政治上，要遵守国际法和国际关系基本原则，秉持公道正义，坚持平等相待。经济上，要立足全局、放眼长远，坚持互利共赢、共同发展，既要让自己过得好，也要让别人过得好。习近平主席指出：义，反映的是我们的一个理念。这个世界上一部分人过得很好，一部分人过得很不好，不是个好现象。真正的快乐幸福是大家共同快乐、共同幸福。中国希望全世界共同发展，特别是希望广大发展中国家加快发展。利，就是要恪守互利共赢原则，不搞我赢你输，要实现双赢。中国有义务对贫穷的国家给予力所能及的帮助，有时甚至要重义轻利、舍利取义，绝不能唯利是图、斤斤计较。正确义利观承继了中国外交的优良传统，体现了中国特色社会主义国家的理念。

8 "亲、诚、惠、容"的周边外交理念 building relations with neighboring countries based on friendship, good faith, mutual benefit, and inclusiveness

2013年10月24日，习近平总书记在周边外交工作座谈会上强调，中国周边外交的基本方针，就是坚持与邻为善、以邻为伴，坚持睦邻、安邻、富邻，突出体现"亲、诚、惠、容"的理念。"亲"是指巩固地缘相近、人缘相亲的友好情谊，要坚持睦邻友好、守望相助，讲平等、重感情，常见面、多走动，多做得人心、暖人心的事，使周边国家对我们更友善、更亲近、更认同、更支持，增强亲和力、感召力、影响力。"诚"是指坚持以诚待人、以信取人的相处之道，要诚心诚意对待周边国家，争取更多朋友和伙伴。"惠"是指履行惠及周边、互利共赢的合作理念，要本着互惠互利的原则同周边国家开展合作，编织更加紧密的共同利益网络，把双方利益融合提升到更高水平，让周边国家得益于我国发展，使我国也从周边国家共同发展中获得裨益和助力。"容"是指展示开放包容、求同存异的大国胸怀，要倡导包容的思想，强调亚太之大容得下大家共同发展，以更加开放的胸襟和更加积极的态度促进地区合作。"亲、诚、惠、容"这四字箴言，是新形势下中国坚持走和平发展道路的一份生动宣言，是对多年来中国周边外交实践的一个精辟概括，也反映了中国新一届中央领导集体外交理念的创新发展。

9 尊重各国人民自主选择发展道路的权利 respecting the rights of all peoples to choose their own development path

一个国家的发展道路合不合适，只有这个国家的人民才最有发言权。习近平用中国民间的俗语做比喻说，"鞋子合不合脚，自己穿了才知道"。意思是说，走什么样的发展道路，是一个国家的内部事务，任何外国无权干涉，无权指手画脚，更无权通过强制或颠覆等手段把别国拉到自己划定的轨道上来。在国际关系中，中国历来坚持国家不分大小、强弱、贫富一律平等，尊重各国人民自主选择发展道路的权利，承认各国文化传统、社会制度、价值观念、发展理念等方面的差异，努力推动不同文明的发展模式取长补短、相互促进、共同发展，反对以一种模式来衡量丰富多彩的世界。

10 交流互鉴的文明观 exchanges and mutual learning between civilizations

中国倡导交流互鉴的文明观，其核心内涵是文明是多彩的，人类文明因多样才有交流互鉴的价值；文明是平等的，人类文明因平等才有交流互鉴的前提；文明是包容的，人类文明因包容才有交流互鉴的动力。当今世界，人类生活在不同文化、种族、肤色、宗教和不同社会制度所组成的世界里，各国人民形成了你中有我、我中有你的命运共同体。应该推动不同文明相互尊重、和谐共处，让文明交流互鉴成为增进各国人民友谊的桥梁、推动人类社会进步的动力、维护世界和平的纽带。应该从不同文明中寻求智慧、汲取营养，为人们提供精神支撑和心灵慰藉，携手解决人类共同面临的各种挑战。

六 外交讲话翻译练习

1. 请将下列外交讲话译成英文，注意外交讲话的翻译原则。

1) 2017年，中国召开了中国共产党第十九次全国代表大会，宣告中国特色社会主义进入新时代，提出外交工作推动构建新型国际关系、推动构建人类命运共同体的总目标，描绘了分两步走全面建设社会主义现代化国家的宏伟蓝图，展现出同世界各国共同创造人类美好未来的坚定信念。

2）开放合作是科技进步和生产力发展的必然逻辑。贸易战不可取，因为不会有赢家。经济霸权主义更要不得，因为这将损害国际社会共同利益，最终也将搬起石头砸自己的脚。

3）潮流来了，跟不上就会落后，就会被淘汰。我们能够做的和应该做的就是要抢抓机遇，加大创新投入，着力培育新的经济增长点，实现新旧动能转换。要全力推进结构性改革，消除一切不利于创新的体制机制障碍，充分激发创新潜能和市场活力。

2. 请将下列外交讲话译成英文，注意修辞手段的处理。

1）我国同美、俄、欧等大国的协调与合作取得新进展，同周边国家互信合作进一步加强，同广大发展中国家伙伴关系的"含金量"得到新提升。"对话不对抗、结伴不结盟"的理念深入人心，国与国交往的新路越走越宽。

2）我们期待，2018年的世界多一些合作、少一些摩擦。我们将扩展深化全球伙伴关系网络，积极构建总体稳定、均衡发展的大国关系框架。践行亲诚惠容理念深化同周边国家关系，合作上做加法，问题上做减法，共同建设亚洲命运共同体。

3）我们应该坚持以开放求发展，深化交流合作，坚持"拉手"而不是"松手"，坚持"拆墙"而不是"筑墙"，坚决反对保护主义、单边主义，不断削减贸易壁垒，推动全球价值链、供应链更加完善，共同培育市场需求。

4）世界多极化、经济全球化在曲折中前行，地缘政治热点此起彼伏，恐怖主义、武装冲突的阴霾挥之不去。单边主义、保护主义愈演愈烈，多边主义和多边贸易体制受到严重冲击。要合作还是要对立，要开放还是要封闭，要互利共赢还是要以邻为壑，国际社会再次来到何去何从的十字路口。

5）今年是曼德拉先生诞辰100周年。他有一句名言："攀上一座高山后，你会发现，还有更多的高山等着你去攀登。"金砖合作的历程，正是五国携手勇攀高峰、不断超越的历程。只要金砖国家携手同心，就能不断攀越险峰峭壁，登顶新的高峰、到达新的高度，为人类和平与发展的崇高事业做出新的更大的贡献！

6）在两国各界人士共同努力下，中国同印尼的关系已驶入发展的快车道，经贸是两国合作中最活跃、最富有成果的领域。

3. 请将下列外交讲话译成英文，注意数据表述的处理。

1）未来10年，将是国际格局和力量对比加速演变的10年。新兴市场国家和发展中国家对世界经济增长的贡献率已经达到 80%。按汇率法计算，这些国家的经济总量占世界的比重接近 40%。保持现在的发展速度，10 年后将接近世界总量一半。

2）中国连续 7 年成为印尼第一大贸易伙伴，两国贸易平衡持续改善，今年一季度双边贸易额同比又增长 28%。中国是印尼主要的外资来源国，去年对印尼投资增长 30% 以上，投资存量超过 100 亿美元。

3）过去五年，中国经济保持年均 7.1% 的中高速增长，2017 年国内生产总值达 82 万亿元人民币，累计城镇新增就业 6600 万人以上，经济结构进一步优化，服务业占国内生产总值比重升至 51.6%。中国经济对世界经济增长年均贡献率超过 30%。今年一季度国内生产总值同比增长 6.8%，平均每天新登记企业 1.5 万户。4 月份采购经理人指数达 51.4%，持续位于扩张区间。今年前四个月货运量、全社会用电量增速分别为 6.3% 和 10.1%，税收收入增速超过 16%，中国经济延续稳中向好发展态势。

第二章

外交署名文章翻译

一、外交署名文章的概念及文体特点

"署名文章"是报纸行业特有词汇。"一般而言，署名文章是指个人或团体署上名字公开发表的文章，而署名是文责自负的承诺。有别于其他体裁的普通署名文章，政治理论性的署名文章通常表明特定权威人士的观点或意见风向，具有宏观指导性"[1]。外交署名文章通常指国家领导人在外访前（国家元首），或访问时（国家总理、副总理等）在到访国主流媒体上发表的署名文章。就我国而言，国家领导人在国外发表署名文章是开展公共外交的重要形式，除了展现个人思想观点、领导举措与风范，更能增进与到访国的关系，拉近与当地民众的距离，使当地民众更加了解中国国情及中国文化，对传达中国声音、表达中国理念、提升国家形象、建构中国特色话语体系发挥重大作用。就内容而言，领导人署名文章"一般包括此次访问的目的，双方将在哪些领域进行合作，对两国未来的展望和期许，向民众表达善意"[2]。

外交署名文章属于政论文体，具有政论文体的鲜明特征，语言严谨正式，展现独特的政治语境，富含时政术语，包括国际通用的时政术语及具有源语特色的时政术语等。比如，"我们愿同吉方密切国际合作，加强在联合国、上海合作组织、亚信等多边框架内的沟通和协调，共同维护以联合国宪章宗旨和原则为基础的国际关系基本准则，支持多边主义，推进经济全球化进程，推动构建新型国际关系和人类命运共同体"。其次，为拉近与当地民众的距离，文内用词也有通俗易懂的一面。此类表达常见于引用到访国的名人名言、日常俗语、诗文典故，回顾两国交往的历史渊源或感人故事，或是分享亲身经历等。比如，"曾两次访问中国的希腊文学巨匠卡赞扎基斯有一句名言，'苏格拉底和孔子是人类的两张面具，面具之下是同一张人类理性的面孔'"；"塔吉克斯坦谚语讲：'有志气的蚂蚁也能把大山搬走'"。再如下例中对两国人民交往及情谊的回顾：

中吉两国人民比邻而居，传统友好源远流长。2000多年前，中国汉代张骞远行西域，古丝绸之路逶迤穿过碎叶古城。数百年后，黠戛斯人跋涉千里远赴唐都长安，返程不仅带回了精美的丝绸和瓷器，也收获了亲切友爱的兄弟般情谊。中国唐代伟大诗人李白的绚丽诗篇在两国家喻户晓、广为传诵。2000多年的历史积淀，铸就了两国人民牢不可破的深情厚谊。

再次，源语蕴含独特的文化特征。署名文章的目的之一是传播本国文化，搭建

---

1 范武邱，胡建. 2017. 我国领导人海外署名文章及其英译研究. 中国外语，（5）：101-107.
2 同上。

沟通和理解的桥梁，因此署名文章中不乏宣传源语文化或思想的语句。比如，"中国的先哲曰：'事虽小，不为不成'"；或引用诗歌"海内存知己，天涯若比邻"；或引用中国谚语"路遥知马力，日久见人心"；或描述中国悠久历史"2000多年前，中国西汉张骞凿空西域之旅，开辟了伟大的丝绸之路，在人类文明交流史上留下了华美乐章"等。最后，外交署名文章风格各异，受出访主体视域的影响，领导人的语体风格各有侧重、各具特色。如上例所示，国家主席习近平的亲民风格就充满吸引力、亲和力和感召力，善用短、实、新的语言贴近民心，同时阐发深刻的思想和观点。比如："我们要做心贴着心的亲密伙伴。双方要以民心相通为宗旨，广泛开展文化、教育、卫生、旅游、新闻等各领域交流，带动两国社会友好大发展"。再如："让我们一起抓住机遇，只争朝夕，使中巴关系实现弯道超车、后来居上，使两国合作行稳致远，为建设更加美好的未来和更加繁荣的世界不断作出新贡献"。习近平主席语言质朴却内涵深刻，表达直白但又让人耳目一新。

二 外交署名文章汉英对照举隅

深化务实合作　共谋和平发展
中华人民共和国主席 习近平

A Shared Commitment to Practical Cooperation and Peaceful Development
By H.E. Xi Jinping President of the People's Republic of China

我很高兴2017年第一次出访就来到瑞士这个美丽的国家。这是我首次以中国国家主席身份访问瑞士，也是新世纪以来中国国家元首对瑞士进行的首次国事访问。

瑞士著名诗人、诺贝尔文学奖获得者施皮特勒说："找到同呼吸、共命运的朋友是人世间最大的幸福。"访问期间，

I am very pleased to come to the beautiful country of Switzerland for my first overseas trip in 2017. This is the first time for me to visit Switzerland as Chinese President and the first state visit by a Chinese head of state in the new century.

The well-known Swiss poet and Nobel laureate Carl Spitteler once said that there is no greater happiness than having friends who share the same outlook and destiny with oneself.

我将同瑞士联邦委员会、联邦议会领导人会谈会见，同社会各界进行广泛接触和交流。我将赴达沃斯出席世界经济论坛2017年年会，并到日内瓦、洛桑访问联合国机构和国际组织总部。我对这次瑞士之行充满期待。

（一）

中瑞两国虽然相距遥远，但瑞士对中国人民来说并不陌生。瑞士被誉为"欧洲屋脊"和"科技创新之国"，风光秀美，人民勤劳，经济发达。

中瑞两国交往合作源远流长。早在上世纪初，瑞士钟表、制药、纺织、机械产品就已经远销中国，瑞士金融保险机构也在华开展业务。

上世纪50年代，瑞士成为最早承认并同新中国建交的西方国家之一。1954年，周恩来总理率团出席日内瓦会议，向世界展示了新中国外交的风格和特色。

中国实行改革开放之初，瑞士企业就在华设立了第一家

During my visit, I will have talks and meetings with leaders of the Swiss Federal Council and Federal Assembly and have extensive contact and discussion with people from various sectors. I will also attend the World Economic Forum (WEF) Annual Meeting 2017 in Davos and visit the headquarters of UN agencies and international organizations in Geneva and Lausanne. I am very much looking forward to this trip.

I

Despite the great distance between our two countries, the Chinese people are no strangers to Switzerland. Known as the roof of Europe and a leader in innovation, Switzerland boasts beautiful landscape, hard-working people and an advanced economy.

The exchange and cooperation between us go back a long way. In the early 20th century, Swiss-made clocks and watches, medicine, textiles and mechanical products were already sold in China, and Swiss financial and insurance services also had presence there.

In 1950, Switzerland was one of the first Western countries to recognize and establish diplomatic relations with New China. In 1954, Premier Zhou Enlai led the Chinese delegation to the Geneva Conference, unveiling to the world the diplomatic style and approach of the young People's Republic.

Shortly after China began its reform and opening-up program in the late 1970s, a Swiss

中外合资工业企业。进入新世纪，瑞士在欧洲国家中率先承认中国完全市场经济地位。

近年来，瑞士成为首个同中国签署并实施自由贸易协定的欧洲大陆国家。在支持人民币国际化、参与创立亚洲基础设施投资银行、互免持外交护照人员签证等方面，中瑞合作展现了与时俱进、敢为人先的创新精神，对中欧合作发挥了示范作用。

中瑞关系保持高水平发展。去年4月，我同来中国进行国事访问的施奈德-阿曼联邦主席一道，宣布建立中瑞创新战略伙伴关系，这是中国首次同外国建立以创新为标志的战略伙伴关系。中瑞关系进入新的发展阶段。

中瑞两国是不同社会制度、不同发展阶段、不同大小国家友好合作的典范。这是因为两国人民彼此怀有友好感情，更是因为双方相互尊重各自选择的社会制度和发展道

company set up the first industrial joint venture in China. At the start of this century, Switzerland was among the first European countries to recognize China as a full market economy.

In recent years, Switzerland became the first European continental country to conclude and implement a free trade agreement with China. Our two countries have taken pioneering and innovative steps in our engagement with each other, such as Switzerland's support for the internationalization of the RMB, its participation in the founding of the Asian Infrastructure Investment Bank (AIIB) and mutual visa exemption for diplomatic passport-holders of our two countries. These have set a good example for cooperation between China and other European countries.

The China-Switzerland relationship is growing from strength to strength. During his state visit to China last April, President Johann Schneider-Ammann and I announced the establishment of an innovative strategic partnership between the two countries, the first of its kind for China featuring innovation. This marked a new phase of our bilateral relations.

The relations between our countries are a model of friendship and cooperation between countries that are different in size, social system and development stage. This is made possible by our people's mutual goodwill, by a shared commitment to growing our bilateral relations

路，秉承平等相待、创新共赢的合作精神发展双边关系。

在当前国际形势复杂多变、世界经济复苏乏力的背景下，中瑞携手合作，全面深化创新战略伙伴关系，可以造福两国人民、带动中欧关系发展，也可以为当今国际关系稳定发展、世界经济复苏、贸易自由化作出积极贡献。

面向未来，我们两国要在以下方面作出努力。

——保持高层交往。发挥两国各层级对话和磋商机制作用，在涉及彼此核心利益和重大关切问题上相互理解和支持。

——创新务实合作。通过建立中瑞高水平创新合作等平台，推动两国企业、高校、科研机构开展创新合作，拓展节能环保、气候变化、知识产权、金融、生态农业、社会保障等领域合作。加强在联合国等国际组织及国际事务中的协调和合作，共同致力于和平解决国际争端，为国际形势注入稳定因素。

——加强人文交流。以签

on the basis of equality, innovation and win-win cooperation, and above all, by our respect for each other's social system and development path.

In a complex and fast-changing world beset by weak economic recovery, China and Switzerland need to work together to deepen the innovative strategic partnership across the board. This will not only benefit our peoples and grow China-Europe relations, but also contribute to the steady progress of international relations, global recovery and fair trade.

Going forward, we need to deepen our engagement in the following areas:

Maintaining high-level exchanges. We should leverage the dialogue and consultation mechanisms at various levels and show mutual understanding and support on issues concerning each other's core interests and major concerns.

Breaking new ground in practical cooperation. The newly established Sino-Swiss High-level Innovative Dialogue will enable us to promote collaboration between our companies, universities and research institutes and in energy conservation, environmental protection, climate change, IPR protection, financial services, eco-agriculture and social security. We may also increase coordination and cooperation at the UN and other multilateral organizations and in international affairs, work for the peaceful settlement of international disputes and promote stability in the world.

Expanding people-to-people exchanges.

署中瑞新的文化合作协议、中国在伯尔尼建立中国文化中心、共同举办中瑞旅游年为契机，扩大两国民间和青年交流，便利两国人员往来，加强两国旅游、冬季运动、职业教育、地方交往等领域合作，巩固中瑞关系社会基础。

——完善中瑞自由贸易区。积极探讨升级中瑞自由贸易协定，发挥其示范作用，共同维护自由开放的国际贸易和投资体系。利用亚洲基础设施投资银行、中国－中东欧国家合作等多边合作平台，助力中欧"一带一路"合作。

（二）

2016年9月，在美丽的西子湖畔，在二十国集团领导人杭州峰会上，中方同各方凝聚共识，为构建创新、活力、联动、包容的世界经济注入了新动力。今年，我首次赴达沃斯，希望在世界经济论坛年会上同各方坦诚深入交流，增强应对挑战的信心，推动世界经济恢复增长。

With the signing of the new cultural cooperation agreement, the establishment of the Chinese cultural center in Bern and the launch of the year of tourism, we are well placed to expand people-to-people and youth exchanges, facilitate personnel visits, and beef up cooperation in tourism, winter sports and vocational education and at the subnational level. All this will help cement public support for China-Switzerland relations.

Improving our Free Trade Area. We may actively explore the possibility of upgrading the Free Trade Agreement, and set a good example of promoting the free and open international trade and investment system. We may also step up China-Europe cooperation on the Belt and Road Initiative through the AIIB and the cooperation mechanism between China and Central and Eastern European countries.

II

In September 2016, the G20 Hangzhou Summit took place by the picturesque West Lake. During the summit, China worked with other parties to strive for consensus and inject momentum into the efforts to build an innovative, invigorated, interconnected and inclusive world economy. As I make my first trip to Davos for the WEF annual meeting, I look forward to candid and in-depth exchanges with the participants. It is a good opportunity to boost confidence in rising to challenges and re-energize world economic

瑞士达沃斯世界闻名。每逢新年伊始，来自世界不同地区、国家、领域的各界人士在此聚会，交流观点，碰撞思想，吸引着世界的目光。特别是国际金融危机爆发以来，世界经济论坛年会成为各方集思广益、对话合作的重要平台。这种同舟共济、共克时艰的精神为促进世界经济复苏发挥了积极作用。

当前，人们普遍对世界经济发展前景感到焦虑，反经济全球化思潮、民粹主义、贸易保护主义明显上升，主张对现行发展道路、分配制度、治理模式进行反思和变革的声音增多，世界经济走向成为各方共同关心的问题。

中国一直同包括欧洲国家在内的世界各国一道，探索应对全球发展面临的挑战。我们主动适应外部环境变化和中国经济发展新常态，以创新、协调、绿色、开放、共享的发展理念为指引，推进供给侧结构性改革，培育增长新动能，取得积极成效。中国将继续为

growth.

Davos is a well-known town. At the start of each new year, people from different regions, countries and backgrounds would come and meet here. Such a meeting of minds has always been under international spotlight. This has been especially so in the wake of the global financial crisis, when the WEF annual meetings have emerged as a major platform for brainstorming, dialogue and cooperation. Sticking together in times of difficulty, this is the very spirit that has helped to put the world economy on the path of recovery.

We meet at a time of angst about the prospects of the world economy, growing backlash against economic globalization, and rising populism and trade protectionism. There is a stronger call for revisiting and changing the current paths of development, systems of wealth distribution and models of governance. The direction of the world economy is a subject of heated discussion.

China has been working with European countries, among others, to address the challenges facing global development. We have taken the initiative to adapt to the fluid external environment and the "new normal" of the Chinese economy. We have followed the vision of innovative, coordinated, green, open and shared development, and made good progress in deepening supply-side structural reform and

世界经济增长提供巨大市场空间，继续成为各国投资的热土，继续为增进各国人民福祉作出贡献。

（三）

日内瓦在近现代国际关系史上具有举足轻重的地位，见证了联合国及其专门机构等政府间国际组织的发展，提供了达成伊朗核、叙利亚、中东和平进程等重要热点问题阶段性协议的平台，促成了《日内瓦公约》《全面禁止核试验条约》等一系列国际条约和法律文书的通过。

1971年，中国恢复在联合国合法席位并重返位于日内瓦的国际机构后，深入参与和平、安全、发展、人权、社会等各领域治理，为人类和平与发展的崇高事业做出了自己的贡献。中国和各国人民通过长期探索特别是在日内瓦的多边外交实践，倡导了主权平等、和平和解、法治正义、开放包容、人道主义等理念和原则。这些既体现了日内瓦多边主义精神的内涵，也是中国外交的传统。

fostering new growth drivers. China will continue to be a huge market supporting world economic growth, a hot destination attracting foreign investment and a contributor to the well-being of people around the world.

Ⅲ

Geneva has a prominent place in the international relations of the modern era. The city has witnessed the development of inter-governmental organizations such as the UN and its specialized agencies, served as the venue for negotiating key agreements on hotspot issues, including the Iranian nuclear issue, Syria and the Middle East peace process, and facilitated the adoption of many international treaties and legal instruments, notably the Geneva Convention and the Comprehensive Test Ban Treaty.

After regaining its lawful seat in the UN and returning to various international organizations in Geneva in 1971, China has deepened its involvement in the governance of peace, security, development, human rights and social agenda, making its due contribution to the lofty cause of peace and development. Decades of hard work, especially multilateral diplomacy practised here in Geneva, has inspired the people in China and elsewhere to establish the notions and principles of sovereign equality, peaceful reconciliation, the rule of law and justice, openness and inclusiveness, and humanitarianism. These reflect both the Geneva

我这次访问联合国日内瓦总部，是想同各方重温历史，弘扬各方公认的外交理念，探索构建人类命运共同体这个重大命题，就建设一个更加美好的世界聆听各方意见。

世界卫生组织是负责卫生事务的联合国专门机构，为完善全球卫生治理、维护世界人民健康作出了重要贡献。卫生既是中国发展的重要方面，又是中国对外合作的重点领域。中国同世界卫生组织的合作，提升了中国卫生与健康事业水平，也对全球卫生事业作出了贡献。我期待着同陈冯富珍总干事就中国同世界卫生组织合作充分交换意见。

国际奥林匹克运动走过了100多年的历程，对实现人的全面发展，增进各国人民友谊，推动世界和平、发展、进步事业发挥了积极作用。中国始终是奥林匹克运动的积极支持者和参与者，举办了2008年北京奥运会、残奥会和2014年南京青奥会，正在积极筹办2022年北京冬奥会、冬残奥会。我

spirit of multilateralism and the fine tradition of Chinese diplomacy.

I will visit the United Nations Office at Geneva with the following goals in mind: reviewing our shared historical journey, championing the widely accepted principles of diplomacy, exploring ways to realize the vision of building a community of shared future for mankind, and seeking ideas on how we can make the world a better place.

The World Health Organization (WHO) is a specialized UN agency dedicated to global health issues. It has done its best to improve global health governance and safeguard the well-being of all people. Health is a high priority on China's development agenda and a key area of its international cooperation. Cooperation with the WHO has helped to improve China's national health programs and represents a contribution to global health endeavors. I look forward to an extensive discussion with Director General Margaret Chan on this subject.

The International Olympic Movement, in its over 100 years, has played a positive role in enhancing all-round human development, deepening friendship between nations and promoting peace, development and progress. China, a long-time supporter and member of the Olympic Movement, has hosted the Beijing 2008 Olympic and Paralympic Games and the Nanjing 2014 Youth Olympic Games, and is actively preparing for the Beijing 2022 Winter Olympic

很高兴有机会访问国际奥委会，听取巴赫主席和国际奥委会关于弘扬奥林匹克精神、推进奥林匹克运动的意见。

我期待着在瑞士同各方人士共商合作、共议创新，推动中瑞关系、中欧关系、中国同联合国的关系、中国同奥林匹克运动的关系在新的一年迎来更好发展。

and Paralympic Games. I am glad to visit the International Olympic Committee (IOC) and learn from President Thomas Bach and the IOC their ideas about promoting the Olympic spirit and advancing the Olympic Movement.

In short, I look forward to my upcoming trip to Switzerland, where I will meet people from different walks of life to promote cooperation and innovation. Hopefully, the trip will give a strong impetus to China's relations with Switzerland, Europe, the UN and the Olympic Movement in the year ahead.

三 外交署名文章的翻译原则与难点

署名文章具有政治外交属性，使用的是政治外交语言，具有典型的政治功能，翻译时需有高度的政治敏锐性，忠实传达原文信息尤为重要，即便看起来无关紧要的内容也不能擅自修改或是随意删除，更不能任意添加有悖原文的内容，以免造成误解或引发麻烦。

署名文章的翻译要尽力再现文本风格及特征，既要展现政论文体的严谨与正式，又要还原易于接受的通俗易懂的文风；既要重视宏观，传达源语文本承载的文化内涵和立场观点，又要兼顾微观，表现领导人的个体风格与思想理念。

在注重源语政治外交属性，确保文本风格再现的同时，翻译时还要具有读者意识，尽力打造读者友好型文本，因为署名文章承载的重要使命就是架起连接世界的桥梁，让世界更好地了解中国，走近中国。因此，满足目标受众期待，提升文本的可读性，符合目的语的流畅性和连贯度也是译者需要遵守的原则和攻克的难点。

综上，署名文章作为传播中国故事的重要形式，翻译时必须具有使命意识，秉承上述三个层次的原则要求，实现讲述中国故事的最佳效果。"'中国故事'蕴含丰富内容、表现多元形式，不仅包含中国的过去、现在和未来，还有中国所秉承的发展理念、所确立的制度、所走过的道路和所坚持的基本原则，更有中华民族的悠久历史、文化积淀，以及中国的基本国情、文明交往、历史传统、最深层次的精神与价值追求"[1]。海外署名文章的翻译效果直接影响到中国方案、中国声音、中国思想能否得到世界的认可，能否走进世界的中心，能否在世界格局中赢得话语权，能否获得更多主动权。署名文章的成功翻译会在很大程度上助力中国软实力的提升和中国外交话语的建构。

四 外交署名文章的英译技巧

本章选取的范例是国家主席习近平在对瑞士进行国事访问、出席世界经济论坛 2017 年年会并访问瑞士国际组织前夕，在瑞士媒体发表的题为《深化务实合作 共谋和平发展》的署名文章，发表时间为 2017 年 1 月 13 日。习近平主席的署名文章以感人肺腑、辞顺理正、入情入理而著称，深刻体现出大国领导人的风范。2014 年 3 月 23 日，习近平就任国家主席后首次在荷兰《新鹿特丹商业报》发表了题为《打开欧洲之门 携手共创繁荣》的署名文章。"据统计，从 2014 年到 2019 年，习近平主席通过 70 余家海外主流媒体在全球 50 多个国家共发表了 57 篇署名文章"[2]。这些署名文章对于增强中国国际地位、传达中国声音、拓展国际合作、获得世界认同、建构国际话语等起到关键作用，得到普遍认同和高度评价。王群认为，"习近平在海外发表署名文章，不仅是个人外交理念、领导风格、语言特色的集中展现，更是为了增加与公众的接触和交流，使其更清楚中国的立场主张、访问目的和文化魅力，更好回应国外舆论的猜测和不安"[3]。张树军、贾亮认为，"综观习近平数十篇海外署名文章，无论内容还是形式，都独具魅力，堪称习近平外交理念、领导思维和语言风格在中国对外传播场域的体现、拓展和延伸"[4]。本章从署名文章的翻译角度出发，重点关注署名文章中的时政术语和四字结构的翻译，在解读中国顶层设计、原则立场、语言特色等的同时，探求相关内容的翻译技巧，总结讲好中国故事的可行性方式，为外交署名文章的英译提供建设性思考。

---

1 张树军，贾亮. 2017. 在当地主流媒体刊发署名文章：彰显对外传播新理念新方法——习近平主席海外署名文章特色解读. 中国记者，（12）：53-58.
2 崔艳红. 2020. 习近平海外署名文章与中国国家形象的国际表达. 区域与全球发展，（1）：63-76.
3 王群. 2019. 习近平海外署名文章外交意蕴与价值旨归. 当代世界社会主义问题，（3）：11-19.
4 张树军，贾亮. 2017. 在当地主流媒体刊发署名文章：彰显对外传播新理念新方法——习近平主席海外署名文章特色解读. 中国记者，（12）：53-58.

1 外交署名文章中时政术语的英译

时政术语是时事政治术语的简称，是国家或世界发展不同时期的政治产物。时政术语主要指出现在时政文体中具有特殊意义的核心关键词，这些关键词相对固定，政策性强，时间性强，严密性强，对传达政治文献的内容和思想起到重要作用。由于中西历史文化背景、政治经济体制、社会意识形态方面差异巨大，译者在翻译时需要根据英语语言特点，选择既符合我国国情又符合英语特点，同时能让目标读者易于理解和接受的处理方法。时政术语包括世界通用的术语以及带有国家特色的术语。以上面范例为例，前者包括"民粹主义""贸易保护主义""完全市场经济地位""自由贸易区""战略伙伴关系"等，而后者包括"创新、协调、绿色、开放、共享的发展理念""供给侧结构性改革""义利观""真、实、亲、诚理念"等。相较而言，前者比较容易处理，因为有全球通用译文，只要利用翻译工具查找对应译文即可；后者则比较复杂，因为涉及中国特色表达，且没有对应目标语可以直接移用，翻译时需要根据实际情况形成标准而恰切的外交话语，保证译文的忠实度、可读性、时效性等。

纵观习近平主席发表的署名文章可见，很多时政术语都是国际通用表达，且已形成相对固定形式。有经验的译者对相关译文耳熟能详，因而无需借助翻译工具，从个人积累或是记忆储存库中直接调用即可。从这些已有对应文本的翻译效果来看，大多译文采用直译法，且多为字对字等值翻译。习近平主席的署名文章《深化务实合作 共谋和平发展》中有不少这样的例子："自由贸易区"译为 Free Trade Area；"自由贸易协定"译为 the Free Trade Agreement；"亚洲基础设施投资银行"译为 the Asian Infrastructure Investment Bank (AIIB)；"民粹主义"译为 populism；"贸易保护主义"译为 trade protectionism；"对话和磋商机制"译为 the dialogue and consultation mechanisms；"全球卫生治理"译为 global health governance。

当然，不可能所有通用术语都能百分百直译，或有绝对的对等译文，在表达形式上会有所差异，差异程度视上下文语境或是语言表达习惯而定。比如，"互免持外交护照人员签证"译为 mutual visa exemption for diplomatic passport-holders of our two countries，"签证"的位置被提前，后接 for 的短语结构，明确免持对象。再如，"人文交流"译为 people-to-people exchanges，强调人与人之间的交流。事实上，人文交流有广义与狭义之分。广义的人文交流指文化交流，人文即人类文化的简称，如在十九大报告中提到的人文交流就是广义："加强中外人文交流，以我为主、兼收并蓄。推进国际传播能力建设，讲好中国故事，展现真实、立体、全面的中国，提高国家文化软实力。"与此不同的是，在《深化务实合作 共谋和平发展》中，人文交流则为狭义，是指人员文化性交流，强调人与人之间的密切交流。

> **原文** 加强<u>人文交流</u>。以签署中瑞新的文化合作协议、中国在伯尔尼建立中国文化中心、共同举办中瑞旅游年为契机，扩大两国民间和青年交流，便利两国人员往来，加强两国旅游、冬季运动、职业教育、地方交往等领域合作，巩固中瑞关系社会基础。

> **译文** Expanding <u>people-to-people exchanges</u>. With the signing of the new cultural cooperation agreement, the establishment of the Chinese cultural center in Bern and the launch of the year of tourism, we are well placed to expand people-to-people and youth exchanges, facilitate personnel visits, and beef up cooperation in tourism, winter sports and vocational education and at the subnational level. All this will help cement public support for China-Switzerland relations.

根据上文语境，人文交流强调的是"扩大两国民间和青年交流，便利两国人员往来"，属于人员之间的交流，故翻译为 people-to-people exchanges。当然，也有出于语言清晰度、流畅度等因素考虑，稍作调整，比如"完全市场经济地位"译成 a full market economy，译文省略了"地位"未翻，但并未影响传达内涵及效果。

此外，值得注意的是，"伙伴关系"（partnership）在我国领导人署名文章中出现频率很高。不同的"伙伴关系"代表了不同的合作与交流领域及程度等，同时也表达出双方的友好及合作立场，体现双方彼此的尊重和认可。中国与他国的"伙伴关系"一般以双方元首联合声明为标志确立。"伙伴关系"源于"冷战"结束之后，北约提出"和平伙伴关系计划"，目的是与非北约国建立"伙伴关系"，由此产生"伙伴关系"的提法。就我国而言，"伙伴关系"强调相互尊重、求同存异、合作共赢。中国一直沿用"伙伴关系"定位双边关系。在《深化务实合作 共谋和平发展》中，习近平主席特别强调了中瑞之间的"创新战略伙伴关系"的特别意义。如下文：

> **原文** 去年4月，我同来中国进行国事访问的施奈德-阿曼联邦主席一道，宣布建立中瑞<u>创新战略伙伴关系</u>，这是中国首次同外国建立以创新为标志的战略伙伴关系。中瑞关系进入新的发展阶段。

> **译文** During his state visit to China last April, President Johann Schneider-Ammann and I announced the establishment of <u>an innovative strategic</u>

partnership between the two countries, the first of its kind for China featuring innovation. This marked a new phase of our bilateral relations.

2016年4月中瑞双方共同发表了《中华人民共和国和瑞士联邦关于建立创新战略伙伴关系的联合声明》，标志着"创新战略伙伴关系"的首次创立。习近平主席会见瑞士联邦主席施奈德–阿曼时指出："开拓创新是中瑞关系最突出的特点。"2016年不但见证了中国"十三五"规划的开局，同样见证了瑞士新一届政府开始执政。创新在我国"十三五"规划中处于国家发展全局的核心位置，外交也围绕这一战略核心为全面发展助力。瑞士素有"创新之国"之称，其经济技术实力连续多年荣登"全球创新指数"榜首。把中国的创新驱动发展战略与瑞士的创新优势相结合，在各个领域展开通力合作，能够力促两国经济发展，创造更多高端技术成果，大大提升双边关系。"创新战略伙伴关系"译为 an innovative strategic partnership，属于对等直译。当然，随着两国合作的深化，关系的深入，这种双边关系也会逐步升级。比如，2019年6月11日，习近平主席在对吉尔吉斯共和国进行国事访问并出席上海合作组织成员国元首理事会第十九次会议前夕，在吉尔吉斯斯坦《言论报》、"卡巴尔"国家通讯社发表题为《愿中吉友谊之树枝繁叶茂、四季常青》的署名文章，其中有这样一句：

原文 6年前，我首次访问美丽的吉尔吉斯斯坦，同吉方共叙友谊、共商合作、共话未来，开启中吉<u>战略伙伴关系</u>新时代。6年后，我欣喜地看到，两国关系已提升至<u>全面战略伙伴关系</u>。中吉友好合作事业正如仲夏时节的山川草原，充满生机和活力。

译文 I first visited this beautiful country six years ago. The discussions I had with Kyrgyz leaders on the friendship and cooperation between our two countries and on the future growth of the China-Kyrgyzstan relationship ushered this relationship into a new era of <u>strategic partnership</u>. Now six years on, it is heartening to see that this relationship has been upgraded further to <u>a comprehensive strategic partnership</u>, and that our friendship and cooperation are brimming with vigor and vitality like the mountains and grasslands in the prime of summer.

习主席特别强调了中吉两国伙伴关系由"战略伙伴关系"（strategic partnership）升级为"全面战略伙伴关系"（comprehensive strategic partnership），表明两国关系的良好发展势头和广阔合作前景。战略合作伙伴关系基于高度信任基础之上，强调伙伴成员间共享竞争优势以及利益的长期性、战略性协同发展。"战略"（strategic）

强调在双边或多边国际活动中，在重大问题上有交集，体现双方关系重要，彼此合作领域高端；而升级后增加的"全面"（comprehensive）（有时也用全方位，all-round）则强调合作领域的多元性、范围的广泛性。以上两种伙伴关系都有标准译文，具有统一性和固定性，可以直接移植。其他类型的"伙伴关系"还有很多种，英汉对照如下：

汉语	英语
全天候战略合作伙伴关系	all-weather strategic partnership of cooperation
全面战略协作伙伴关系	comprehensive strategic partnership of coordination
全面战略合作伙伴关系	comprehensive strategic partnership of cooperation
全方位战略伙伴关系	all-round strategic partnership
创新全面伙伴关系	innovative comprehensive partnership
睦邻友好合作关系	the good-neighborly relations and cooperation
全方位友好合作伙伴关系	all-round partnership of friendship and cooperation
全面友好合作伙伴关系	comprehensive friendly partnership of cooperation
友好合作伙伴关系	friendly cooperative partnership
全方位合作伙伴关系	all-round partnership of cooperation
全面合作伙伴关系	comprehensive cooperative partnership
面向未来的新型合作伙伴关系	future-oriented new-type cooperative partnership

国际通用时政术语翻译相对容易，只需准确掌握通用译文，翻译时直接移植即可。时政术语翻译的复杂性主要在于其国别属性。时政术语往往紧跟时代发展，基于国情产生，具有很强的政策性，体现国别的差异性。各国政治、经济、文化等在不同时期的发展变化在时政术语中得以体现。因此，如果没有相关背景知识，目标受众将很难理解其中内涵。以中国为例，在进行对外政治、经济等宣传时，必然使用具有中国特色的时政术语。由于英文词典中罕见对应表达，译者在翻译过程中不能随意增删其中措辞和内容，也不能避而不译，而应依照目标语言的习惯用法，用适恰易懂的语言反映中国政策内涵。比如，本章范例中的典型翻译：

原文 中国一直同包括欧洲国家在内的世界各国一道，探索应对全球发展面临的挑战。我们主动适应外部环境变化和中国经济发展新常态，以创新、协调、绿色、开放、共享的发展理念为指引，推进供给侧结构性改革，培育增长新动能，取得积极成效。

> **译文** China has been working with European countries, among others, to address the challenges facing global development. We have taken the initiative to adapt to the fluid external environment and the "new normal" of the Chinese economy. We have followed <u>the vision of innovative, coordinated, green, open and shared development</u>, and made good progress in deepening <u>supply-side structural reform</u> and fostering new growth drivers.

2015年10月，习近平总书记在制定"十三五"规划的建议说明中指出："发展理念是发展行动的先导，是管全局、管根本、管方向、管长远的东西，是发展思路、发展方向、发展着力点的集中体现。发展理念搞对了，目标任务就好定了，政策举措也就跟着好定了。"随后，中共十八届五中全会首次鲜明提出创新、协调、绿色、开放、共享的发展理念，其中创新被确立为五大发展理念之首，成为引领国家全局发展的第一动力。五大发展理念不但是全面建成小康社会的重要保障，也对中国外交具有重要指导作用，在中国外交战略中具有充分体现。上文译例中，"创新、协调、绿色、开放、共享"的发展理念译为 the vision of innovative, coordinated, green, open and shared development，基本遵循了忠实原则，准确传达原文内涵。就表达形式而言，因语言结构差异，译文采用后置定语修饰中心词，而汉语惯用前置修饰语修饰中心词。因此，译文既兼顾了内涵准确，又确保了可读易懂效果。

上例中另外一个典型的富有中国政策性内涵的术语是"供给侧结构性改革"。2016年1月26日，国家主席习近平主持召开中央财经领导小组第十二次会议，研究供给侧结构性改革方案。2017年10月18日，习近平主席在十九大报告中强调了深化供给侧结构性改革的重要性。2018年3月5日，李克强总理在2018年《政府工作报告》中将"发展壮大新动能"和"加快制造强国建设"列为供给侧改革任务前两位，加快制造业升级，培育经济新动能。在中央财经领导小组第十二次会议的讲话中，习近平主席强调，供给侧结构性改革的根本目的是提高社会生产力水平，落实好以人民为中心的发展思想。要在适度扩大总需求的同时，去产能、去库存、去杠杆、降成本、补短板，从生产领域加强优质供给，减少无效供给，扩大有效供给，提高供给结构适应性和灵活性，提高全要素生产率，使供给体系更好适应需求结构变化。"供给侧结构性改革"采用直译法译为 supply-side structural reform。尽管译文没有具体解释术语的政策内涵，但根据译文传达的意思能够看出改革的关键所在。其他类似兼顾中国理念及清晰易懂要求的译例还有"真、实、亲、诚理念"（the principle of sincerity, real results, affinity, and good faith）、"推进精准扶贫、精准脱贫"（implement targeted poverty reduction and alleviation measures）、"互联互通"（connectivity）、"新型国际关系"（the new type of international relations）等，这些翻译皆明晰晓畅，便于接受，不易产生歧义和误解。

在习近平主席的署名文章中还有一个关键术语出现率特别高，即"命运共同体"。2011年中国政府公布《中国的和平发展》白皮书中首次提出："不同制度、不同类型、不同发展阶段的国家相互依存、利益交融，形成'你中有我、我中有你'的命运共同体。"2012年12月5日，习近平主席在北京人民大会堂同在华工作的外国专家代表座谈时，再次强调："国际社会日益成为一个你中有我、我中有你的命运共同体。"人类共享一个地球，各国共处一个世界。面对世界经济的复杂形势和全球性问题，任何国家都不可能独善其身。2017年中共十九大明确指出："坚持和平发展道路，推动构建人类命运共同体"，正式将"命运共同体"的理念写入大会报告。2018年3月11日，第十三届全国人民代表大会第一次会议通过宪法修正案，将序言中"发展同各国的外交关系和经济、文化的交流"修改为"发展同各国的外交关系和经济、文化交流，推动构建人类命运共同体"。"命运共同体"是中国政府反复强调的关于人类社会的新理念，是中国特色大国外交关键词，在很多国际重大场合得以宣扬和阐发，理论内涵逐步丰富，从最初国家之间的命运共同体，深化到区域内命运共同体，再到人类命运共同体。比如，在题为《深化务实合作 共谋和平发展》的署名文章中，习近平主席指出：

原文 我这次访问联合国日内瓦总部，是想同各方重温历史，弘扬各方公认的外交理念，探索构建<u>人类命运共同体</u>这个重大命题，就建设一个更加美好的世界聆听各方意见。

译文 I will visit the United Nations Office at Geneva with the following goals in mind: reviewing our shared historical journey, championing the widely accepted principles of diplomacy, exploring ways to realize the vision of building <u>a community of shared future for mankind</u>, and seeking ideas on how we can make the world a better place.

"人类命运共同体"追求本国利益时兼顾他国合理关切，在谋求本国发展中促进各国共同发展。这一全球价值观包含相互依存的国际权力观、共同利益观、可持续发展观和全球治理观。译文 a community of shared future for mankind 对术语内涵把握到位，表达恰切，尤其 community 和 shared 准确再现内涵，表达中国坚持合作共赢，推动和平发展，倡导相互联系、相互依存的外交理念。这一理念在习近平主席署名文章中多次强调，为应对全球共同挑战和建设美好世界提供"中国方案"。再以下面几例为证：

原文 中希应该挖掘古老文明的深邃智慧，展现文明古国的历史担当，共同推动构建相互尊重、公平正义、合作共赢的新型国际关系，共同推动构建<u>人类命运共同体</u>。

译文 China and Greece, each with a strong sense of history and responsibility, can tap our civilizations for wisdom and build a new type of international relations featuring mutual respect, equity, justice and mutually beneficial cooperation. Together, we can usher in <u>a community with a shared future for all mankind</u>.

原文 我们要做休戚与共的发展伙伴。中国和巴拿马同为发展中国家，有着相同历史遭遇，面临共同的发展任务。双方要同心协力，推动构建相互尊重、公平正义、合作共赢的新型国际关系，推动构建<u>人类命运共同体</u>。

译文 Let us be development partners, come rain or shine. Both being developing countries, China and Panama have similar historical experiences and face common development tasks. We need to work together to promote a new type of international relations featuring mutual respect, fairness, justice and win-win cooperation and build <u>a community with a shared future for mankind</u>.

原文 加强双方在联合国、二十国集团、世界贸易组织、七十七国集团等多边框架内协作，支持经济全球化和多边贸易体制，维护新兴市场国家和广大发展中国家根本利益，为维护世界和平、建设开放型世界经济、推动构建<u>人类命运共同体</u>作出应有贡献。

译文 Coordination under multilateral frameworks will be strengthened, including at the United Nations, G20, WTO and the Group of 77, to underline support for economic globalization and the multilateral trading system and safeguard the fundamental interests of emerging markets and developing countries. Together, we will make our contributions to maintaining world peace and building an open world economy and <u>a community with a shared future for mankind</u>.

上述可见,"人类命运共同体"理念在外交领域中得以广泛阐释,除一例译文稍有不同,翻成 a community with a shared future for all mankind 外,其余一律译为 a community with a shared future for mankind,体现术语的统一性、固定性和规范性。其他"命运共同体"相关的术语表述还有很多,比如习近平在吉尔吉斯斯坦《言论报》、"卡巴尔"国家通讯社发表题为《愿中吉友谊之树枝繁叶茂、四季常青》的署名文章中有"上海合作组织命运共同体"(SCO community with a shared future),在阿根廷《号角报》发表题为《开创中阿关系新时代》的署名文章中有"中拉命运共同体"(a community with a shared future between China and Latin American countries),在塞内加尔《太阳报》发表题为《中国和塞内加尔团结一致》的署名文章中有"中非命运共同体"(China-Africa community with a shared future),在卢旺达《新时代报》发表题为《中卢友谊情比山高》的署名文章中有"中卢、中非命运共同体"(a community with a shared future between our two countries and between China and Africa as a whole)等等,展现出"命运共同体"理念在不同外交场合的广泛延伸和丰富发展。

同样值得一提的是,2017年11月13日,在对老挝人民民主共和国进行国事访问之际,习近平主席在老挝《人民报》《巴特寮报》《万象时报》发表题为《携手打造中老具有战略意义的命运共同体》的署名文章。文中从四个方面强调了中老构建命运共同体的重大意义,具体如下:

原文	我们要加强战略沟通,打造互尊互信的命运共同体。
译文	We need to strengthen strategic communication and build a community of shared future based on mutual respect and mutual trust.
原文	我们要深化战略对接,打造互帮互助的命运共同体。
译文	We need to enhance the complementarity of our development strategies and build a community of shared future through mutual assistance.
原文	我们要拓展务实合作,打造互惠互利的命运共同体。
译文	We need to expand practical cooperation and build a community of shared future for mutual benefit.
原文	我们要扩大人文交流,打造互学互鉴的命运共同体。

译文 We need to increase people-to-people exchange and build a community of shared future featuring mutual learning.

围绕战略沟通、战略对接、务实合作、人文交流四大方面，习主席提出建构中老"互尊互信""互帮互助""互惠互利""互学互鉴"的命运共同体的宏伟蓝图。译文考虑到原文工整对称的表达形式，保留了由"我们""打造"两个关键词引领的字数相等、结构相同的平行结构，准确传达了原文内涵。与此同时，受英文表达习惯所限，兼顾目标语接受效果，"互尊互信""互帮互助""互利互惠""互学互鉴"由前置修饰语挪移成后置修饰语，译文"based on mutual respect and mutual trust, through mutual assistance, for mutual benefit, featuring mutual learning"打破了原文工整的四字结构，以多样化方式灵活传达原意。总体而言，译文通顺晓畅，虽未百分百传达原文的形与神，但效果接近，易于读者接受。

时政术语另一值得探讨的一点是缩略语的频繁使用。缩略词的特点是简洁凝练、高度概括，常用数字词的缩写方式。翻译缩略词时需要考虑深层内涵，而不能单纯停留在词汇的字面意义。翻译重点是要首先将缩写表达法的内容领会彻底，然后直接将其所包含的具体内容全部译出，避免直译缩写词汇或数字所带来的歧义。对于国际常用缩略语而言，因其广泛的普遍性和认知度，翻译时用通用全称或是缩略词皆可。而针对中国特色缩略语而言，使用全称或者解释性翻译的处理方式比较普遍。再看上述习近平主席署名文章《愿中吉友谊之树枝繁叶茂、四季常青》中的译文：

原文 我们愿同吉方密切国际合作，加强在联合国、上海合作组织、亚信等多边框架内的沟通和协调，共同维护以联合国宪章宗旨和原则为基础的国际关系基本准则，支持多边主义，推进经济全球化进程，推动构建新型国际关系和人类命运共同体。

译文 China wants to step up international cooperation with Kyrgyzstan. We will strengthen communication and coordination at the United Nations, the Shanghai Cooperation Organization (SCO), the Conference on Interaction and Confidence Building Measures in Asia (CICA) and other multilateral frameworks, uphold basic norms governing international relations based on the purposes and principles of the UN Charter, support multilateralism, advance economic globalization, and promote a new type of international relations and a community with a shared future for mankind.

"亚信"的全称是"亚洲相互协作与信任措施会议"，也经常简称为"亚信会议"。亚信是1992年10月5日由哈萨克斯坦首任总统纳扎尔巴耶夫在第47届联合国大会上倡议建立的亚洲安全问题论坛，致力于制定和落实旨在增进亚洲和平、安全与稳定的多边信任措施，加强相关领域合作。译文the Conference on Interaction and Confidence Building Measures in Asia (CICA) 将会议全称和简称一并给出，信息清晰准确，体现鲜明的受众意识，便于目标读者掌握。此外，上海合作组织也用同样方式译为the Shanghai Cooperation Organization (SCO)，同具清晰明了的效果。当然，如果下文再次出现同一术语名称时，翻译常常运用CICA与SCO等缩略语形式。与以上两例不同，"联合国宪章"译为the UN Charter，直接用UN缩略方式，而未给出全称the United Nations，一是因为UN已达普及化国际认知度，二是因为在联合国网站公布的官方名称用的是UN缩略形式。综上，如果缩略语已达国际普及程度，世界各地的受众都耳熟能详，完全可以直接使用缩略形式，再如EU、WTO、WHO等，但如果尚未形成国际普遍认知度，翻译时用全称或是全称加缩略语的形式更便于受众理解和接受。

此外，数字类缩略词在外交时政术语中也比较常见，也是中国政策表达的独特之处。在翻译这类缩略语时，不能仅仅停留形式表层，直译字面意思，而应根据内涵和语境采用适当翻译技巧。如"三股势力"在习近平主席署名文章中经常出现：

原文	我们要全力深化打击"<u>三股势力</u>"和跨国有组织犯罪、禁毒、网络安全等领域合作，更好维护两国和本地区安全稳定。
译文	We need to do all we can to deepen cooperation on fighting the three forces of <u>terrorism, separatism and extremism</u> as well as transnational organized crime, and on narcotics control and cybersecurity, thus providing greater security and stability for both our countries and our region.
原文	吉方也在台湾、涉疆、打击"<u>三股势力</u>"等问题上一贯给予中方坚定支持和有力配合。
译文	Likewise, Kyrgyzstan has rendered China full support and cooperation on issues related to Taiwan, Xinjiang and the fight against <u>terrorism, separatism and extremism</u>.
原文	我们愿同吉方加强安全合作，践行共同、综合、合作、可持续的安全观，合力打击"<u>三股势力</u>"、贩毒、跨国有组织犯罪，维护两国人民生命财产安全，共同营造地区和谐稳定的安全环境。

译文 China wants to strengthen security cooperation with Kyrgyzstan. We will follow the vision for common, comprehensive, cooperative and sustainable security in our joint fight against <u>terrorism, separatism and extremism</u> and against drug-trafficking and transnational organized crime to protect the life and property of our people and foster a regional security environment defined by harmony and stability.

原文 上海合作组织高度重视安全、经济、人文、对外交往等领域合作，严厉打击"三股势力"，着力深化共建"一带一路"同各国发展战略和地区合作倡议对接，不断加强贸易、投资、互联互通、能源、创新、人文等领域合作，大力拓展同观察员国、对话伙伴以及联合国等国际组织的伙伴关系，致力于打造更加紧密的上海合作组织命运共同体。

译文 The SCO has prioritized cooperation in security, economy, people-to-people exchanges, and outreach to non-SCO members. It has taken tough measures to crack down on <u>terrorism, separatism and extremism</u>. With a focus on deepening the synergy between Belt and Road cooperation, development strategies of individual countries, and regional cooperation initiatives, the SCO has kept scaling up cooperation in trade, investment, connectivity, energy, innovation and people-to-people exchanges. It has also been expanding partnerships with observer states, dialogue partners, and international organizations like the United Nations. All these efforts have contributed to our vision of a closer SCO community with a shared future.

上述四例文将"三股势力"皆译为 terrorism, separatism and extremism，采用解释性意译，选择易懂的方式直接表明具体内容，让受众直接获得术语所指，清晰明了，增强阅读和理解效果。典型的解释性意译还有"三去一降一补"的翻译：five priority tasks—cutting overcapacity, reducing excess inventory, deleveraging, lowering costs, and strengthening areas of weakness—thereby improving the composition of supply。"三去一降一补"的政策指的是去产能、去库存、去杠杆、降成本、补短板五大任务。five priority tasks 点明政策涉及五大任务，随后对数字缩略词的解释性处理更能让目标语受众清晰了解中国政策，降低表达的复杂性，使译文更加易懂。还有一种常用的方式是直译加括号注释，比如"两个一百年"奋斗目标译为 the two "centenary goals" (to complete the building of a society of initial prosperity in all respects when the CPC celebrates its centenary in 2021 and turn China into a modern socialist country that is prosperous, strong, democratic, culturally advanced and harmonious when China marks its centennial in 2049)。括号中的解释性内容虽然篇幅较长，但有传达中国政策内涵的必要性，让目标受众更加清楚中国发展的规划蓝图，从而了解中国发展趋势和潜能。

当然，时政术语的稳定性和固定性特征是相对的，随着改革深入推进，社会不断发展，时政术语的内涵也会与时俱进，发生相应改变。因此，译文也得随之做出调整，准确传达新增内涵。比如"小康社会"的翻译就经过几次修订。中国改革开放初期，邓小平同志率先提出"小康"的概念及在20世纪末我国达到"小康社会"的构想。党的十二大正式引用了"小康"概念，并将其定为20世纪末的战略目标。在"小康社会"人民的生活达到"小康水平"，这是指在温饱的基础上，深入提升生活质量，最终达到丰衣足食。2002年，党的十六大提出全面建设惠及十几亿人口的更高水平的小康社会的奋斗目标，设定的实现时间为2020年。2012年党的十八大再次进行全面部署，把"全面建设"改为"全面建成"。虽只一字之差，但却体现出着重点从建设过程向实现结果转变的战略提升。早期的"小康社会"多翻译成 a relatively comfortable society，强调在温饱基础上生活质量的进一步提升，但随着十六大全面建设惠及十几亿人口的更高水平的小康社会的奋斗目标的设定，到十八大将"全面建设"改为"全面建成"，"小康社会"的内涵发生改变，故而翻译相应调整，前后出现的译文包括 the building of a well-off society in an all-round way，the building of a moderately prosperous society in all respects，the building of a society of initial prosperity in all respects。后两种是当下领导人外交或国际活动中比较通用的翻译版本，其概念阐释更为具体清晰，对内涵把握更为贴近。

综上，时政术语翻译因其特殊的政治内涵，承载了宣传国家思想、政策的重任，翻译时需特别慎重，尤其是外交时政术语，涉及中国故事的讲述，中国声音的传达，中国话语的建构，任何译者都应切忌盲走两端：要么极端追求译文的流畅而牺牲原文真意或者原文风格；要么极端追求忠于原文而造成译文晦涩难懂，难以品味。因此，优秀的译者需要在归化（domestication）和异化（foreignization）之间做好权衡，争取最大化保持原风原意，同时赢得受众的认同。

2 外交署名文章中四字结构的英译

四字结构是汉语一种独特的语言现象，沿袭了古汉语的语法特点，结构多变，简洁明快，音节整齐，富含音韵，生动形象，常具修辞功能。四字结构在政论文体中非常多见，包括四字成语、四字词组和四字时政术语三种类型。常见的四字成语有"与时俱进""同舟共济""休戚与共""集思广益"等；四字词组有"绿色环保""平等相待""世代友好""创新共赢"等；四字时政术语有"简政放权""社会保障""主权平等""一带一路""减税降费""互联互通"等。四字成语和四字时政术语都是固定结构，具有稳定性，不能随意改动。因外交署名文章具有政治文体的严谨性，四字结构的使用能够体现时政语言准确性、简明性、概括性、严密性等特点，同时可以产生一定的修辞效果。本章习近平主席署名文章范文中，使用了不少四字结构，举例如下：

原文	中瑞两国虽然<u>相距遥远</u>，但瑞士对中国人民来说并不陌生。瑞士被誉为"欧洲屋脊"和"科技创新之国"，<u>风光秀美</u>，<u>人民勤劳</u>，<u>经济发达</u>。
译文	Despite <u>the great distance</u> between our two countries, the Chinese people are no strangers to Switzerland. Known as the roof of Europe and a leader in innovation, Switzerland boasts <u>beautiful landscape</u>, <u>hard-working people</u> and <u>an advanced economy</u>.
原文	在支持人民币国际化、参与创立亚洲基础设施投资银行、互免持外交护照人员签证等方面，中瑞合作展现了<u>与时俱进</u>、<u>敢为人先</u>的创新精神，对中欧合作发挥了示范作用。
译文	Our two countries have taken <u>pioneering</u> and <u>innovative</u> steps in our engagement with each other, such as Switzerland's support for the internationalization of the RMB, its participation in the founding of the Asian Infrastructure Investment Bank (AIIB) and mutual visa exemption for diplomatic passport-holders of our two countries. These have set a good example for cooperation between China and other European countries.
原文	——创新务实合作。推动两国企业、高校、科研机构开展创新合作，拓展<u>节能环保</u>、<u>气候变化</u>、知识产权、金融、<u>生态农业</u>、<u>社会保障</u>等领域合作。
译文	The newly established Sino-Swiss High-level Innovative Dialogue will enable us to promote collaboration between our companies, universities and research institutes and in <u>energy conservation, environmental protection</u>,

climate change, IPR protection, financial services, eco-agriculture and social security.

原文 瑞士达沃斯世界闻名。每逢新年伊始，来自世界不同地区、国家、领域的各界人士在此聚会，交流观点、碰撞思想，吸引着世界的目光。特别是国际金融危机爆发以来，世界经济论坛年会成为各方集思广益、对话合作的重要平台。这种同舟共济、共克时艰的精神为促进世界经济复苏发挥了积极作用。

译文 Davos is a well-known town. At the start of each new year, people from different regions, countries and backgrounds would come and meet here. Such a meeting of minds has always been under international spotlight. This has been especially so in the wake of the global financial crisis, when the WEF annual meetings have emerged as a major platform for brainstorming, dialogue and cooperation. Sticking together in times of difficulty, this is the very spirit that has helped to put the world economy on the path of recovery.

原文 这是因为两国人民彼此怀有友好感情，更是因为双方相互尊重各自选择的社会制度和发展道路，秉承平等相待、创新共赢的合作精神发展双边关系。

译文 This is made possible by our people's mutual goodwill, by a shared commitment to growing our bilateral relations on the basis of equality, innovation and win-win cooperation, and above all, by our respect for each other's social system and development path.

原文 中国和各国人民通过长期探索特别是在日内瓦的多边外交实践，倡导了主权平等、和平和解、法治正义、开放包容、人道主义等理念和原则。

译文 Decades of hard work, especially multilateral diplomacy practised here in Geneva, has inspired the people in China and elsewhere to establish the notions and principles of sovereign equality, peaceful reconciliation, the rule of law and justice, openness and inclusiveness, and humanitarianism.

考察上述译文可见，四字结构尽管短小精悍，朗朗上口，言简意丰，具有艺术表现力和音乐美感，但因其独特的汉语特色翻译时很难保留原有结构或字对字直译。汉语是语义型、分析型语言，句子与句子、短语与短语之间并无明显的连接词，需要依靠上下文语境理解表达内涵。与汉语不同,英语是语法型语言,素有"链语"之称,主要依靠介词、从句等建构的衔接来实现连贯效果。因此,简单直译会使英语译文直接变成中式英语,使其附带汉语散句特点,这样有违目标语言习惯,造成受众接受困难,最终导致信息传达失败。

相较而言,偏正结构,尤其是"定语 + 中心词"的偏正结构,采用直译法翻译的情况较多,如气候变化(climate change)、知识产权(IPR protection)、生态农业(eco-agriculture)、社会保障(social security)、重要平台(a major platform)、社会制度(social system)、发展道路(development path)、和平和解(peaceful reconciliation)。除知识产权(IPR protection)采用增译法,添加了 protection,使源语内涵清晰化外,上述其他"定语 + 中心词"四字结构都采用直译移植方式处理。当然也有特殊情况,比如友好情感(goodwill)和人道主义(humanitarianism)用单个词语译出,前者根据理解采用意译,而后者则是固定术语,采用通用译文。至于"状语 + 中心词"的偏正结构的翻译则根据上下文和英语表达习惯灵活处理。为了与"创新共赢"的译文(innovation and win-win cooperation)形成平行结构,"平等相待"(equality)采用了词性转换法和简化法译成名词 equality。此外,并列四字结构使用直译的情况也较多。比如"法治正义"译为 the rule of law and justice,"开放包容"译为 openness and inclusiveness,"创新共赢"译为 innovation and win-win cooperation 等,三个结构前后两部分都采用并列名词或名词词组进行翻译,中间用 and 连接,直接传达原文内涵和结构信息。

动宾、动补和主谓四字结构整体处理比较灵活,根据上下文语境需求选择适当的处理方法,常常涉及合并、简化、转换等翻译技巧。比如"风光秀美,人民勤劳,经济发达"主谓结构转换成偏正结构,译为 beautiful landscape, hard-working people and an advanced economy。再如下例中的"繁花似锦,绿草如茵"也是主谓结构,同样译成偏正结构 blooming flowers and lush grass:

原文 六月的天山<u>繁花似锦,绿草如茵</u>。

译文 Strewn with <u>blooming flowers</u> and <u>lush grass</u>, the Tianshan Mountains offer an enchanting view at this time of the year.

上述本章范例中还可见政治文体中常用的汉语四字排比结构,又称"连珠四字句"。这种排比结构气势恢宏、词义丰富、文采生动、表达连贯,常能营造强烈的修辞效果。但是,如果英译时直译照搬这种结构,会违背"链语"思维,造成表现力欠佳,语句不地道。如果要简洁、流畅、准确地传递信息,翻译时须先弄清语篇中各信息之间的逻辑关系，如果直译移植影响接受效果，可以采取简化、合并、重组等方式处理，达到语义上的准确和连贯。如上例中"中瑞合作展现了与时俱进、敢为人先的创新精神"的处理就比较典型，译为"Our two countries have taken pioneering and innovative steps in our engagement with each other"，"与时俱进、敢为人先"同为"创新精神"的定语，根据上下文语境及结构特征，简化合并译为 pioneering and innovative，构成单字平行结构。译文简洁易懂，避免四字直译的冗长和繁琐。事实上，并非所有四字结构都要简化译为单字，四字结构的翻译可长可短，关键要把握上下文语境，根据英语表达习惯和可读性译出。

> **原文** 中国唐代伟大诗人李白的绚丽诗篇在两国<u>家喻户晓</u>、<u>广为传诵</u>。2000多年的<u>历史积淀</u>，铸就了两国人民<u>牢不可破</u>的<u>深情厚谊</u>。

> **译文** The great poet Li Bai, living some 1,300 years ago in the Tang Dynasty, <u>is a household name in our two countries and his poems are widely quoted</u> by the Chinese and Kyrgyz alike. In the <u>course</u> of over two millennia, interactions like these have forged <u>an unbreakable bond of amity</u> between our peoples.

在此例中，"家喻户晓、广为传诵"的译文较长，比较充分地忠于原意，而"历史积淀""牢不可破"和"深厚情谊"则采用简化法"短译"，分别译为 course 和 an unbreakable bond of amity。当然，要按英语思维方式组织语言，除了简化法，也会采用重组法对源语结构进行调整，典型的例子有：

> **原文** 只要我们秉持<u>世代友好</u>，<u>矢志不渝</u>推进合作，中吉友好事业必将如<u>巍巍天山</u>上<u>苍劲挺拔</u>的<u>雪岭云杉</u>，<u>枝繁叶茂</u>、<u>四季常青</u>。

> **译文** I believe that as long as we <u>stay committed to our longstanding amity</u> and cooperation, the friendship between China and Kyrgyzstan will <u>endure and thrive like the mighty, evergreen spruce trees on the majestic Tianshan Mountains</u>.

"世代友好，矢志不渝"被简化合并译为"stay committed to our longstanding amity"，"巍巍天山""苍劲挺拔""雪岭云杉""枝繁叶茂""四季常青"则根据英语思维方式进行了重组，译为"endure and thrive like the mighty, evergreen spruce trees on the majestic Tianshan Mountains"，其中"苍劲挺拔""枝繁叶茂""四季常青"又简化译为单个词 might、thrive 及 endure。

此外，有时受汉语思维和欣赏习惯的影响，四字平行结构具有"同义反复"的特点。再以本章范例中的句子为例：

原文 每逢新年伊始，来自世界不同地区、国家、领域的各界人士在此聚会，<u>交流观点，碰撞思想</u>，吸引着世界的目光……这种<u>同舟共济、共克时艰</u>的精神为促进世界经济复苏发挥了积极作用。

译文 At the start of each new year, people from different regions, countries and backgrounds would come and meet here. <u>Such a meeting of minds</u> has always been under international spotlight… <u>Sticking together in times of difficulty</u>, this is the very spirit that has helped to put the world economy on the path of recovery.

"交流观点，碰撞思想"和"同舟共济、共克时艰"构成"同义反复"平行结构，前一对属于普通四字结构，两个四字结构意思相近，后一对是由成语和新造词构成。"同舟共济"是成语，表层意思是坐一条船，共同渡河，常用来比喻团结互助，同心协力，战胜困难。"共克时艰"首次由新华社使用，利用缩略式造词方式，表示共同克服时下艰难，在当前比较流行。其常用意思与"同舟共济"非常相近，指团结一致，同心协力，一起克服当前面临的灾害或者困苦。在处理此类"同义反复"四字结构时，可采用简化法英译共同表达的意思。与此同时，根据英语表达习惯，重组或者转换也是必要之举。两句因"同义反复"四字结构做了较大调整，前者首先采用切分法用两句话译出，然后将"交流观点，碰撞思想"简化译为 Such a meeting of minds，同时由原来的动词谓语成分转换为名词主语成分；后者同样采用简化法译为 Sticking together in times of difficulty，虽未进行分句处理，但一样进行了成分和词性转换，"同舟共济、共克时艰"由原来的定语成分转换为名词性主语成分。对"同义反复"结构采用简化加转换／重组进行处理，在署名文章英译中比较普遍，再如下面几例：

原文 这些都充分表明，两国人民<u>血脉相连，心心相印</u>。

译文 All these attest to <u>the fraternal bonds connecting the people</u> of our two countries.

原文 实践表明，中塔两国已携手走出一条<u>优势互补</u>、<u>共谋发展</u>、<u>共享繁荣</u>的道路。

译文 All of these are prime examples of our two countries <u>pursuing shared prosperity on the basis of mutual complementarity</u>.

上述两例都涉及"同义反复"结构的简化处理。与此同时，第一例在此基础上做了成分转换，由原来的谓语成分变为宾语结构；第二例将"共谋发展、共享繁荣"简化译为 shared prosperity，同时将三组四字结构重组，打破了原来的并列结构，译为 pursuing shared prosperity on the basis of mutual complementarity。尽管这些处理方式会弱化源语通过反复产生的强调或者修辞效果，但更符合英语简洁直观的特点。由上可见，四字结构作为汉语的独特表达在应用中功能多样，充当的句子成分灵活多变，翻译时针对每一种功能都要仔细理解和斟酌，挑选最佳翻译方式。最后再举两例：

| 原文 | 中塔已成为<u>山水相连</u>的好邻居、<u>真诚互信</u>的好朋友、<u>合作共赢</u>的好伙伴、<u>彼此扶持</u>的好兄弟。 |

| 译文 | Indeed, our two countries are good neighbors <u>linked by mountains and rivers</u>, good friends <u>who trust each other with all sincerity</u>, good partners <u>engaged in win-win cooperation</u> and good brothers <u>who support each other all the time</u>. |

| 原文 | 6年前，我首次访问美丽的吉尔吉斯斯坦，同吉方<u>共叙友谊</u>、<u>共商合作</u>、<u>共话未来</u>，开启中吉战略伙伴关系新时代。 |

| 译文 | I first visited this beautiful country six years ago. <u>The discussions I had with Kyrgyz leaders on the friendship and cooperation between our two countries and on the future growth of the China-Kyrgyzstan relationship</u> ushered this relationship into a new era of strategic partnership. |

上文第一例的四组四字结构充当定语修饰语，与中心词"好邻居""好朋友""好伙伴""好兄弟"构成平行结构，彰显汉语工整对仗的审美修辞效果，译文"good neighbors linked by mountains and rivers, good friends who trust each other with all sincerity, good partners engaged in win-win cooperation and good brothers who support each other all the time"在一定程度保留了这种平行结构，但并未完全移植，而是将前置定语后置化，以便符合目标语读者的表达习惯。第二例中"共叙友谊、共商合作、共话未来"同样工整对仗，在原句中并列充当谓语成分，但译文"The discussions I had with Kyrgyz leaders on the friendship and cooperation between our two countries and on the future growth of the China-Kyrgyzstan relationship"不但打破了原有平行结构，追求语义的明晰，而且转换了句子成分，由原来的谓语变为主语。

五 中国关键词加油站

1 中国道路 the Chinese road

中国道路是中国共产党把马克思主义基本原理同中国实际和时代特征结合起来走出的新路。中国特色社会主义道路是中国道路在当代的集中体现。中国道路，从制度前提上看，中国特色社会主义制度以人民代表大会为根本政治制度，实行多党合作和政治协商等基本政治制度；以公有制为主体，多种经济成分并存和共同发展。从指导思想上看，中国的社会主义市场经济高度重视宏观调控，强调发挥计划与市场两个手段的长处。从政府在经济活动中的作用来看，它不仅拥有一个"大政府"，而且拥有一个"好政府"。此外，中国道路还有一些鲜明的特点，如出口导向型政策、高储蓄率和投资率、重视教育和人力资源开发，等等。这些特征，共同构成了中国道路的主要内涵。

2 中国精神 the Chinese spirit

中国精神的主要内涵就是以爱国主义为核心的民族精神，以改革创新为核心的时代精神。中国的爱国主义，并不是狭隘的民族主义，而是国际视野和国际胸怀的爱国主义。以改革创新为核心的时代精神，为中华民族实现中国梦提供强大的精神动力。

3 中国力量 the Chinese strength

中国力量就是中国各族人民大团结的力量，是包括作为主力军的工人阶级和一切非公有制经济人士和其他新的社会阶层人士的力量，包括中国共产党同民主党派和无党派人士团结合作的力量，包括平等团结互助和谐的各民族大团结的力量，包括大陆、港澳台以及海外同胞等一切可以调动起来的积极因素、一切可团结起来的力量。中国力量，是14亿中国人、九千多万党员汇聚起来推动实现中国梦的智慧和力量。

4 顶层设计 top-level design

2010年10月18日,中国共产党十七届五中全会通过的《关于制定国民经济和社会发展第十二个五年规划的建议》提出"更加重视改革顶层设计和总体规划"。由此,"顶层设计"被引入中国的改革领域,并在此后一些中央文件和会议中进一步得到强调。"顶层设计"是中国重要的改革逻辑——由中央政府从全局的角度,系统地对改革任务进行统筹规划,调配资源,高效实现目标。

5 不忘初心 remain true to our original aspiration

2016年2月初,习近平在调研考察时强调,"行程万里、不忘初心";2016年7月1日,他在中国共产党成立95周年庆祝大会上号召全党:"面向未来,面对挑战,全党同志一定要不忘初心、继续前进。"此后,"不忘初心"迅速成为社会各界高度关注的热词。简单来说,"初心"就是中国共产党人自建党之初就树立的奋斗精神和对人民的赤子之心。"不忘初心",就是不能忘记党的理想、信念、宗旨。坚持不忘初心,就要坚持马克思主义的指导地位,就要牢记中国共产党从成立起就把为共产主义、社会主义而奋斗确定为自己的纲领,就要坚持中国特色社会主义道路自信、理论自信、制度自信、文化自信,就统筹推进"五位一体"总体布局,协调推进"四个全面"战略布局,就要坚定不移高举改革开放旗帜,就要坚信党的根基在人民、党的力量在人民,就要始终不渝走和平发展道路、奉行互利共赢的开放战略,就要保持党的先进性和纯洁性。

6 创新发展 innovative development

作为"五大发展理念"之首,创新发展注重的是解决中国发展的动力问题。中国把创新作为引领发展的第一动力,期望以此实现从要素驱动转向创新驱动、从依赖规模扩张转向提高质量效益,加快形成以创新为主要引领和支撑的经济体系和发展模式。创新发展的基本要求是,把创新摆在国家发展全局的核心位置,不断推进理论创新、制度创新、科技创新、文化创新等各方面创新,让创新贯穿党和国家一切工作,让创新在全社会蔚然成风。"十三五"期间,中国将把发展基点放在创新上,增强自主创新能力,并从培育发展新动力、拓展发展新空间、深入实施创新驱动发展战略、大力推进农业现代化、构建产业新体系、构建发展新体制、创新和完善宏观调控方式等七个着力点，绘制、实施创新发展的路线图。

7 绿色发展 green development

作为"五大发展理念"之一，绿色发展注重的是解决人与自然和谐相处的问题。"十三五"期间，中国将遵循绿色发展理念，"像保护眼睛一样保护生态环境，像对待生命一样对待生态环境"，在促进人与自然和谐共生、加快建设主体功能区、推动低碳循环发展、全面节约和高效利用资源、加大环境治理力度、筑牢生态安全屏障等六个方面下功夫，推动建立绿色低碳循环发展产业体系，致力于把生态文明建设融入经济、政治、文化、社会建设的各方面和全过程，让中华大地青山常在、绿水长流、蓝天永驻，也为全球生态安全做出中国的新贡献。

8 共享发展 development for the benefit of all

作为"五大发展理念"之一，共享发展注重的是解决社会公平正义问题。让人民群众共享改革发展成果，是社会主义的本质要求，是社会主义制度优越性的集中体现，也是中国共产党坚持全心全意为人民服务根本宗旨的必然选择。共享发展的明确指向，在于促进公平正义，实现人的全面发展。中国就共享发展作出增加公共服务供给、实施脱贫攻坚工程、提高教育质量、促进就业创业、缩小收入差距、建立更加公平更可持续的社会保障制度、推进健康中国建设、促进人口均衡发展等八个方面的部署。这既是有效的制度安排，也是中国"十三五"期间推动共享发展的重要着力点。

9 开放发展 development for global progress

作为"五大发展理念"之一，开放发展注重的是解决中国发展内外联动的问题。中国从六个方面对开放发展进行了部署：完善对外开放战略布局，形成对外开放新体制，推进"一带一路"建设，深化内地和港澳、大陆和台湾地区合作发展，积极参与全球经济治理，积极承担国际责任和义务。这显示出深度融入世界的中国期望以开放发展实现合作共赢，有效促进中国和世界的共同发展。

10 协调发展 coordinated development

作为"五大发展理念"之一,协调发展注重的是解决中国发展中的不平衡问题。中国以往高速发展过程中出现和积累的不平衡、不协调、不可持续问题,已经成为继续发展的"短板"。"十三五"期间,中国将会增强发展协调性,其重点有三:促进城乡区域协调发展,旨在破解城乡二元结构难题;促进经济社会协调发展,旨在改变"一条腿长、一条腿短"失衡问题;促进新型工业化、信息化、城镇化、农业现代化同步发展,致力于在增强国家硬实力的同时注重提升国家软实力,增强发展整体性。

六 外交署名文章翻译练习

1. 将下列署名文章译成英语,注意下画线时政术语的翻译。

1)习主席多次利用出席经济峰会的重要国际场合,从历史和现实的角度、从国内外比较的视角阐释中国道路,演绎创新、协调、绿色、开放、共享五大发展理念,揭示中国发展奇迹的奥秘所在,与世界分享中国发展的成功经验,让"中国故事"在全球范围内引起共鸣,充分展现了中国的道路自信、理论自信、制度自信和文化自信。

2)在建设有本国特色社会主义的伟大征程中,中老两国"志同而气和"。上个月,中国共产党成功召开第十九次全国代表大会。这次大会制定了中国党和国家未来发展的总体方针和行动纲领。大会绘制了从现在到本世纪中叶中国建设发展的宏伟蓝图。到 2020 年,将全面建成小康社会;从 2020 年到 2035 年,基本实现社会主义现代化;从 2035 年到本世纪中叶,把中国建设成为富强民主文明和谐美丽的社会主义现代化强国。我们有能力、有信心带领中国人民朝着实现中华民族伟大复兴的中国梦迈进。

3)2005 年中塞复交后,两国关系翻开新的一页。中方支持塞方走适合本国国情的发展道路,塞方在涉及中国核心利益问题上给予中方坚定支持。两国政治互信水平不断提升,互利合作成果实实在在,在重大国际和地区问题上保持密切协调。中塞关系实现了从长期友好合作伙伴关系到全面战略合作伙伴关系的跨越。

2．将下列署名文章译成英语，注意下画线四字结构的翻译。

1）我曾两次到访老挝，<u>热情友善</u>的老挝人民、<u>金碧辉煌</u>的万象塔銮、<u>风光旖旎</u>的湄公河畔给我留下深刻而美好的印象。我期待同老挝的新老朋友们<u>畅叙友谊</u>、<u>共谋发展</u>，共辟两国关系美好未来。

2）卢旺达有"千丘之国"美誉。这里风景秀丽、四季如春、物产丰饶，这里人民<u>勤劳勇敢</u>、<u>自强不息</u>，是非洲大陆上一片充满生机的土地。

3）去年6月，我和巴雷拉总统共同作出重大政治决断，中巴正式建交。对两国，这是一件<u>功在当今</u>、<u>利在千秋</u>的盛事。对世界，这是一面昭示<u>大势所趋</u>、<u>人心所向</u>的旗帜。国际社会倾听巴拿马恪守一个中国政策的正义宣言，两国人民一致支持中巴关系发展。

3．将下列署名文章译成英语，注意时政术语及四字结构的翻译。

1）主办 G20 杭州峰会是中国深度参与全球经济治理、加快推进全球经济治理体制改革的一次成功实践。习近平主席在 G20 工商峰会（B20）开幕式上首次系统提出以平等为基础、以开放为导向、以合作为动力、以共享为目标的全球经济治理观，倡导共同构建公正高效的全球金融治理格局、开放透明的全球贸易和投资治理格局、绿色低碳的全球能源治理格局、包容联动的全球发展治理格局，为完善全球经济治理体系描绘了路线图。在办会过程中，中国全力推动 G20 因时而变，与时俱进，为 G20 从危机应对向长效治理机制转型、从侧重短期政策向短中长期政策并重转型奠定了坚实基础，巩固了 G20 国际经济合作主要论坛的地位，也为世界经济稳定复苏提供了坚实的机制保障。

2）中阿关系全面快速发展正是中拉关系蓬勃生机的缩影。中拉是发展中国家和新兴市场国家的重要代表，都面临前所未有的机遇和挑战。我们需要深化合作，携手共进。为此，我提出构建中拉命运共同体，倡议中拉描绘共建"一带一路"新蓝图，得到拉美和加勒比朋友们积极响应。我们愿同拉美和加勒比国家一道，秉持共商共建共享原则，以政策沟通、设施联通、贸易畅通、资金融通、民心相通为合作重点，通过共建"一带一路"给中拉人民带来更多实惠，促进中拉合作优化升级、创新发展。

第三章 外交新闻翻译

一　外交新闻的概念及文体特点

外交新闻首先具有新闻的特点。新闻的定义可见多种，根据《辞典》定义，指"报社、广播电台、电视台等，对任何足以引起民众兴趣或造成影响力的事件，所作的最新而及时的报道。其形式包括消息、通讯稿、特写、调查报告、图片等"。新闻的主要特点包括真实性、客观性、时效性、准确性、公开性、广泛性等。外交新闻主要指对外交领域新近发生的事件进行的报道。除了具备新闻的所有特征，外交新闻尤其强调政治性，讲究原则性、严谨性和分寸感，常常涉及我国外交立场、外交理念、决策主张等，是外交话语构成的重要方面。

通常而言，外交新闻跟新闻一样，由标题、导语、主体三部分构成，有时也会有背景和结语两部分，但二者起辅助作用。标题除主标题外，还可有副标题；导语主要用于概括新闻的主要内容，一般位于新闻开头的第一段；主体是对导语内容的进一步拓展，用具体事实或者细节表现新闻主题；背景主要指与新闻事件关联的社会、自然环境等；结语是对整个新闻的总结。就新闻报道形式而言，主要分为四种：倒金字塔式、正金字塔式、折衷式、平铺直叙式。倒金字塔式使用广度最高，其特点是将最重要的消息放在最前面，然后按照重要性递减的顺序报道相关事实或者具体细节，目的主要是为了迎合受众期待，便于受众快速抓住新闻要点。与倒金字塔式相反，正金字塔形式主要以时间顺序报道事件发生过程，采取重要性递增的方式叙述，在新闻结尾处展现高潮，多用于特写之中。折衷式介于倒金字塔式与正金字塔式之间，亦即将二者折衷，将最重要的信息放在导言中，主体内容则按照时间顺序叙述，也可称为新华体。平铺直叙式多用于声明之中，强调语言表达的准确性和流畅性。总体而言，倒金字塔式在外交新闻报道中应用频率较高。

外交新闻是关于外交领域的报道，国际性比较突出，经常涉及两国或者多国之间的对话、会见、交涉、磋商、会谈、条约、协议、宣言、声明、公报、备忘录等。因此，在翻译时必须注重不同场合、不同事件中使用的外交语言的特征。语言是国与国之间交流、谈判等的重要工具。在外交互动中，恰当使用语言能够促进合作，推进和平；反之，则会引发分裂，制造仇恨。外交语言具有国别属性，不同国家的外交语言呈现不同的风格特征。中国外交一直倡导和平发展，反对霸权主义，奉行和平共处五项原则，因此在涉及国家独立、主权和领土完整问题时政治立场非常坚定，语言表达非常明确。与此同时，由于国际形势复杂多变，国与国之间存在不同程度的矛盾分歧，在处理国际问题时也要因势而行，语言表达有时也会婉约含蓄，以便调和矛盾或者避免冲突。以上两点表明,外交语言既要讲究原则,也要适度灵活,从中又可见分寸掌握的重要性。根据外交事件严重程度的不同,在表明态度立场时,分为不同的等级,如抗议、强烈抗议、最强烈抗议;遗憾,深表遗憾;关切,严重关切;谴责,强烈谴责等,翻译时必须注意表达的等级,恰当再现源语的分寸。外交语言还有一点尤需注意的是信息传达的准确性。如上所述,新闻报道具有客观性、真实性等特征,外交新闻因与政治的密切关联更是如此,违背这些属性就会抹杀外交新闻文体的存在本质。准确性要求翻译同样客观、真实再现报道内容,即便因为思维差异或者文化空缺等问题进行改写,也不能随意歪曲事实,增删关键内容,任何情况下都需保证信息的准确性,避免信息的误传。

 外交新闻汉英对照举隅

范例一:

各国代表"云聚一堂",共庆首个"国际茶日"
——常驻联合国代表张军大使参加"国际茶日"线上庆祝活动
Virtual Celebration of the First International Tea Day Was Held
2020/05/21

2020年5月21日,常驻联合国代表团和联合国粮农组织共同举办首个"国际茶日"线上庆祝活动,主题是"茶与可持续发展"。常驻联合国代表张军大使同联大主席班迪,俄罗斯、埃及、斯里兰卡、哈萨克斯坦、尼泊尔、肯尼亚、孟加拉国、匈牙利、黎巴嫩、荷兰等20多国常驻联合国代

On 21 May, the Permanent Mission of the People's Republic of China to the United Nations and the Food and Agriculture Organization co-organized a virtual celebration of the first International Tea Day with the theme of "Tea for Sustainable Development". Ambassador Zhang Jun, Permanent Representative of China to the United Nations, Tijjani Muhammad-Bande, President of the 74th Session of the United Nations General Assembly, Permanent

表及近 200 位嘉宾"云聚一堂",共同纪念这一节日。

联大主席班迪发表致辞,表示茶产业关系减贫、消除饥饿、气候行动及提升包容性等第 74 届联大关注的重点领域,是许多最不发达国家的主要经济来源。班迪呼吁国际社会携手促进茶产业可持续发展,帮助相关国家落实可持续发展目标。中国农业农村部部长韩长赋向庆祝活动致视频贺辞,预祝活动圆满成功,呼吁各国为民兴茶、健康饮茶、开放促茶。

张军大使在开幕辞中表示,第 74 届联大通过决议确定 5 月 21 日为"国际茶日",充分肯定了茶对人类社会、经济、文化的珍贵价值,为深化茶领域合作提供了新的契机。习近平主席专门向"国际茶日"系列活动致贺信,表示中方愿同各方一道,推动全球

Representatives of over 20 countries, including Russian Federation, Egypt, Sri Lanka, Kazakhstan, Nepal, Kenya, Bangladesh, Hungary, Lebanon and Netherlands, and nearly 200 delegates joined the celebration of this International Day.

In his remarks, President Bande said that the tea industry is related to the prioritized action on key areas of the 74th Session of the General Assembly, including poverty eradication, zero hunger, climate action and inclusion, and is also a main source of income and export revenues for many least developed countries. He called on the international community to jointly promote the sustainable development of the tea industry and help relevant countries implement the Sustainable Development Goals. Minister of Agriculture and Rural Affairs of China Mr. Han Changfu offered his congratulations and good wishes through a video message. He called upon all countries to put people first in developing the tea sector, advocate healthy ways to drink tea, and develop the tea sector through opening-up.

In his opening remarks, Ambassador Zhang Jun said that the 74th Session of the General Assembly adopted a resolution that designated May 21st as the International Tea Day, which fully affirmed the great value of tea to human society, economy and culture and provided a fresh opportunity for deepening cooperation in the field of tea. President Xi Jinping sent a letter expressing warm congratulations on a series of activities

茶产业持续健康发展，深化茶文化交融互鉴，让更多的人知茶、爱茶，共品茶香茶韵，共享美好生活。

张军大使指出，茶是人与自然和谐共生的写照。茶让人们增进健康、丰富生活，人们也通过对茶的种植、经营和生产来滋养和回报自然，这是"天人合一"思想的生动诠释。茶是人类经济生活的重要支柱。茶作为经济作物，养育了一辈又一辈人，是许多国家和民众的主要收入来源，创造了无数新的就业良机。茶是人类文明交流的纽带。茶穿越历史、跨越国界，有力促进了文明的沟通交融，不同国家和民族相识相知，践行着"和而不同、多元并存"的重要理念。

张军大使强调，"国际茶日"的设立，为茶赋予了新生命、新活力。各国人民应该在对茶的共赏共鉴中，共同建设更加美好和谐的世界。要以茶为伴，促进人与自然和谐共生，走绿色发展之路。要以茶兴业，实现减贫等可持续发展目标，"绿水青山就是金山银

marking the first International Tea Day and said that China is willing to work with all sides to nurture the sustained and healthy development of the global tea industry, deepen cultural exchange on tea, and allow more people to relish lives accompanied by tea.

Ambassador Zhang pointed out that tea is a symbol of harmony between man and nature. As a gift of nature, tea is good for health and enriches human life. Meanwhile, through tea planting, production and operation, people nourish and give back to nature. This cycle of man and nature is a vivid testament to the philosophy of "Unity of Heaven and Man". Tea is an important pillar of human economic activities, and has been an economic crop that nurtured generation after generation. Tea is also a main source of income for many households and has created tremendous job opportunities for many countries and people.

Ambassador Zhang emphasized that the inception of International Tea Day has given tea new life and vitality. With the shared love for tea, people of all countries could work together to build a better and more harmonious world. Tea is a good partner in our endeavor to promote the harmonious coexistence between man and nature and achieve green development. Tea is a good business that can help more farmers shake

山"。要以茶会友，促进贸易交往和互联互通，让世界更紧密联系起来。要充分发挥茶的作用，有效应对疫情冲击，维护产业链供应链稳定畅通，积极为恢复世界经济增添动力。

张大使还呼吁大家利用当前特殊时期，隔空相约，共同品茗、共同思考，共同为多边主义、为人类的共同未来探寻方向。等到再见面时，将思考变成行动，为构建人类命运共同体作出新的贡献。

俄罗斯、埃及、斯里兰卡、哈萨克斯坦、尼泊尔、肯尼亚、孟加拉国、匈牙利、黎巴嫩常驻代表，阿根廷常驻团临时代办，土耳其常驻副代表等纷纷发言表示，茶从中国传出，成为仅次于水、最受世界人民欢迎的饮品，饮茶也已成为许多国家世代相传的传统文化。茶产业是许多发展中国家的重要经济来源，茶产业可持续发展对各国经济发展、落实可持续发展目标有重要影响。新冠肺炎疫情对茶产业造成冲击，国际社会应凝聚力量，帮助茶产业和从业者渡过难关。

off poverty and attain the SDGs, as lucid waters and lush mountains are invaluable assets. Tea is a catalyst of friendship that can bring people closer together, promote trade and build an interconnected world. Tea can also help us tackle the challenges posed by the COVID-19, maintain stable and unimpeded industrial and supply chains, and facilitate the recovery of world economy.

Ambassador Zhang also called for using this special period to invite each other from distance to drink tea together, think together, and explore together the future for multilateralism and humanity so as to turn thinking into action and make new contributions to a better future shared by all.

The Permanent Representatives of the Russian Federation, Egypt, Sri Lanka, Kazakhstan, Nepal, Kenya, Bangladesh, Hungary and Lebanon, the Charge D'affaire of Argentina, and the Deputy Permanent Representatives of Turkey made interventions and said that tea, originated in China, has become the world's most popular drink second only to water. Drinking tea has also become a traditional cultural heritage in many countries. Tea industry is an important source of income for many developing countries. The sustainable development of tea industry has important effect on economic development and implementation of the SDGs. Given the negative impact of COVID-19 on tea industry, the international community should strengthen solidarity to help tea industry

联合国粮农组织总干事屈冬玉通过视频致闭幕辞，祝贺"国际茶日"活动圆满成功，表示饮茶文化源远流长，茶产业支撑着数百万农村地区人口的生计，希望各方携起手来，促进茶产业可持续发展。

在活动现场，中方展示了传统青瓷、紫砂茶具和各式茶叶，并通过穿插播放精美视频，同与会嘉宾"云分享"中国茶产业可持续发展的生动景象。茶文化视频展示了六大茶系各自特色，描绘了一片茶叶从大山深处走进百姓茶杯，从茶树嫩芽经过采、制、冲、泡成为美味茶汤的奇妙历程。茶与减贫视频讲述了种茶制茶助力数十万茶农脱贫增收，诠释了"绿水青山就是金山银山"的重要理念。茶产业应对疫情视频则展现了地方政府和从业者齐心协力，依托网络平台销售产品、积极开展复工复产的抗疫图景。有关视频受到各方一致称赞，大家对历史悠久的中国茶文化兴致盎然，认为茶叶促进减贫、茶产业抗击疫情

and its practitioners get through the difficulties.

Director General of the FAO Mr. Qu Dongyu delivered closing remarks. He extended congratulations on the full success of the virtual celebration and said that the culture of drinking tea enjoys a long history and the tea industry provides livelihood for millions in rural areas. He expressed the hope that all parties could join hands to promote the sustainable development of tea industry.

During the celebration, China presented the traditional celadon, purple clay teapots and various varieties of tea. Short videos were played to show the sustainable development of tea industry in China. Audiences could see the unique features of the six major varieties of tea in China, the journey of a tea leaf, the whole process of picking and making tea, and the role of tea in increasing household incomes and reducing poverty. The idea of "lucid waters and lush mountains are invaluable assets" was emphasized. Stories were told about how Chinese local governments and practitioners of tea industry worked to fight COVID-19, including selling tea via e-commerce and promoting the recovery of tea sector. The participants showed great interest in the time-honored Chinese tea culture, saying that these true stories provide a useful reference for other countries, especially developing countries. The Russian Federation, Nepal and Kenya also showed, via video, their own tea-drinking customs and

的"中国故事"为其他国家特别是发展中国家提供了有益借鉴。俄罗斯、尼泊尔、肯尼亚也以视频形式展示了本国饮茶习俗和茶产业抗击疫情情况。

在纽约疫情形势依然严峻、联合国继续实行居家办公的背景下,首个"国际茶日"庆祝活动依托网络,通过新颖的交流方式、丰富的展示内容,营造出非常时期特有的温馨气氛。整场活动持续近两个小时,结束之际各国嘉宾互相挥手告别,都感到意犹未尽。会后,多国大使纷纷通过社交媒体转发照片和视频,对庆祝活动给予高度评价。

their fight against the COVID-19.

Due to the impact of COVID-19 on New York and the continuation of remote working of UN staff, the first International Tea Day was celebrated online. It was a heart-warming and informative event and lasted nearly two hours. Many ambassadors posted photos and videos on social media afterwards, expressing high appreciation of the celebration.

范例二:

王毅同爱尔兰外交与国防部长科文尼举行会谈
Wang Yi Holds Talks with Irish Minister for Foreign Affairs and Minister for Defence Simon Coveney
2020/05/31

2021年5月30日,国务委员兼外长王毅在贵阳同爱尔兰外交与国防部长科文尼举行会谈。

王毅表示,中爱关系始终

On May 30, 2021, State Councilor and Foreign Minister Wang Yi held talks with Irish Minister for Foreign Affairs and Minister for Defence Simon Coveney in Guiyang.

Wang Yi said, China-Ireland relations have

保持健康稳定发展，并在不断走向成熟。最重要的经验就是，尽管双方历史文化、社会制度各异，但我们尊重各自选择的发展道路，包容彼此存在的不同，不断巩固互信、扩大共识，为促进两国合作和国际和平稳定作出积极贡献，这一宝贵经验值得继承和弘扬。

王毅表示，中爱务实合作的本质是互利共赢，动力是互通有无。爱尔兰是为数不多连续十多年保持对华贸易顺差的欧盟成员国，中国已成为爱乳制品、猪肉第二大市场。中国对外开放的大门将越开越大。中国每年召开进口博览会，就是向世界表明我们不搞贸易保护主义，而是与世界共享发展机遇。要用好中爱科技创新联委会等机制，加强科技创新、优质农业、高等教育、文化产业等领域交流合作。希望爱方一如既往为中国企业提供公平、透明、非歧视性的营商环境。双方要加强人文交流，夯实中爱关系的民意基础。中方将努力办好明年北京冬奥会，期待爱运动员在赛场上取得好成绩。

maintained sound and steady growth, and become more mature. The most important experience is that, despite their difference in history, culture, social system, China and Ireland respect each other's choice of development path, tolerate each other's differences, strengthen mutual trust, and expand common ground, contributing to bilateral cooperation and world peace and stability. This precious experience should be carried forward.

Wang Yi expressed, the essence of China-Ireland practical cooperation is mutually beneficial, and the major driver is complementarity. Ireland is one of the few EU member states that maintain trade surpluses with China for over ten consecutive years, and China has become the second biggest market of Irish meat and dairy products. China will open its door wider to the outside world. The China International Import Expo annually held is to show the world that we do not engage in trade protectionism, but share development opportunities with the world. We should leverage mechanisms such as China-Ireland Technological Innovation Joint Commission, strengthen exchange and cooperation in fields such as technological innovation, quality agriculture, higher education, and cultural industry. China hopes that the Irish side will, as always, provide an open, transparent and non-discriminatory business environment for the Chinese companies investing and operating in Ireland. Both sides should continue to strengthen cultural and people-to-people exchanges and further consolidate the social basis of the bilateral ties. China will endeavor to prepare for Beijing Winter Olympic Games, and expect the excellent performance of Irish athletes.

王毅表示，抗疫是"遭遇战"，更是"持久战"。中国在自身需求紧张，供需矛盾突出情况下，已累计向其他国家提供3.4亿剂疫苗，以实际行动履行将新冠疫苗作为全球公共产品的承诺。未来3年，中国还将再提供30亿美元，支持发展中国家抗疫和恢复经济社会发展。中爱双方可发挥各自优势，加强抗疫国际合作，维护产业链供应链顺畅稳定，助力世界经济加快复苏。

Wang Yi said, the fight against the pandemic is both an "unexpected" and "protracted" war. Despite the enormous demand at home and the serious imbalance between supply and demand, China has supplied 340 million doses of vaccines to the world, honoring its pledge to turn vaccines into a global public good with practical actions. China will provide an additional 3 billion U.S. dollars over the next three years to support COVID-19 response and economic and social recovery in other developing countries. China and Ireland can leverage respective strengths and strengthen international cooperation against COVID-19, keep the industrial and supply chains smooth and stable, and facilitate the faster recovery of the world economy.

王毅表示，中方历来主张，国家不分大小、强弱、贫富，都是平等一员，世界上的事情应由各国商量着办，这才是多边主义的真谛。而推进多边主义必须维护以联合国为核心的国际体系，维护联合国宪章的宗旨和原则，维护普遍认同的国际法和国际关系基本准则。少数几个国家或国家集团

Wang Yi expressed, China always believes that all countries, big or small, strong or weak, rich or poor, are equal members of the international community, and that world affairs should be handled through extensive consultation. This is the essence of multilateralism. To advance multilateralism, all countries should uphold the international system with the United Nations at its core, the purposes and principles of the UN Charter, and universally recognized international

制定的所谓"规则"并不是真正的多边主义。中方重视爱方在国际和地区事务中的独特作用和影响，愿同爱方加强在联合国安理会等多边框架内的协调合作，共同坚持和践行真正的多边主义。

王毅说，中欧是全面战略伙伴而不是对手，双方合作大于竞争，共识多于分歧。存在分歧并不可怕，完全可以通过平等对话增进了解，搞清真相，消除疑虑，明辨是非。更重要的是，欧方应客观全面认识中国所处的发展阶段，实事求是评价中国取得的发展进步，更加冷静理性处理对华关系。爱尔兰是欧盟内部的稳健力量，相信爱方会继续为中欧关系健康稳定发展发挥积极作用。

王毅还应询全面介绍了中国新疆的真实情况以及香港局势由乱转治的发展历程，阐明了中方在涉疆、涉港问题上的原则立场。安全，防止此类事

laws and basic norms governing international relations. The so-called "rules" formulated by a few countries or groups of countries are not real multilateralism. China values the Irish unique role and influence in the regional and international affairs, and it stands ready to enhance coordination and cooperation with Ireland under multilateral frameworks such as the UN Security Council, and jointly adhere to and practice the true multilateralism.

Wang Yi said, China and Europe Union (EU) are comprehensive strategic partners, not rivals. The bilateral cooperation far outweighs competition, and we agree much more than we disagree. We should not be afraid of differences, but enhance understanding, clarify matters, remove misgivings and distinguish right from wrong through equal dialogues. More importantly, the EU should understand China's development stages in an objective and unbiased manner, assess China's progress based on facts, and deal with its relations with China in a calm and evidence-based manner. Ireland is a stable force within the EU, and China believes that Ireland will continue to play a positive role in promoting the sound and stable development of the China-EU relations.

As a reply, Wang Yi also talked about the true situation in Xinjiang, and the process of Hong Kong's transition from chaos to stability, and expounded China's position on Xinjiang and Hong Kong-related issues.

件再次发生。

科文尼祝贺中国经过艰苦努力成功控制疫情,感谢中方为爱抗疫提供的宝贵支持和帮助,表示爱尔兰是世界上最开放的经济体、中国是世界上最大的消费市场,爱高度重视推进与中国的务实合作,愿继续深化与中方在网络安全、航空、地方等领域合作,克服疫情影响积极推动人员往来和人文交流。在爱尔兰,华人深受尊重,为爱的经济社会发展作出了重要贡献,爱对中方投资持欢迎和开放态度,希望成为中国企业进入欧洲的门户。

科文尼表示,爱方坚定支持联合国及其专门机构发挥作用,赞赏中方面对单边主义逆流时坚定维护多边主义,这样做很不容易,对广大中小国家尤为重要。爱方积极评价中方今年5月担任联合国安理会轮值主席国期间勇于承担责任,在非洲、中东等问题上发挥了积极引领作用。爱方愿加强双方在气候变化、维和等领域的协调合作,同中方共同推

Coveney congratulates on China's successful control of the COVID-19 after making arduous efforts, and thanks China for offering valuable support and sincere assistance in Irish fight against the pandemic. He said, Ireland is the most open economy, and China is the largest consumer market. Ireland prioritizes its practical cooperation with China, and stands ready to deepen cooperation with China in fields such as cyber security, and aviation, as well as at local levels to overcome the impact of the pandemic and actively promote people-to-people exchanges. Overseas Chinese are highly respected in Ireland, and they make a significant contribution to Irish social and economic development. Ireland welcomes the investment from China, and hopes to become a gateway of Chinese enterprises to the European market.

Coveney said, Ireland firmly supports the role of the UN and its institutions, and praises China's firm safeguarding of multilateralism despite headwinds of unilateralism. It is indeed not easy, but multilateralism is vital to small and medium-sized countries. Ireland evaluates positively that China courageously undertook its responsibilities in its presidency of the UN Security Council this May, and played a leading role on the issues related to Africa and the Middle East. Ireland is willing to strengthen coordination and cooperation with China in fields such as climate change and peacekeeping,

动世界卫生组织履行应有职能。国际社会应合作抗疫而不是相互指责。欧洲和中国都在世界上发挥着重要作用，在气候变化、可持续发展、全球治理等领域有广泛共同利益。加强对华合作仍是欧洲各国的普遍愿望。欧中双方如果因为某些人为障碍而渐行渐远，将铸成历史性错误。欧中签署全面投资协定符合双方利益，希望通过坦诚对话克服当前出现的困难。爱尔兰是中方在欧盟内的诚实朋友，也愿做可靠的伙伴，期待欧中关系得到进一步改善和发展。

and jointly promote the WHO to play its due role. The international community should focus on anti-virus cooperation rather than point fingers. Both Europe and China play a vital role in the world and share broad interests in areas such as climate change, sustainable development, and global governance. It is still the shared aspiration of European countries to strengthen cooperation with China. Both sides will make irrevocable mistakes of historic consequences if each side goes its way due to certain man-made obstacles. The EU-China comprehensive investment agreement serves the common interests, so both sides should overcome the current difficulties through candid dialogues. As a good friend of China in the EU, Ireland is willing to be China's trustworthy partner, and it expects further progress of the EU-China relations.

三　外交新闻的翻译原则与难点

外交新闻是外宣的重要构成，翻译时需要熟知外交新闻涵盖的多领域知识体系，包括政治、经济、文化、军事、科技等，需要具备高度的政治敏感性，把握好方针政策、原则立场等，拿捏好话语的分寸，还要与时俱进，掌握外交新闻中出现的新词汇、新术语，再现新闻的语体风格等。毋庸置疑，外交新闻翻译的好坏直接影响中国话语和中国形象建构，在翻译时必须遵循恰当的原则，正确处理难点，通过各种方式最大化提升译文的可读性和接受度。

就外宣翻译而言，黄友义曾指出，"外宣翻译更需要翻译工作者熟知并运用'外宣三贴近'（贴近中国发展的实际，贴近国外受众对中国信息的需求，贴近国外受众的思维习惯）的原则"[1]。作为中国外宣的重要构成，"外宣三贴近"原则同样适用于外交新闻翻译。在外交新闻翻译中，要想达到"外宣三贴近"原则，译者必须具备关于中国发展的多领域知识，比如"命运共同体"相关理念以及"交流互鉴文明观""中国特色大国外交""军民融合发展战略""社会主义核心价值体系""中国制造2025""战略性新兴产业""中国经济新常态"的内涵等。在翻译中国的国情、政策、体制、制度等时，必须字斟句酌、反复推敲，深度领会原文本中的核心思想、主张或关键词，正确阐释中国对外话语，如实传达外交新闻涵盖的各类信息。除此之外，译者还必须具备高度的跨文化素养，了解目标受众的期待，满足目标受众的思维习惯。事实上，这是外交新闻翻译的一大难点。外交新闻翻译涉及很多具有中国话语特色的表达，如何将这些具有国别特征的语言翻译成地道流畅的目标语是译者面临的巨大挑战。

外交新闻中涉及很多严肃的政治话题，涉及的话语具有政治、外交、新闻三重特性，翻译时"最应该注意的是要潜心研究外国文化和外国人的心理思维模式，善于发现和分析中外文化的细微差异和特点，时刻不忘要按照国外受众的思维习惯去把握翻译"[2]。因此，在翻译"中国表达""中国话语"时，除了一贯倾向的异化策略，采用音译、音译+解释、直译、直译+解释的方法外，在处理文化鸿沟、文化差异或文化空缺问题时也需适当改写，运用西方的语言思维习惯传达中国声音，传输外交信息，明确中国立场，实现外交新闻域外接受的最大化。常用改写方式包括词性转换、适度删减、弃修辞变意译、替换套用、调整语序、显化逻辑或成分、结构重组等。

四　外交新闻的英译技巧

1 国际组织或外交职务的恰当翻译

外交新闻中由于经常报道国际组织或外交官员处理外交事务或事件、参与外交活动、发表外交领域相关讲话、对外表明态度立场等，因而不可避免涉及相关官员的职务身份。对于外交领域译者而言，掌握这些职务的国际通用译法尤为重要：一

---

[1] 黄友义.2004.坚持"外宣三贴近"原则，处理好外宣翻译中的难点问题.中国翻译，（6）：27-28.

[2] 同上。

是确保翻译的准确性，二可避免目标受众的认知混淆，三能防止翻译错误引发的尴尬或矛盾。因此，就国际或外交职务翻译而言，译者必须遵循通用原则，同时与时俱进，随时掌握相关变化，及时更新知识储备。下面以本章范例一中的职务描述为例具体说明。

> **原文** 常驻联合国代表张军大使同联大主席班迪，俄罗斯、埃及、斯里兰卡、哈萨克斯坦、尼泊尔、肯尼亚、孟加拉国、匈牙利、黎巴嫩、荷兰等20多国常驻联合国代表及近200位嘉宾"云聚一堂"，共同纪念这一节日。

> **译文** Ambassador Zhang Jun, Permanent Representative of China to the United Nations, Tijjani Muhammad-Bande, President of the 74th Session of the United Nations General Assembly, Permanent Representatives of over 20 countries, including Russian Federation, Egypt, Sri Lanka, Kazakhstan, Nepal, Kenya, Bangladesh, Hungary, Lebanon and Netherlands, and nearly 200 delegates joined the celebration of this International Day.

本例主要涉及两个职务，一个是"常驻联合国代表"，另一个是"联大主席"。前者出现两次，第一次采用完整翻译，同时显化中国国别，译为 Permanent Representative of China to the United Nations；第二次为了避免重复烦琐，译者采取简化翻译，只译了 Permanent Representatives，符合上下文语境，不影响受众理解。"联大主席"是"联合国大会主席"的简称。联合国大会主席任期为1年，每年6月份会进行下一届联大主席的选举。译者此处同样采用显化策略，将班迪74届联大主席的身份清晰化，增加了信息的准确性和清晰性。此外，人名与职务翻译的顺序也值得注意。就英语表达习惯而言，如果职务名称较短，可以放在人名前面，如 President Xi Jinping、Prime Minister Li Keqiang 等，如果职务名称较长，常采用人名在前，职务和国籍/组织在后的顺序。因此，"常驻联合国代表张军大使"译为 Ambassador Zhang Jun, Permanent Representative of China to the United Nations，"联大主席班迪"译为 Tijjani Muhammad-Bande, President of the 74th Session of the United Nations General Assembly。当然，职务的翻译也具有灵活性，并非固定，有时也会发现职务名称较长，但仍然放在人名前面的情况，如"中国农业农村部部长韩长赋"译为 Minister of Agriculture and Rural Affairs of China Mr. Han Changfu。

熟练掌握各类外交职务是外交领域译员必具的知识储备，除上例外，范例中的相关表达还有"阿根廷常驻团临时代办"（the Charge D'affaire of Argentina）、"土耳其常驻副代表"（the Deputy Permanent Representatives of Turkey）、"联合国粮农组织总干事屈冬玉"（Director General of the FAO Mr. Qu Dongyu）等。政治职衔中的副职经常使用 deputy，如副司长/局长（Deputy Director-General）、副国务卿（Deputy Secretary）、副助卿（Deputy Assistant Secretary）等。FAO 的英文全称是 Food and Agriculture Organization of the United Nations，国际通用的很多组织名称都用缩写形式。

此外，其他联合国职务名称的翻译，同样需要译者具有丰富的知识积累，掌握官方正规翻译方式，确保译文的精确性。比如"联合国副秘书长兼裁军事务高级代表"（UN Under-Secretary-General and High Representative for Disarmament Affairs）、"联合国秘书长技术特使办公室代理负责人"（Officer in Charge of Office of the Secretary-General's Envoy on Technology）、"联合国经社事务部助理秘书长"（UN Assistant Secretary-General for Policy Coordination and Inter-Agency Affairs of Department of Economic and Social Affairs）等。

在翻译实践中，必须掌握的常识性外交职务名称还有：特命全权大使（Ambassador Extraordinary and Plenipotentiary）、公使（Minister）、公使衔参赞（Minister-Counselor）、参赞（Counselor）、一等秘书（First Secretary）、二等秘书（Second Secretary）、三等秘书（Third Secretary）、专员（attaché）等。

2 外交新闻报道文中主题句的翻译

在外交新闻报道中，经常会涉及领导人讲话或者发表官方文件的要点，文内经常使用简洁精悍、结构工整的主题句，主要交代某一部分/段落的中心思想、核心内容、主要任务等。在中国外交文本中，文内主题句以无主句结构为主，整体结构相似，工整鲜明。如下例所示：

> **原文** 李克强就深化三国合作提出以下建议：
>
> ——夯实互信根基，维护合作大局。要客观理性地看待彼此的发展，秉承正视历史、开辟未来的精神，尊重彼此核心利益和重大关切，聚焦互利共赢合作，坚持通过对话协商解决分歧，为深化合作创造有利条件。
>
> ——加强顶层设计，明确合作方向。要着眼未来，从战略高度和长远角度规划三国合作，明确发展方向和重点领域，深化务实合作，打造伙伴关系。
>
> ——加速自贸谈判，推动区域经济一体化。中日韩三国都是区域全面经济

伙伴关系协定（RCEP）的坚定支持者，应推动明年如期签署协议。加速中日韩自贸区谈判，早日建成更高标准的自贸区，实现更高水平的贸易和投资自由化便利化。

——促进创新合作，打造新增长点。中日韩都是创新大国，优势互补。三方要提升创新能力，分享创新成果。

——密切人文交流，筑牢友好纽带。加强三国体育、奥运、青少年等交流合作。

——开展环保合作，推动可持续发展。加强在卫生、老龄化、气候变化等领域的政策交流和务实合作，增强人民的获得感和幸福感。

译文 Li Keqiang made the following suggestions on deepening cooperation among the three countries.

Solidifying mutual trust to uphold the larger interest of cooperation. We need to view each other's development in an objective and rational light. In the spirit of facing history squarely and shaping a brighter future, we need to respect each other's core interests and major concerns, stay focused on mutually beneficial cooperation, and keep to dialogue and consultation in addressing differences. This will create enabling conditions for deeper cooperation.

Enhancing overall planning to set the direction for future cooperation. We need to be future-minded and plan our cooperation from a strategic and long-term perspective. We need to set out the direction and priorities of our cooperation, deepen practical cooperation and forge partnership.

Accelerating FTA negotiations to boost regional economic integration. Our three countries are all staunch supporters of the RCEP. We need to make the agreement ready for formal signing next year as scheduled. We need to speed up the trilateral FTA negotiations and work for its early conclusion. A trilateral FTA with higher standards will bring about trade and investment liberalization and facilitation at a higher level.

> Boosting innovation cooperation to cultivate a new growth area. All three countries are major innovators with complementary advantages. We need to share the fruits of innovation and raise the capabilities to innovate.
>
> Increasing people-to-people exchanges to forge a closer bond of friendship. The three countries should enhance exchanges and cooperation in sports, the Olympic Games and youth.
>
> Carrying out cooperation in environmental protection to advance sustainable development. We need to intensify policy exchange and practical cooperation on health, aging and climate change with a view to bringing greater benefits and happiness to our people.

上例是 2019 年 12 月 24 日李克强总理出席第八次中日韩领导人会议时就中日韩合作及地区、国际问题交换看法的部分内容。根据原文可见，李克强总理就深化三国合作提出六条建议，每条建议都有主题句。六个主题句结构一致，都分为前后两部分，且前后皆为动宾结构。译者在处理这六个句子时，再现了原文无序号导引方式，用破折号引出主题句和具体建议内容。就前后两部分逻辑而言，存在因果关系，需要在翻译时进行逻辑显化。通过主题句的译文可以看出，译者对前后两部分的结构关系显化处理，即运用不定式结构，将后半部分充当目的状语，体现前后两部分的目的关系。可见，译者考虑了汉英不同的思维习惯，突显了英语的形合特征，对汉语的意合结构进行显化，符合英语表达习惯和目标受众期待。变换后的结构同样整齐工整，表达凝练清晰，体现了主题句的概括和导引功能。除此之外，六个主题句的另一显著特征是都没有主语。汉语是主题显著的语言，不像英语强调主语显著，因而在主语的使用上存在诸多差异。无主句结构在政治外交文本中非常常见，翻译时可根据上下文语境采用多种方法，比如变主动结构为被动结构，常借 it 形式主语，如用 it is hoped/ believed that...结构，或者采用分词短语结构，或者通过添加主语等。就上例主题句而言，译文采用分词短语结构翻译六个主题句，尽量贴合源语形式，动词 -ing+ 宾语 + 不定式结构整齐再现了原文的形式美。另外，上例中第一、二及五、六条建议也是无主句，译文大部分都添加了主语 we，表示中日韩三方，第五句添加 the three countries，更加明确主语所指。另外，由于具体阐述的建议较长，有些句子译者采用切分法，用添加主语的方式译成两至三句话，使表达更为清晰明了。以第一条建议为例，第二句话切分成三句话：We need to view each other's development in an objective and rational light. In the spirit of facing history squarely and shaping a brighter future, we need to respect each other's core interests and major concerns, stay focused on mutually beneficial cooperation, and keep to dialogue and consultation in addressing differences. This will create enabling conditions for deeper cooperation. 前两句用 we 做主语，主干部分统一用 we need to 结构完成翻译；第三句话用 This 做主语，明确与前两句的逻辑关系，体现由前两方面举措带来的结果，符合英语思维方式。用 we need to 结构翻译无主语主题句在外交文本中比较常见，再如下例：

原文 李克强指出，当前国际格局正经历深刻调整。中日韩应加强团结合作，发扬同舟共济精神，坚定支持多边主义和自由贸易，共同应对挑战，为地区乃至世界的繁荣稳定作出贡献。

第一，要共同维护地区和平稳定。实现半岛无核化、建立和平机制符合三国的共同利益。要继续推进对话取得进展，妥善处理各方合理关切，推动半岛问题政治解决，实现地区长治久安。

第二，要共同践行新的安全理念。坚持共同、综合、合作、可持续的新安全观，基于共同安全利益，追求本地区的整体安全。国家间加强安全合作不应针对第三方，不应影响地区稳定。

第三，要共同坚持开放包容。秉持相互尊重、公平正义、合作共赢的原则，维护自由贸易，推进世界贸易组织改革，反对"脱钩"和分割。

第四，要共同引领区域合作。三国要加强在地区合作中的协调配合，引领区域合作聚焦东亚、聚焦发展，维护和完善东亚现有区域合作架构，使之更加符合地区国家需要。

译文 Li Keqiang pointed out, the current international landscape is undergoing profound adjustment. Our three countries must step up unity and cooperation in a spirit of mutual help and partnership. We must stand firmly by multilateralism and free trade, jointly address challenges and make contributions to regional and global prosperity and stability.

First, we need to jointly safeguard regional peace and stability. Realizing denuclearization and establishing a peace mechanism on the Peninsula is in the interest of all three countries. We need to continue to facilitate progress in the talks, properly address the legitimate concerns of all parties and push for the political settlement of the Korean Peninsula issue, with a view to achieving enduring peace and security of our region.

Second, we need to jointly apply a new vision of security. We need to follow a new vision of common, comprehensive, cooperative and sustainable security, and work for the security of the whole region proceeding from our common security interests. Moves to enhance security cooperation should neither target third parties nor undermine regional stability.

Third, we need to jointly pursue openness and inclusiveness. We need to keep with the principles of mutual respect, fairness, justice and win-win cooperation, safeguard free trade, promote the reform of the World Trade Organization and oppose "decoupling" and segmentation.

Fourth, we need to jointly drive regional cooperation. We need to strengthen coordination and collaboration in regional cooperation. We need to keep the focus of regional cooperation on East Asia and on development, and preserve and improve the existing East Asian cooperation architecture to better serve the needs of countries in this region.

在此例中，李克强总理从四大方面强调了中日韩加强团结合作的重要性："第一，要共同维护地区和平稳定"；"第二，要共同践行新的安全理念"；"第三，要共同坚持开放包容"；"第四，要共同引领区域合作"。因为"第一""第二""第三"及"第四"在目标语中存在对等表达方式，所以直接译成 first、second、third、fourth 即可。当然，序号的使用存在国别差异，汉语有自己独特的标序体系，除了上述方式，也常常使用"一、二、三"罗列顺序，而英语则习惯使用罗马数字标序，翻译时需要采用归化策略，使用英语标序方式，便于目标读者接受。上述四句都是运用无主语结构阐明四个段落的核心内容，译者统一采用增译法，将隐性主语显化，利用 we need to 结构引出四个方面的核心观点。因此，上面四句主题句分别译为"First, we need to jointly safeguard regional peace and stability. Second, we need to jointly apply a new vision of security. Third, we need to jointly pursue openness and inclusiveness. Fourth, we need to jointly drive regional cooperation."，四个主题句的翻译传神达意，结构整齐一致，用词准确到位。四个主题句中的"共同"统一用 jointly 译出，强调"联合""携手"

的重要性。事实上，"共同"在此例中是个高频词，李克强总理在不同方面强调了三方团结协作的重要性，其他使用情况包括："共同应对挑战""实现半岛无核化、建立和平机制符合三国的共同利益""坚持共同、综合、合作、可持续的新安全观，基于共同安全利益，追求本地区的整体安全"，分别译为"jointly address challenges"，"Realizing denuclearization and establishing a peace mechanism on the Peninsula is in the interest of all three countries"以及"We need to follow a new vision of common, comprehensive, cooperative and sustainable security, and work for the security of the whole region proceeding from our common security interests."。第一例为短语，"共同"译为 jointly。第二例和第三例为句子，在"三国共同利益"中，"共同"根据上下文语境译为 all；最后一例中，"共同"出现两次，全部译为 common，表示"共有"或者"共用"。因此，"共同"在不同的上下文语境意义会有所不同，务必正确领会内涵。总体而言，四句主题句的翻译大体遵循了忠实原则，实现了政治文本翻译的准确性和严谨性。

3 外交新闻报道中观点与立场表达的翻译

本章两个范例都从不同方面涉及观点或立场的表达，体现外交新闻报道中经常涉及的重要方面，即报道某一活动、会议或事件中参与者或相关者的看法、立场等。事实上，这也是外交文本总体上的重要特征之一。国家领导人或外交官员在参加不同场合的重要外交活动，或者面对各类外交事件时，时常会有针对性地发表观点或者立场。

统计可见，两个范例中最常用的引出观点或者立场的表达包括"表示""说""提出""指出""强调""呼吁""希望"等，几种表达都有常用英语表达方式，"表示"出现率最高，共 11 次，其中 9 次译为 say，2 次译为 express；"呼吁"出现 2 次，分别采用 call on/upon sb. to do sth. 结构和 call for doing sth. 结构进行翻译；"期待"2 次皆译为 expect；"指出""说""强调""相信"都出现 1 次，分别直译为 point out, say, emphasize 和 believe；"希望"出现 3 次，采用三种翻译方式，分别为 express the hope that…, hope that…以及 should…结构，最后一种翻译比较特殊，并未采用常见的直译法进行翻译。

原句 欧中签署全面投资协定符合双方利益，<u>希望</u>通过坦诚对话克服当前出现的困难。

译文 The EU-China comprehensive investment agreement serves the common interests, so both sides <u>should</u> overcome the current difficulties through candid dialogues.

译者选用 should 翻译"希望",表示提出的建议,更符合上下文语境折射的内涵。"认为"译成 say 也比较特殊,此类译法通常用于转述观点语境之中。此外,还有"一致认为"(agree that...),"普遍认为"(generally believe that...)等表达在此类文本中也比较常见。有时也会用 it is...结构引出观点,比如"大家普遍主张"可译为"It was a prevailing view among participants that...",体现语言表达的多样性,如下例:

原文 <u>大家普遍主张</u>要秉持开放包容精神,积极开展国际交流合作,促进新兴科技发展并实现成果互惠共享,<u>防</u>止科技鸿沟。

译文 <u>It was a prevailing view among participants that</u> all parties need to advocate the development and benefit-sharing of emerging technologies in the spirit of openness and inclusiveness and through international exchange and cooperation, and prevent digital gap.

本章两个范例中多处可见表示支持立场的典型表达。比如,有关意愿的表达有"愿同……",出现 2 次,其中 1 次译为 be willing to...,1 次译为 stand ready to...。两者在外交文本中在表达意愿时使用频率都很高,单独的"愿"字出现 3 次,其中译为 be willing to... 2 次,stand ready to... 1 次。此外,"将与"也可用于传达意愿,同样可用 stand ready to...或 be willing to...进行翻译。范例中与评价相关的表达包括"评价",译为 assess,"积极评价"译为 evaluates positively,"充分肯定"译为 fully affirm,"给予高度评价"译为 express high appreciation,其他外交文本也常见"高度评价"译为 speak highly of sth.。表示支持立场的表达还有很多,比如表示"同意"的表达译成 approve, accept 等,"双方同意"译为 the two sides agreed to...,"双方一致同意"译为 the two sides agreed to...;"高度一致"译为 be highly consistent in...,"达成新的重要共识"译为 reach new and important consensus 等。"支持"在范例中出现 3 次,皆译为 support,表达"公开支持"还可用 endorse。值得一提的是,有时为了表示支持态度的坚决,经常会用"坚定"加强语气,表明不可撼动的决心,如本章范例二中的句子:

原文 科文尼表示,爱方<u>坚定</u>支持联合国及其专门机构发挥作用,赞赏中方面对单边主义逆流时<u>坚定</u>维护多边主义,这样做很不容易,对广大中小国家尤为重要。

| 译文 | Coveney said, Ireland firmly supports the role of the UN and its institutions, and praises China's firm safeguarding of multilateralism despite headwinds of unilateralism. It is indeed not easy, but multilateralism is vital to small and medium-sized countries. |

在本例中,"坚定"出现2次,前者表示爱方对联合国及其专门机构的"坚定支持",译为firmly support,保留了偏正结构;后者指中方对多边主义的"坚定维护",译为firm safeguarding of。受上下文语法结构影响,前者使用副词firmly,后者用形容词firm,尤其译文praises China's firm safeguarding of multilateralism despite headwinds of unilateralism变换了原句结构,打破原文"中方面对单边主义逆流时坚定维护多边主义"的宾语从句结构,改用名词短语做宾语,更加简洁清晰。其他类似的表达还有"坚定奉行"(firmly adhere to)、"坚定站在"(firmly stand on the side of)等。再如,

| 原文 | 在爱尔兰,华人深受尊重,为爱的经济社会发展作出了重要贡献,爱对中方投资持欢迎和开放态度,希望成为中国企业进入欧洲的门户。 |

| 译文 | Overseas Chinese are highly respected in Ireland, and they make a significant contribution to Irish social and economic development. Ireland welcomes the investment from China, and hopes to become a gateway of Chinese enterprises to the European market. |

本例强调了华人及中国企业在爱尔兰的认同地位,不但用"深受尊重"表达华人在爱尔兰的重要地位,而且用"持欢迎和开放态度"欢迎中方企业在爱投资。前者用be highly respected直译原文内涵,后者采用简化翻译,单用welcome表达欢迎和开放的态度,基本传达了原文信息。

翻译中也会经常涉及汉英思维习惯差异问题的处理,除上文无主句的处理方式外,还会涉及诸多其他方面。如下文有关爱尔兰对中方支持态度的例子:

| 原文 | 科文尼祝贺中国经过艰苦努力成功控制疫情,感谢中方为爱抗疫提供的宝贵支持和帮助,表示爱尔兰是世界上最开放的经济体、中国是世界上最大的消费市场,爱高度重视推进与中国的务实合作,愿继续深化与中方在网络安全、航空、地方等领域合作,克服疫情影响积极推动人员往来和人文交流。 |

| 译文 | Coveney congratulates on China's successful control of the COVID-19 after |

> making arduous efforts, and thanks China for offering valuable support and sincere assistance in Irish fight against the pandemic. He said, Ireland is the most open economy, and China is the largest consumer market. Ireland prioritizes its practical cooperation with China, and stands ready to deepen cooperation with China in fields such as cyber security, and aviation, as well as at local levels to overcome the impact of the pandemic and actively promote people-to-people exchanges.

本例是典型的中式长句，具有汉语意合特征，体现竹节式结构，句子流散疏放，一个主语可以引出多个动词结构。因强调主题突出，源语读者理解起来比较容易。然而，翻译成英语时，就得按照形合思维，尽量满足目标受众表达习惯，使用树状结构，或明晰不同成分之间的关系。必要时，还要对这样的长句进行拆分，使信息更加清晰易懂。上例译文可见，译者首先根据原文传达的信息，将原文的一句话译成三句话，明晰了科文尼传达的三层含义：一是对中国的祝贺和感谢，二是强调了中国与爱尔兰的重要地位，三是表明爱方与中方合作的重视与意愿。通过运用拆分法，译文迎合英语表达习惯，逻辑关系更为清晰。除此之外，译文同样考虑了英汉语序差异问题，在本例中主要体现在修饰语的翻译上。与英文不同，汉语没有后置定语，但可以有较长的前置定语，翻译时必须根据英语思维和语法厘清哪些修饰成分前置，哪些后置，否则会影响译文的可读性和可接受度。思维习惯不同，必然会引发表达语序或逻辑差异。比如本例中，状语"经过艰苦努力"和"为爱抗疫"都做了后置处理，"最开放的经济体""最大的消费市场""务实合作"中的定语则仍保留前置位置。一般而言，较短的定语不会后置，较长的定语大都会后置处理，如翻译"愿继续深化与中方在网络安全、航空、地方等领域合作"中的定语就需调整表达顺序，将"在网络安全、航空、地方等领域"后置化，整个部分译为"stands ready to deepen cooperation with China in fields such as cyber security, and aviation, as well as at local levels"。再如，

原文 要用好中爱科技创新联委会等机制，加强科技创新、优质农业、高等教育、文化产业等领域交流合作。

译文 We should leverage mechanisms such as China-Ireland Technological Innovation Joint Commission, strengthen exchange and cooperation in fields such as technological innovation, quality agriculture, higher education, and cultural industry.

在此例中，"中爱科技创新联委会""科技创新、优质农业、高等教育、文化产业"作为定语同样采用后置化处理，根据英语表达习惯用 such as 引出，表示列举。值得一提的是，有时定语的后置也会涉及词性转化，比如：

> **原文** 要共同追求和平、发展、公平、正义、民主、自由的全人类共同价值。

> **译文** We should all pursue the common values of peace, development, fairness, justice, democracy and freedom.

本句中的定语修饰语较长，"和平、发展、公平、正义、民主、自由的全人类共同"修饰"价值"，译文采用形容词名词化处理方式，除了"共同"保留形容词词性并保留前置位置外，"和平""发展""公平""正义""民主""自由"六个形容词全部转化为名词并后置，放在 the common values of 后面，译为 peace, development, fairness, justice, democracy and freedom。译文地道清晰，可读性较强。

本章范例中还涉及通过贺辞（congratulations）、贺信（a letter expressing warm congratulations）表达支持立场。除此之外，有时领导人也会通过贺电（a congratulatory message/message of congratulation）表示祝贺和支持。外交文本中跟祝贺相关的动词结构常用 congratulate somebody on something 或者 send/extend/offer congratulations to somebody on something 等，如下例：

> **原文** 中国农业农村部部长韩长赋向庆祝活动致视频贺辞，预祝活动圆满成功，呼吁各国为民兴茶、健康饮茶、开放促茶。

> **译文** Minister of Agriculture and Rural Affairs of China Mr. Han Changfu offered his congratulations and good wishes through a video message. He called upon all countries to put people first in developing the tea sector, advocate healthy ways to drink tea, and develop the tea sector through opening-up.

在本例中，译者在翻译"向庆祝活动致视频贺辞"和"预祝活动圆满成功"时采用合并方式，用一个动词 offer 引出两方面内容，同时将"预祝活动圆满成功"简化翻译为 offer good wishes，打破原有汉语表达习惯，使行文更为简洁易懂，满足目标受众期待。更值得一提的是，翻译韩部长的呼吁"为民兴茶、健康饮茶、开放促茶"时，译者根据上下文语境显化三个"茶"字的真正内涵，极大增强了译文的可读性。第一、第三个"茶"指"茶产业"，故译成 tea sector；第二个"茶"指"茶叶"，故译成 tea。整体内容译为"put people first in developing the tea sector, advocate healthy ways to drink tea, and develop the tea sector through opening-up"，其中"为民""健康""开放"的词性也因目的语习惯进行了适当转换,译文可读性得到增强。

> **原文** 习近平主席专门向"国际茶日"系列活动致贺信,表示中方愿同各方一道,推动全球茶产业持续健康发展,深化茶文化交融互鉴,让更多的人知茶、爱茶,共品茶香茶韵,共享美好生活。

> **译文** President Xi Jinping sent a letter expressing warm congratulations on a series of activities marking the first International Tea Day, and said that China is willing to work with all sides to nurture the sustained and healthy development of the global tea industry, deepen cultural exchange on tea, and allow more people to relish lives accompanied by tea.

在此例中,习近平主席通过贺信(sent a letter expressing warm congratulations)表达了中方愿同世界各方共同推动茶产业发展的立场。译文多半忠于原文,在结尾部分进行了简化改写,将"让更多的人知茶、爱茶,共品茶香茶韵,共享美好生活"译为 allow more people to relish lives accompanied by tea,省略"知茶、爱茶、共品茶香茶韵"具体信息,而是采用模糊方式简单翻成 accompanied by tea。就忠实原则而言,译文实有一定缺憾,但相对简单易懂,便于接受。除省略外,拆分也是实现译文简单易懂的有效方法,见下例:

> **原文** 联合国粮农组织总干事屈冬玉通过视频致闭幕辞,祝贺"国际茶日"活动圆满成功,表示饮茶文化源远流长,茶产业支撑着数百万农村地区人口的生计,希望各方携起手来,促进茶产业可持续发展。

> **译文** Director General of the FAO Mr. Qu Dongyu delivered closing remarks. He extended congratulations on the full success of the virtual celebration and said that the culture of drinking tea enjoys a long history and the tea industry provides livelihood for millions in rural areas. He expressed the hope that all parties could join hands to promote the sustainable development of tea industry.

译文可见,译者总体采用直译法,原意传达比较全面准确,但在形式上尚未完全对等。如前面所述,汉语与英语结构存在鲜明差异,前者为竹节结构,常见流水长句,整体比较松散;后者为树形或是葡萄结构,句子与句子之间相互逻辑关联紧密。竹节式松散长句在中国外交文体中比较常见,此例就是典型之一。主语"联合国粮农组织总干事屈冬玉"的后面是由"致""祝贺""表示""希望"四个谓语动词构成的动宾结构,且除了第一个宾语外,其余三个宾语都是句子。如不厘清意群关联，而按原有结构简单直译，势必造成句式复杂冗余，影响受众理解和接受。解决此类问题的常用方法是将长句拆分成几个句子，以确保信息和意义传达的清晰性。根据译文可见，译者在翻译本句时将原句拆分为三句话。第一句点明发表致辞；第二句表达祝贺并点明茶产业的重要性；第三句提出希望。三句中第一句为简单句，第三句为复杂句，保留了源语宾语形式。第二句前半句将原有的宾语从句结构（"国际茶日"活动圆满成功）变成名词短语充当宾语，译为"congratulations on the full success of the virtual celebration"，后半部分直译再现宾语从句，译为"the culture of drinking tea enjoys a long history and the tea industry provides livelihood for millions in rural areas"。总体而言，拆分处理恰当合理，译文清晰明了，利于理解。

　　上述分析绝大多数皆与支持或者中立（希望、呼吁、指出等）立场的典型翻译相关。与此同时，也需注意的是，外交新闻中也可见"决不接受"（never bow to）、"反对"（oppose）等否定立场的例子，翻译时也要做到忠实精确。外交事务中常常涉及违背国际政策、原则、条约、利益等的不当行为，对此会表达不满，提出反对、抗议、交涉等，行为严重时会提出强烈反对、强烈谴责、严正交涉等。比如，"提出交涉"译为 lodges representations to，"提出严正交涉"译为 lodge stern representations，"坚决反对"译为 firmly oppose，"强烈谴责"译为 strongly condemn 等。强调"公开谴责"或者"强烈谴责"有时也用 deplore。除此之外，常用表达还有"遗憾"（regret）、"强烈不满"（be strongly dissatisfied）、"表达强烈不满"（express strong disapproval/discontent/dissatisfaction）、"表示关切"（express concern）、"表示严重关切"（express grave concern）等。另外，还有一些表示敦促与命令的常用表达也需掌握，如"敦促"（urge）、"要求"（demand, request）、"命令"（order）等。

五　中国关键词加油站

1　人民至上 *put the people in the first place*

　　人民至上，坚持以人民为中心的发展思想，是习近平始终不变的执政理念。人民至上，就是要"在任何时候都把群众利益放在第一位"。中国共产党根基在人民、血脉在人民。党团结带领人民进行革命、建设、改革，根本目的就是让人民过上好日子，无论面临多大挑战和压力，无论付出多大牺牲和代价，这一点都始终不渝、毫不动摇。人民至上，就是要"紧紧依靠人民"。人民是千千万万的普通人。然而，正是千千万万普通人的奋斗造就了极不平凡的事业。人民当家作主是社会主义民主政治的本质特征。我国社会主义民主是维护人民根本利益最广泛、最真实、最管用的民主。我们要坚持人民民主，更好把人民的智慧和力量凝聚到党和人民事业中来。人民至上，就是要"把为民造福作为最重要的政绩"。党员、干部特别是领导干部要清醒地认识到，自己手中的权力、所处的岗位，是党和人民赋予的，是为党和人民做事用的，只能用来为民谋利。要求真务实、真抓实干，把老百姓的安危冷暖时刻放在心上，以造福人民为最大政绩，想群众之所想，急群众之所急，让人民生活更加幸福美满。

2 全球公共卫生安全 global public health security

全球化时代，有人说"文明与病毒之间，只隔了一个航班的距离"。防控不力，病毒对人类的杀伤力轻易地就能成千上万倍地扩散和放大。全球命运与共，没有谁能独善其身。2020年1月28日，习近平主席会见世界卫生组织总干事谭德塞时指出，疫情是魔鬼，我们不能让魔鬼藏匿。中国政府始终本着公开、透明、负责任的态度及时向国内外发布疫情信息，积极回应各方关切，加强与国际社会合作。世界卫生组织在协调全球卫生事务方面发挥着重要作用，中方高度重视同世界卫生组织的合作。中方愿同世界卫生组织和国际社会一道，共同维护好地区和全球的公共卫生安全。

3 外防输入、内防扩散 preventing the coronavirus from entering and spreading within a region

控制新增、防止扩散是疫情防控工作的关键所在。以习近平同志为核心的党中央多次要求各省市采取针对性措施，做到外防输入、内防扩散。这是针对非疫情防控重点地区、人口流动大省大市的一项差异化防控策略。

社区是疫情联防联控的第一线，也是外防输入、内防扩散最有效的防线。通过把好入口关，强化网格化管理，守好社区防控，筑牢安全防线，可以有效切断传染源，控制新增输入性病例，防止疫情扩散蔓延。

疫情防控期间，中共中央、国务院还发出了减少人员流动、协同抗击疫情的号召，通过及时延长春节假期，提前部署延迟开学、灵活复工、错峰出行，并在健康监测、人员管理等方面采取严格措施，坚决抓好外防输入、内防扩散两大环节。

4 出入境防疫 epidemic prevention at borders

2020 年 3 月 9 日召开的中央应对新冠肺炎疫情工作领导小组会议指出，为有效防范疫情跨境传播，要加强国际合作，做好出入境防疫工作。要推动关口前移，加强出入境相关信息共享，协调推动对来华人员在离境国进行健康检测，做好航空器清洁消毒、机组防护、健康申报、体温检测、飞行途中防控等，采取分区分级分类输入风险管控措施。严格实施出入境人员口岸卫生检疫和防控工作，在严控疫情输出的同时，对卫生检疫部门判定的确诊病例、疑似病例、密切接触者等入境人员，按规定落实检测、转运、治疗、隔离、留观等措施，并加强人文关怀。与有关国家教育部门建立协调机制，暂缓或减少留学人员等双向流动。做好对我国在境外公民疫情防控的指导帮扶工作。北京等出入境人员较多的口岸，要依法实施缜密的出入境防疫管理。

5 重大疫情防控体制机制 mechanism for major epidemic prevention and control

国家治理能力是指运用国家制度管理社会事务的能力，包括改革开放发展、社会稳定运行、内政外交国防、治党治军治国等多方面内容。治理体系和治理能力是一体两面，只有完备的体系，而缺乏应有的执行能力，落实就会不到位；拥有完备的体系，还必须具有较强的治理能力才能充分发挥制度的优越性。要着力完善重大疫情防控救治体系、医疗保险和救助制度。我们既要健全重大疫情应急响应机制，建立集中统一高效的领导指挥体系，全面提升应急管理能力，增强应急救援的协同性、整体性、专业性，又要健全重大疾病医疗保险和救助制度，完善应急医疗救助机制，在突发疫情等紧急情况时，确保医疗机构先救治、后收费，解除群众的后顾之忧。疫情防控是对国家治理体系和治理能力的一次大考、一堂大课。完善国家治理体系、提高治理能力关系到党和国家安危及人民的命运，是当前的头等重要工作，也是今后需长期加强的紧迫任务。

6 教育扶贫 poverty alleviation through education

新中国成立以来，党和国家十分重视发展教育事业，开展普及九年制义务教育、扫除青壮年文盲、均衡发展优质教育资源、精准帮扶贫困家庭子女等一系列教育扶贫措施和行动，对扶贫攻坚作出了卓越贡献。中共十八大以来，习近平围绕"全面建成小康社会"提出了一系列新思想、新论断、新要求，对扶贫工作作出了一系列重要部署，对教育扶贫提出了明确要求。2015 年 11 月，习近平在中央扶贫开发工作会议上强调，教育是阻断贫困代际传递的治本之策，贫困地区教育事业是管长远的，必须下大力气抓好，扶贫既要富口袋，也要富脑袋。

根据《关于实施教育扶贫工程的意见》，基础教育主要解决贫困地区办学条件差、教育基础设施薄弱、优质师资队伍欠缺、教育经费不足等造成的基础教育办学质量不达标以及基础教育普及程度不达标等问题；职业教育要提高促进脱贫致富的能力，提高贫困地区贫困人群的自主发展能力，发展贫困地区区域性经济，解决贫困地区"造血能力"不足等问题；高等教育一方面要与贫困地区的经济、产业、科技发展相结合，促进贫困地区产业结构升级，另一方面要通过"继续实施高校招生倾斜政策"，保障和增加贫困地区学生接受高等教育的机会。

7 易地扶贫搬迁 relocation of rural poor for poverty alleviation

易地搬迁是"五个一批"精准脱贫的重要内容，是中共中央发出脱贫攻坚战总动员后的第一仗，也是中国打赢脱贫攻坚战的重要内容。《中共中央 国务院关于打赢脱贫攻坚战的决定》提出，实施易地搬迁脱贫，对居住在生存条件恶劣、生态环境脆弱、自然灾害频发等地区的农村贫困人口，加快实施易地扶贫搬迁工程。

易地搬迁属于生态扶贫和绿色减贫的范畴，其主要原因就是易地搬迁应遵循自然规律与经济规律，对于生态环境较差的地区，实施保护型减贫策略，通过搬迁、因地制宜确定安置方式来改善贫困人口的客观生存环境，有效缓解扶贫开发造成的环境破坏，促进当地经济社会的可持续发展。根据规划，"十三五"时期中国将对约 1000 万建档立卡贫困人口实施易地扶贫搬迁。截至 2019 年年末，易地扶贫搬迁建设任务基本完成。

8 金融扶贫 financial measures for poverty alleviation

金融扶贫是脱贫攻坚适应市场经济要求、拓展资金渠道的新举措，是扶贫投入的重大创新，是脱贫攻坚最强有力的支撑。具体来说，金融扶贫是指在中央政府主导下，各级政府、金融机构、各类企业或非企业社会组织参与扶贫开发，主要面向贫困地区和贫困人群提供综合金融服务，扶持低收入和贫困农户生产和经营，帮助其摆脱贫困、增加收入，实现自力更生，提高经济社会地位。

在长期扶贫开发探索和实践中，金融扶贫政策和机制不断完善和创新，从最开始实施扶贫贴息贷款到推广小额信贷（微型金融），从探索金融扶贫模式到初步形成金融扶贫政策体系，再到普惠金融、金融科技的发展支持下的精准扶贫战略，金融扶贫被越来越广泛地应用于中国扶贫开发的各个领域，在中国扶贫开发过程中发挥着越来越重要的作用。金融扶贫已成为推进中国扶贫开发的一项有效工具和重要手段。

9 健康扶贫 the health program for poverty alleviation

国务院扶贫办建档立卡数据显示，截至2015年年底，因病致贫、因病返贫的贫困人口近2000万人，占贫困人口总数的44.1%。其中，患大病的和慢性病的是734万人。在各种致贫原因中，因病致贫在各地区都排在最前面。健康不良的状态容易导致贫困，贫困又容易滋生疾病，贫困人口极易陷入"疾病—贫困—疾病"的恶性循环。

因此，保障贫困人口的健康权利，防止因病致贫、因病返贫，开展健康扶贫，成为脱贫攻坚的重点领域。健康扶贫是国家精准扶贫精准脱贫方略的重要组成部分，是确保打赢脱贫攻坚战、实现全面建成小康社会目标的重要举措。为此，国家卫生计生委、国务院扶贫办等部门联合印发《关于实施健康扶贫工程的指导意见》，强调健康扶贫工程要按照脱贫攻坚"两不愁三保障"的要求，聚焦贫困人口"基本医疗有保障"这一总体目标，落实健康中国和乡村振兴两大战略，通过大病集中救治一批、慢病签约服务管理一批、重病兜底保障一批"三个一批"行动计划，努力让贫困人口"看得起病、看得好病、看得上病、少生病"。

10 精准扶贫 targeted poverty alleviation

精准扶贫是中国贫困治理的重大理论创新，是中共中央治国理政新理念新思想新战略的重要组成部分。中共十八大以来，基于习近平关于精准扶贫的一系列重要论述，中国共产党治理贫困工作翻开新篇章：脱贫攻坚战在全国全面打响，国家贫困治理体系日渐完善，减贫实践取得历史最好成绩。从政策设计层面来看，精准扶贫有着明确的减贫目标，是问题导向的贫困治理创新，是提高中国减贫成效的策略性选择。从新时代中国特色社会主义的背景以及习近平有关扶贫工作重要论述的整体来看，精准扶贫不仅是减贫事业的创新，更是治国理政思想的重要发展。

这种创新性的贫困治理理念及严谨的政策体系，使得脱贫攻坚取得了亮眼的减贫成绩，并对中国经济社会发展产生了诸多积极而深远的影响，充分显示了其实践价值。在贫困治理方面，精准扶贫不仅破解了贫困治理固有的若干难题，而且提升了扶贫开发的效能；在经济社会发展方面，精准扶贫一方面激活了农村基层社会治理，另一方面促进了区域经济社会的整体发展。此外，精准扶贫还在激活基层农村社会治理、提升扶贫资源配置的公正性等方面产生了积极影响。

脱贫攻坚彰显了中国特色减贫之路的新发展，精准扶贫方略包含了反贫困的中国智慧与中国方案，对于中国打赢脱贫攻坚战以及完善贫困治理体系具有非凡的意义。同时，作为科学的理论创新，其对于国际减贫事业同样具有重要的启示意义。

六　外交新闻翻译练习

1．将下列外交新闻翻译成英语，注意标题或主题句的恰当翻译。

1）与会领导人经过友好、深入交流，达成以下共识：

一、对新冠肺炎疫情在全球范围内扩散蔓延，给世界各国人民带来前所未有的迫切挑战，给非洲人民的生命健康安全造成巨大冲击深表关切。

二、高度评价和积极支持世界卫生组织在谭德塞总干事带领下为世界各国应对疫情发挥引领和协调作用，呼吁国际社会加大对世界卫生组织政治支持和资金投入。

三、非方高度评价中国政府采取坚决果断措施阻遏疫情蔓延，本着公开、透明和负责任态度及时向世界卫生组织及相关国家通报疫情信息，为全球抗疫赢得宝贵时间。

四、充分肯定中非投融资合作为非洲发展和民生改善发挥积极作用，呼吁国际社会通过团结合作，分享抗疫经验，向非洲国家提供更多物资、技术、资金和人道支持，帮助非方克服疫情影响、实现自主可持续发展。

五、重申坚定支持多边主义，反对单边主义，维护以联合国为核心的国际体系，捍卫国际公平正义。

六、祝贺中非合作论坛成立20周年，肯定中非合作论坛北京峰会成果落实行动取得重要进展，支持中非合作"八大行动"更多向公共卫生领域倾斜。

七、赞赏中国、南非和塞内加尔在非洲抗疫关键时期倡议发起此次峰会。

2）如何更好地开发、利用、治理新兴科技，既更好造福世界人民，又有效管控风险，是摆在我们面前的重大课题，值得国际社会深入思考。中方提出五点主张：

首先，推动创新发展，全面提高各国科技发展和应用能力，缩小数字鸿沟。

第二，营造良好环境，鼓励良性竞争，防止科技垄断。

第三，加强全球治理，更好规范新兴科技开发利用。

第四，认清新兴科技的潜在风险挑战，更好维护国际和平与安全。

第五，加强统筹协调，切实发挥联合国的核心作用。

2．将下列外交新闻翻译成英语，注意观点及立场的恰当翻译。

1）与会各方一致认为新兴科技发展事关人类前途命运，各方应高度重视、抓住机遇、充分利用、管控风险，确保新兴科技造福各国人民。大家普遍主张要秉持开放包容精神，积极开展国际交流合作，促进新兴科技发展并实现成果互惠共享，防止科技鸿沟。大家支持奉行多边主义，充分利用联合国平台，加强对话交流，探讨新兴科技开发利用，推进新兴科技全球治理。

2）杨洁篪会见德国总理默克尔

当地时间2020年1月19日，习近平主席特别代表、中共中央政治局委员、中央外事工作委员会办公室主任杨洁篪在出席利比亚问题柏林峰会期间会见德国总理默克尔。

杨洁篪表示，当前世界形势复杂多变，中德作为两个重要国家，应该相互尊重，加强合作，共同践行多边主义，携手应对全球性挑战，推动双边关系不断健康稳定向前发展。中方愿同德方保持密切高层交往，赞赏默克尔总理积极致力于推动欧盟加强对华合作，愿同德方及新一届欧盟机构一道，推动中欧全面战略伙伴关系取得新发展。

默克尔感谢习近平主席派代表出席利比亚问题峰会，赞赏中方支持多边主义和国际合作，为解决国际和地区问题发挥建设性作用。默克尔表示，德方将积极努力推动德中关系改善和发展，我本人正在为今年德中、欧中一系列重要政治议程作认真准备，将同中方保持密切沟通，确保取得积极成果。

3．将下列外交新闻翻译成英语，注意职务翻译的正确性。

1）2019年12月24日上午，国务院总理李克强在成都与韩国总统文在寅、日本首相安倍晋三共同出席第八次中日韩领导人会议，就中日韩合作以及地区和国际问题交换看法。

2）近日，中华人民共和国主席习近平根据全国人民代表大会常务委员会的决定任免下列驻外大使：

一、免去邢海明的中华人民共和国驻蒙古国特命全权大使职务；

任命柴文睿为中华人民共和国驻蒙古国特命全权大使。

二、免去邱国洪的中华人民共和国驻大韩民国特命全权大使职务；

任命邢海明为中华人民共和国驻大韩民国特命全权大使。

3）2020年1月21日，中共中央政治局委员、中央外事工作委员会办公室主任杨洁篪在京会见第74届联大安理会改革政府间谈判机制共同主席、阿联酋常驻联合国代表努赛贝和波兰常驻联合国代表维罗涅卡。

杨洁篪说，联合国安理会改革的目标是增强安理会的权威和效力，增加发展中国家和中小国家的代表性和发言权，体现国际关系民主化和世界多极化趋势。中方将积极支持两位主席工作，确保改革朝着符合联合国宪章和广大会员国共同利益的方向前进。

第四章

外交公报翻译

一、外交公报的概念及文体特点

外交是指一个国家与国际关系相关的所有活动，如参加国际组织和会议，与他国互派使节、谈判、签订条约和协定等；公报是公开发表的、关于重大的会议决议、国际谈判、国际协议、军事行动等的正式文稿，或者是由政府编印的刊物，专门刊载法律、法令、决议、命令、条约、协定及其他官方文件。由此可见，外交公报（diplomatic communiqué）即为某个国家、政府、政党或团体组织向国内外公布其在国际关系事务上的重大事件、重要情况、重要决议等的正式通告或官方文件。

从发布公告的主体来看，外交公报一般包括两类，单发公报和联发公报。单发公报是指产生国际关系的若干国家中的单个国家，以其国家或政府的名义，正式向外报道关于国家领导人出访、来访等消息。联发公报又称为联合公报，是指产生国际关系的两个或两个以上国家、政府、政党、团体组织就某一国际重大问题或事件进行会谈和磋商情况的联合报道，共同发布的达成一致意见和看法的文书，以及最终形成的、需要各方承担一定权利与义务的协议。另外，从公告的内容来看，外交公报又可分为新闻和会议公报，以及条约公报。新闻和会议公报主要报道对国际重大问题的讨论情况，属于对礼节性友好往来的正式报道，不需双方代表签署，仅由双方议定文稿，在各自首都的重要报刊上发表。条约性公报反映双方或多方对共同关心的事件经过谈判达成的协议，规定各方承担的权利与义务等，须经各自全权代表签署，以昭信守。

外交公报发布的都是新近发生的事件或最新的决议等，充分利用广播、电视、报刊、网络等现代媒体进行广泛宣传，在制作和发布时要求迅速及时，宣传的内容完全公开，因此具有及时宣传性。从外交公报的发布主体来看，大多涉及某个或某几个国家、政府、政党或团体组织，包含了该主体的某种政治倾向、立场和主张，具有一定的政治性，外交公报所发布的内容关涉到重大的事件或决议，具有绝对的权威性。另外，就外交公告的语言而言，一方面语言使用特别讲求庄重严肃以体现公告主体的特殊性，另一方面措辞实事求是，力求真实、准确、可靠。综上所述，外交公报的主要特点包括及时宣传性、政治权威性、高度真实性。

二 外交公报汉英对照举隅

"一带一路"国际合作高峰论坛圆桌峰会联合公报
Joint Communiqué of Leaders Roundtable of Belt and Road Forum

我们，中华人民共和国主席习近平、阿根廷总统马克里、白俄罗斯总统卢卡申科、智利总统巴切莱特、捷克总统泽曼、印度尼西亚总统佐科、哈萨克斯坦总统纳扎尔巴耶夫、肯尼亚总统肯雅塔、吉尔吉斯斯坦总统阿坦巴耶夫、老挝国家主席本扬、菲律宾总统杜特尔特、俄罗斯总统普京、瑞士联邦主席洛伊特哈德、土耳其总统埃尔多安、乌兹别克斯坦总统米尔济约耶夫、越南国家主席陈大光、柬埔寨首相洪森、埃塞俄比亚总理海尔马里亚姆、斐济总理姆拜尼马拉马、希腊总理齐普拉斯、匈牙利总理欧尔班、意大利总理真蒂洛尼、马来西亚总理纳吉布、蒙古国总理额尔登巴特、缅甸国务资政昂山素季、巴基斯坦总理谢里夫、波兰总理希德沃、塞尔维亚总理、当选总统武契奇、西班牙首相拉霍伊、斯里兰卡总理维克勒马辛

We, President Xi Jinping of the People's Republic of China, President Mauricio Macri of the Republic of Argentina, President Alexander Lukashenko of the Republic of Belarus, President Michelle Bachelet Jeria of the Republic of Chile, President Milos Zeman of the Czech Republic, President Joko Widodo of the Republic of Indonesia, President Nursultan Nazarbayev of the Republic of Kazakhstan, President Uhuru Kenyatta of the Republic of Kenya, President Almazbek Atambayev of the Kyrgyz Republic, President Bounnhang Vorachith of the Lao People's Democratic Republic, President Rodrigo RoaDuterte of the Republic of the Philippines, President Vladimir Putin of the Russian Federation, President Doris Leuthard of the Swiss Confederation, President Recep Tayyip Erdogan of the Republic of Turkey, President Shavkat Mirziyoyev of the Republic of Uzbekistan, President Tran Dai Quang of the Socialist Republic of Viet Nam, Prime Minister Hun Sen of the Kingdom of Cambodia, Prime Minister Hailemariam Desalegn of the Federal Democratic Republic of Ethiopia, Prime Minister Josaia Voreqe Bainimarama of the Republic of

哈于2017年5月15日出席在北京举行的"一带一路"国际合作高峰论坛圆桌峰会。我们也欢迎联合国秘书长古特雷斯、世界银行行长金墉、国际货币基金组织总裁拉加德出席。会议由中华人民共和国主席习近平主持。

时代背景

当前，世界经济深度调整，机遇与挑战并存。这是一个充满机遇的时代，各国都在追求和平、发展与合作。联合国2030年可持续发展议程为国际发展合作描绘了新蓝图。

Fiji, Prime Minister Alexis Tsipras of the Hellenic Republic, Prime Minister Viktor Orban of Hungary, Prime Minister Paolo Gentiloni of the Italian Republic, Prime Minister Najib Razak of Malaysia, Prime Minister Jargaltulgyn Erdenebat of Mongolia, State Counsellor Aung San SuuKyi of the Republic of the Union of Myanmar, Prime Minister Muhammad Nawaz Sharif of the Islamic Republic of Pakistan, Prime Minister Beata Szydlo of the Republic of Poland, Prime Minister and President-elect Aleksandar Vucic of the Republic of Serbia, President of the Government Mariano Rajoy Brey of the Kingdom of Spain, and Prime Minister Ranil Wickremesinghe of the Democratic Socialist Republic of Sri Lanka, attended the Leaders Roundtable of the Belt and Road Forum for International Cooperation on 15 May 2017 in Beijing. We also welcome the participation of Secretary General Antonio Guterres of the United Nations, President Jim Yong Kim of the World Bank Group, Managing Director Christine Lagarde of the International Monetary Fund. The Leaders Roundtable was chaired by President Xi Jinping of the People's Republic of China.

General Context

We are mindful that the world economy is undergoing profound changes, presenting both opportunities and challenges. This is an era of opportunity, where countries continue to aspire for peace, development and cooperation. The UN 2030 Agenda for Sustainable Development with

在此背景下,我们欢迎各国积极开展双边、三方、区域和多边合作,消除贫困,创造就业,应对国际金融危机影响,促进可持续发展,推进市场化产业转型,实现经济多元化发展。我们高兴地注意到,各国发展战略和互联互通合作倡议层出不穷,为加强国际合作提供了广阔空间。

我们进一步认识到,世界经济面临诸多挑战,虽在缓慢复苏,但下行风险犹存。全球贸易和投资增长依然低迷,以规则为基础的多边贸易体制有待加强。各国特别是发展中国家仍然面临消除贫困、促进包容持续经济增长、实现可持续发展等共同挑战。

我们注意到,"丝绸之路经济带"和"21世纪海上丝绸之路"("一带一路"倡议)能够在挑战和变革中创造机遇,我们欢迎并支持"一带一路"

the set of Sustainable Development Goals at its core provides a new blueprint of international cooperation.

In this context, we welcome bilateral, triangular, regional and multilateral cooperation where countries place emphasis on eradicating poverty, creating jobs, addressing the consequences of international financial crises, promoting sustainable development, and advancing market-based industrial transformation and economic diversification. We note with appreciation that various development strategies and connectivity cooperation initiatives have been put forward, providing broad space for strengthening international cooperation.

We further recognize the challenges that the world economy faces. While it is currently experiencing modest recovery, downside risks remain. The growth of global trade and investment remains tempered, and the rules-based multilateral trading regime is yet to be strengthened. All countries, especially developing ones, still face common challenges of eradicating poverty, promoting inclusive and sustained economic growth, and achieving sustainable development.

Noting that the Silk Road Economic Belt and the 21st Century Maritime Silk Road (The Belt and Road Initiative) can create opportunities amidst challenges and changes, we welcome and support the Belt and Road Initiative to enhance

倡议。该倡议加强亚欧互联互通，同时对非洲、拉美等其他地区开放。"一带一路"作为一项重要的国际倡议，为各国深化合作提供了重要机遇，取得了积极成果，未来将为各方带来更多福祉。

我们强调，国际、地区和国别合作框架和倡议之间沟通协调能够为推进互联互通和可持续发展带来合作机遇。这些框架和倡议包括：2030年可持续发展议程、亚的斯亚贝巴行动议程、非洲2063年议程、文明古国论坛、亚太经合组织互联互通蓝图、东盟共同体愿景2025、亚欧会议及其互联互通工作组、商旅驿站关税倡议、中国和中东欧国家合作、中欧海陆快线、中间走廊倡议、中国–欧盟互联互通平台、欧盟东部伙伴关系、以平等、开放、透明为原则的欧亚伙伴关系、南美洲区域基础设施一体化倡议、东盟互联互通总体规划2025、欧亚经济联盟2030年经济发展基本方向、气候变化巴黎协定、跨欧洲交通运输网、西巴尔干六国互联互通议程、世界贸易组织贸易便利化协议等。

connectivity between Asia and Europe, which is also open to other regions such as Africa and South America. By providing important opportunities for countries to deepen cooperation, it has achieved positive outcomes and has future potential to deliver more benefits as an important international initiative.

We also emphasize the opportunities which can be created by communication and coordination among other global, regional and national frameworks and initiatives for promoting cooperation in connectivity and sustainable development, such as 2030 Agenda for Sustainable Development, Addis Ababa Action Agenda, Agenda 2063 of the African Union, Ancient Civilizations Forum, APEC Connectivity Blueprint, ASEAN Community Vision 2025, Asia-Europe Meeting and its group on path-finder of connectivity, Caravanserai Customs Initiative, China and Central and Eastern European Countries Cooperation, China-Europe Land-Sea Express Route, East-West Middle Corridor Initiative, EU-China Connectivity Platform, EU Eastern Partnership, Eurasian partnership based on the principles of equality, openness and transparency, Initiative for the Integration of Regional Infrastructure in South America, Master Plan on ASEAN Connectivity 2025, Main Directions for Economic Development of the Eurasian Economic Union until 2030, Paris Agreement on Climate Change, Trans-

我们重申,在"一带一路"倡议等框架下,共同致力于建设开放型经济、确保自由包容性贸易、反对一切形式的保护主义。我们将努力促进以世界贸易组织为核心、普遍、以规则为基础、开放、非歧视、公平的多边贸易体制。

合作目标

我们主张加强"一带一路"倡议和各种发展战略的国际合作,建立更紧密合作伙伴关系,推动南北合作、南南合作和三方合作。

我们重申,在公平竞争和尊重市场规律与国际准则基础上,大力促进经济增长、扩大贸易和投资。我们欢迎推进产业合作、科技创新和区域经济一体化,推动中小微企业深入融入全球价值链。同时发挥税收和财政政策作用,将增长和生产性投资作为优先方向。

我们主张加强各国基础设

European Transport Networks, Western Balkans 6 Connectivity Agenda, WTO Trade Facilitation Agreement.

We reaffirm our shared commitment to build open economy, ensure free and inclusive trade, oppose all forms of protectionism including in the framework of the Belt and Road Initiative. We endeavor to promote a universal, rules-based, open, non-discriminatory and equitable multilateral trading system with WTO at its core.

Cooperation Objectives

We stand for enhancing international cooperation including the Belt and Road Initiative and various development strategies, by building closer collaboration partnerships, which include advancing North-South, South-South, and triangular cooperation.

We reiterate the importance of expanding economic growth, trade and investment based on level-playing field, on market rules and on universally recognized international norms. We welcome the promotion of industrial cooperation, scientific and technological innovation, and regional economic cooperation and integration so as to increase, inter alia, the integration and participation of micro, small and medium enterprises in global value chains. Attention should be paid to tax and fiscal policies, prioritizing growth and productive investment.

We stand for strengthening physical,

施联通、规制衔接和人员往来。需要特别关注最不发达国家、内陆发展中国家、小岛屿发展中国家和中等收入国家，突破发展瓶颈，实现有效互联互通。

我们致力于扩大人文交流，维护和平正义，加强社会凝聚力和包容性，促进民主、良政、法治、人权，推动性别平等和妇女赋权；共同打击一切形式的腐败和贿赂；更好应对儿童、残疾人、老年人等弱势群体诉求；完善全球经济治理，确保所有人公平享有发展机遇和成果。

我们决心阻止地球的退化，包括在气候变化问题上立即采取行动，鼓励《巴黎协定》所有批约方全面落实协定；以平等、可持续的方式管理自然资源，保护并可持续利用海洋、淡水、森林、山地、旱地；保护生物多样性、生态系统和野生生物，防治荒漠化和土地退化等，实现经济、社会、环境三大领域综合、平衡、可持续发展。

institutional and people-to-people connectivity among all countries. The least developed countries, landlocked developing countries, small island developing states and middle-income countries deserve special attention to remove bottlenecks of development and achieve effective connectivity.

We endeavor to expand people-to-people exchanges, promote peace, justice, social cohesion, inclusiveness, democracy, good governance, the rule of law, human rights, gender equality and women empowerment; work together to fight against corruption and bribery in all their forms; to be more responsive to all the needs of those in vulnerable situations such as, children, persons with disabilities and older persons; and help improve global economic governance, and ensure equal access by all to development opportunities and benefits.

We are determined to protect the planet from degradation, including through taking urgent action on climate change and encouraging all parties which have ratified it to fully implement the Paris Agreement, managing the natural resources in an equitable and sustainable manner, conserving and sustainably using oceans and seas, freshwater resources, as well as forests, mountains and drylands, protecting biodiversity, ecosystems and wildlife, combating desertification and land degradation so as to achieving sustainable development in its three dimensions in a balanced

我们鼓励政府、国际和地区组织、私营部门、民间社会和广大民众共同参与,建立巩固友好关系,增进相互理解与信任。

合作原则

我们将秉持和平合作、开放包容、互学互鉴、互利共赢、平等透明、相互尊重的精神,在共商、共建、共享的基础上,本着法治、机会均等原则加强合作。为此,我们根据各自国内法律和政策,强调以下合作原则:

(1)平等协商。恪守《联合国宪章》宗旨和原则,尊重各国主权和领土完整等国际法基本准则;协商制定合作规划,推进合作项目。

(2)互利共赢。寻求利益契合点和合作最大公约数,兼顾各方立场。

(3)和谐包容。尊重自然和文化的多样性,相信所有文化和文明都能够为可持续发展作贡献。

(4)市场运作。充分认识

and integrated manner.

We encourage the involvement of governments, international and regional organizations, the private sector, civil society and citizens in fostering and promoting friendship, mutual understanding and trust.

Cooperation Principles

We uphold the spirit of peace, cooperation, openness, transparency, inclusiveness, equality, mutual learning, mutual benefit and mutual respect by strengthening cooperation on the basis of extensive consultation and the rule of law, joint efforts, shared benefits and equal opportunities for all. In this context we highlight the following principles guiding our cooperation, in accordance with our respective national laws and policies:

(1) Consultation on an equal footing: Honoring the purposes and principles of the UN Charter and international law including respecting the sovereignty and territorial integrity of countries; formulating cooperation plans and advancing cooperation projects through consultation.

(2) Mutual benefit: Seeking convergence of interests and the broadest common ground for cooperation, taking into account the perspectives of different stakeholders.

(3) Harmony and inclusiveness: Acknowledging the natural and cultural diversity of the world and recognizing that all cultures and civilizations can contribute to sustainable development.

(4) Market-based operation: Recognizing

市场作用和企业主体地位，确保政府发挥适当作用，政府采购程序应开放、透明、非歧视。

（5）平衡和可持续。强调项目的经济、社会、财政、金融和环境可持续性，促进环境高标准，同时统筹好经济增长、社会进步和环境保护之间的关系。

合作举措

我们重申需要重点推动政策沟通、设施联通、贸易畅通、资金融通、民心相通，强调根据各国法律法规和相关国际义务，采取以下切实行动：

（1）加强对话协商，促进各国发展战略对接，注意到"一带一路"倡议与第六段所列发展计划和倡议协调发展，促进欧洲、亚洲、南美洲、非洲等地区之间伙伴关系的努力。

（2）就宏观经济问题进行深入磋商，完善现有多双边合作对话机制，为务实合作和大

the role of the market and that of business as key players, while ensuring that the government performs its proper role and highlighting the importance of open, transparent, and non-discriminatory procurement procedures.

(5) Balance and sustainability: Emphasizing the importance of economic, social, fiscal, financial and environmental sustainability of projects, and of promoting high environmental standards, while striking a good balance among economic growth, social progress and environmental protection.

Cooperation Measures

We affirm the need to prioritize policy consultation, trade promotion, infrastructure connectivity, financial cooperation and people-to-people exchanges, and we highlight concrete actions, in accordance with our national laws and regulations and international obligations where applicable, such as:

(1) Pursuing dialogue and consultation in order to build synergies in development strategies among participating countries, noting the efforts to strengthen cooperation in coordinating development of the Belt and Road Initiative with other plans and initiatives as mentioned in Paragraph 6 and to promote partnerships among Europe, Asia, South America, Africa and other regions.

(2) Conducting in-depth consultation on macroeconomic issues by optimizing the existing multilateral and bilateral cooperation and

型项目提供有力政策支持。

（3）加强创新合作，支持电子商务、数字经济、智慧城市、科技园区等领域的创新行动计划，鼓励在尊重知识产权的同时，加强互联网时代创新创业模式交流。

（4）推动在公路、铁路、港口、海上和内河运输、航空、能源管道、电力、海底电缆、光纤、电信、信息通信技术等领域务实合作，欢迎新亚欧大陆桥、北方海航道、中间走廊等多模式综合走廊和国际骨干通道建设，逐步构建国际性基础设施网络。

（5）通过借鉴相关国际标准、必要时统一规则体制和技术标准等手段，实现基础设施规划和建设协同效应最大化；为私人资本投资基础设施建设培育有利、可预测的环境；在有利于增加就业、提高效率的领域促进公私伙伴关系；欢迎国际金融机构加强对基础设施建设的支持和投入。

dialogue mechanisms, so as to provide robust policy support for practical cooperation and the implementation of major projects.

(3) Strengthening cooperation on innovation, by supporting innovation action plans for e-commerce, digital economy, smart cities and science and technology parks, and by encouraging greater exchanges on innovation and business startup models in the Internet age in respect of intellectual property rights.

(4) Promoting practical cooperation on roads, railways, ports, maritime and inland water transport, aviation, energy pipelines, electricity, fiber optic including trans-oceanic cable, telecommunications and information and communication technology, and welcoming the development of interconnected multimodal corridors, such us a new Eurasian Land Bridge, Northern Sea Route, the East-West Middle Corridor etc., and major trunk lines to put in place an international infrastructure network over time.

(5) Maximizing synergies in infrastructure planning and development by taking into account international standards where applicable, and by aiming at harmonizing rules and technological standards when necessary; fostering a favorable environment and predictability for infrastructure investment by private capital; promoting public-private partnership in areas that create more jobs and generate greater efficiency; welcoming international financial institutions to increase

（6）深化经贸合作，维护多边贸易体制的权威和效力；共同推动世界贸易组织第11次部长级会议取得积极成果；推动贸易投资自由化和便利化；让普通民众从贸易中获益。

（7）通过培育新的贸易增长点、促进贸易平衡、推动电子商务和数字经济等方式扩大贸易，欢迎有兴趣的国家开展自贸区建设并商签自贸协定。

（8）推动全球价值链发展和供应链联接，同时确保安全生产，加强社会保障体系；增加双向投资，加强新兴产业、贸易、工业园区、跨境经济园区等领域合作。

（9）加强环境、生物多样性、自然资源保护、应对气候变化、抗灾、减灾、提高灾害风险管理能力、促进可再生能源和能效等领域合作。

（10）加强通关手续等方面信息交流，推动监管互认、

support and investment for infrastructure development.

(6) Deepening economic and trade cooperation; upholding the authority and effectiveness of the multilateral trading system, and working together to achieve positive outcomes at the 11th WTO ministerial conference; promoting trade and investment liberalization and facilitation; enabling the general public to benefit from trade.

(7) Expanding trade by nurturing new areas of trade growth, promoting trade balance and promoting e-commerce and digital economy, welcoming the development of free trade areas and signing of free trade agreements by interested countries.

(8) Advancing global value chains development and supply chain connectivity, while ensuring safer work places and strengthening social protection systems; increasing two-way investment, and enhancing cooperation in emerging industries, trade and industrial parks and cross-border economic zones.

(9) Enhancing cooperation in ensuring the protection of the environment, of bio-diversity and of natural resources, in addressing the adverse impacts of climate change, in promoting resilience and disaster-risk reduction and management, and in advancing renewable energy and energy efficiency.

(10) Regarding the process of customs clearance, strengthening cooperation on information

执法互助、信息共享；加强海关合作，通过统一手续、降低成本等方式促进贸易便利化，同时促进保护知识产权合作。

（11）合作构建长期、稳定、可持续的融资体系；加强金融设施互联互通，创新投融资模式和平台，提高金融服务水平；探寻更好服务本地金融市场的机会；鼓励开发性金融机构发挥积极作用，加强与多边开发机构的合作。

（12）为构建稳定、公平的国际金融体系作贡献；通过推动支付体系合作和普惠金融等途径，促进金融市场相互开放和互联互通；鼓励金融机构在有关国家和地区设立分支机构；推动签署双边本币结算和合作协议，发展本币债券和股票市场；鼓励通过对话加强金融合作，规避金融风险。

exchange and on developing mutual recognition of control, mutual assistance of enforcement, and mutual sharing of information; enhancing customs cooperation with a view to facilitating trade including by harmonizing procedures and reducing costs, and in this regard, strengthening cooperation in protecting intellectual property rights.

(11) Jointly working on a long-term, stable and sustainable financing system; enhancing financial infrastructure connectivity, by exploring new models and platforms of investment and financing and improving financial services; assessing the opportunity to better serve local financial market; and encouraging development-oriented financial institutions to play an active role and strengthen cooperation with multilateral development institutions.

(12) Contributing to a stable and equitable international financial system; promoting openness and connectivity among financial markets, including through mutual cooperation on payment systems and the promotion of financial inclusion; encouraging financial institutions to establish commercial presence in relevant countries and regions; promoting bilateral local currency settlement and cooperation agreements, and facilitating the development of local currency bonds and stock markets; encouraging dialogues to enhance financial cooperation and fend off financial risks.

（13）加强人文交流和民间纽带，深化教育、科技、体育、卫生、智库、媒体以及包括实习培训在内的能力建设等领域务实合作。

（14）鼓励不同文明间对话和文化交流，促进旅游业发展，保护世界文化和自然遗产。

愿景展望

我们携手推进"一带一路"建设和加强互联互通倡议对接的努力，为国际合作提供了新机遇、注入了新动力，有助于推动实现开放、包容和普惠的全球化。

我们重申，促进和平、推动互利合作、尊重《联合国宪章》宗旨原则和国际法，这是我们的共同责任；实现包容和可持续增长与发展、提高人民生活水平，这是我们的共同目标；构建繁荣、和平的人类命运共同体，这是我们的共同愿望。

我们祝贺中国成功举办"一带一路"国际合作高峰论坛。

(13) Promoting people-to-people exchanges and bonds by deepening practical cooperation on education, science, technology, sport, health, think-tank, media, capacity building including through internships.

(14) Encouraging dialogues among civilizations, cultural exchanges, promoting tourism and protecting the world's cultural and natural heritage.

Our Vision for the Future

Our joint endeavor on the Belt and Road Initiative and seeking complementarities with other connectivity initiatives provide new opportunities and impetus for international cooperation. It helps to work for a globalization that is open, inclusive and beneficial to all.

We reiterate that promoting peace, mutually-beneficial cooperation, and honoring the purposes and principles of the UN Charter and international law are our shared responsibilities; achieving inclusive and sustainable growth and development, and improving people's quality of life are our common goals; creating a prosperous and peaceful community with shared future for mankind is our common aspiration.

We congratulate China on successfully hosting the Belt and Road Forum for International Cooperation.

三 外交公报的翻译原则与难点

如上文所述，外交公报的主要特点包括及时宣传性、政治权威性和高度真实性。翻译外交公报时必须考虑外交公报的文体特点，这些特点如果能在译文中体现就尽可能在译文中体现。

首先，外交公报的及时宣传性给译者提出了翻译的时效要求，意味着译者必须在最短时间内提供高质量的译文。其次，外交公报的政治权威性和高度真实性要求译者翻译时高度再现文本语言特点。外交公报是政治语言的一种，有着极高的政治性和极强的政策性，这些性质落实在公告的具体措辞中。"重点推动、鼓励、为……提供有力政策支持"等话语说明公报主体的支持态度，"打击、维护、阻止、对……表示很遗憾"的表达则表明公报主体的否定态度，而"重申、强调"等词语则体现公报主体对某个现象、问题或事物的重视。面对这些能够反映主体立场、态度、语气的词语，译者要有一种"求真"的精神，牢牢把握住公报主体的立场和态度，在此基础上再三揣摩词语所包含的"真"意义和"真"意图，从而获得准确无误的译文。另外，从外交公报主体的身份来看，一般都是国家、政府、政党或团体组织，因此外交公报中使用的语言都是比较正式的书面语，庄重而严肃；外交公报译文的目标读者不但有相关领域的专业人士，也有不具备专业知识的普通读者。译者在翻译时要有读者意识，既要保持原文正式、庄重、严肃的语体特征，也要考虑目标语的习惯和特点，做到行文流畅，通俗易懂，避免晦涩，使读者能够轻松了解公报的内容。

外交公报体现了我国对国际关系的立场和态度，翻译时要求措辞准确而精练，语气庄重而严肃，在维护我国外交原则和立场的基础上，尽量采用各方都能接受的措辞。如何准确措辞是译者翻译外交公报必须面对的一个难题，如"中华人民共和国主席习近平、阿根廷总统马克里"译为 President Xi Jinping of the People's Republic of China, President Mauricio Macri of the Republic of Argentina。尽管中国是中华人民共和国的简称，两者所指基本相同，但各自的隐含意义却略有不同。"中国"更偏向指涉地理概念以及在这个地方生活的人们和人们创造的文化，而"中华人民共和国"却更强调这个国家的国体和政体，体现政府和政权。联合公报的主体是代表国家的政府，因此在翻译时应将"中国"译成 the People's Republic of China，"阿根廷"译成 the Republic of Argentina，体现外交措辞的严谨和准确。另外，翻译领导人称谓时也要注意庄重礼貌，"中华人民共和国主席习近平"可以翻译为 H.E. Xi Jinping, President of the People's Republic of China。H.E. 是 His/Her Excellency 的缩写，表示"阁下"之意，常常用在总统、总督、大使等共和制国家领导人名字之前，多在比较正式的场合或信函中提到第三人称时使用。

其次，外交公报中包含一些专业术语或者涉及特殊的历史或文化背景，对于译者而言也是不小的挑战，必须对相关知识充分了解和把握。比如，在2016年以前，对于"一带一路"战略和"一带一路"倡议的使用比较随意，后来新华社公布了新闻信息报道中的禁用词和慎用词，其中"一带一路"战略赫然在列。"战略"这一字眼在国际关系领域颇为敏感，因为包含着对抗性的意味，容易引起其他国家的疑虑、警惕和焦虑，因此翻译时使用 initiative 而非 strategy 更为妥当。另外新华社在国际关系领域还公布了一系列的禁用或慎用词。比如有的国际组织成员中，既包括一些国家也包括一些地区，在涉及此类国际组织时，不使用"成员国"，而应用"成员"或"成员方"。因此，不使用"世界贸易组织成员国"和"亚太经合组织成员国"，而应用"世界贸易组织成员""世界贸易组织成员方""亚太经合组织成员（members）""亚太经合组织成员经济体（member economies）"。此外，不能用"北朝鲜"（英文 North Korea）来称呼"朝鲜民主主义人民共和国"，英文应用 the Democratic People's Republic of Korea 或缩写 DPRK；充分尊重有关国家自己的界定，不主动使用"穆斯林国家"或"穆斯林世界"，代之以"伊斯兰国家"或"伊斯兰世界"；在达尔富尔报道中不使用"阿拉伯民兵"，而应使用"民兵武装"或"部族武装"；不能将撒哈拉沙漠以南的地区称为"黑非洲"，而应称为"撒哈拉沙漠以南非洲"；在涉及阿拉伯和中东等报道中，不使用"十字军（东征）"等说法；一般情况下不使用"前苏联"，而使用"苏联"；在报道社会犯罪和武装冲突时，一般不刻意突出犯罪嫌疑人和冲突参与者的肤色、种族和性别特征等。

外交公报翻译的原则与难点与其本身所具有的政治性特征密切相关，需要特别考虑外交效应问题，尽可能避免触及外交禁忌。与此同时，外交公报翻译与其他文本翻译一样，不可避免会涉及各类语言转换翻译技巧，本章关注的核心是词类转换法的使用。

四 外交公报英译技巧

翻译过程中，如果完全按照原语词性翻译，译文有时会与译入语的表达习惯不符，从而变得晦涩难懂，因此有必要进行词类转换。所谓词类转换是指在翻译过程中，根据译入语特征及其规范要求，把原语中某个词的词类转换成译入语中另一词类。

英语和汉语的显著差异之一在于句子中动词使用频率的高低,汉语中动词用得比较多,一个句子中可以存在几个动词或者动词性结构的连用,动词(或动词词组)可以充当汉语句子的各种成分,动词的重复、重叠、合成、合并在汉语中比比皆是,使得汉语倾向于动态。与之相比,英语中动词的使用就比较有限,一般的英语句子只能存在一个谓语动词,较多使用名词、形容词、副词、介词等其他词类替代动词。英语喜静,汉语好动这一显著区别使得汉译英时要将汉语动词转换为名词等动作意味较弱的词类。

1 汉语动词转译为英语名词

英语中特别偏好使用名词这一现象被英国语言学家波特称为"名词病"(noun disease)。他认为西方人偏爱名词而不喜欢动词。比如,在 John's arrival was premature 和 John came too soon 两个表达类似意义的句子中做出抉择时,人们往往更倾向前者[1]。英语是一种屈折语(inflectional language),时态、数、格等语法概念可以通过词形变化来表达,因此派生法(derivative)是英语中重要的构词方法。人们可以在词根之前加上前缀或者是在词根之后加上后缀制造出派生词(derivative words)。英语中有一类名词正是以动词为基础,加上相应的后缀转换为同源名词。汉译英时,可以借助这一构词法将汉语的动词转换为相应的英语派生名词。下面首先结合本章范例进行解析:

| 原文 | 我们也欢迎联合国秘书长古特雷斯、世界银行行长金墉、国际货币基金组织总裁拉加德<u>出席</u>。 |

| 译文 | We also welcome <u>the participation</u> of Secretary General Antonio Guterres of the United Nations, President Jim Yong Kim of the World Bank Group, Managing Director Christine Lagarde of the International Monetary Fund. |

| 原文 | 需要特别<u>关注</u>最不发达国家、内陆发展中国家、小岛屿发展中国家和中等收入国家,突破发展瓶颈,实现有效互联互通。 |

| 译文 | The least developed countries, landlocked developing countries, small island |

---

[1] Potter, S. 1969. *Changing English*. London: André Deutsch, 101.

developing states and middle-income countries deserve special <u>attention</u> to remove bottlenecks of development and achieve effective connectivity.

原文 我们鼓励政府、国际和地区组织、私营部门、民间社会和广大民众共同<u>参与</u>，建立巩固友好关系，增进相互理解与信任。

译文 We encourage the <u>involvement</u> of governments, international and regional organizations, the private sector, civil society and citizens in fostering and promoting friendship, mutual understanding and trust.

在上述三个汉英例文中，"出席""关注""参与"在原文中都是动词，在翻译过程中根据上下文语境需要，全都采用名词形式翻译，分别译为 participation, attention 以及 involvement。第一例和第三例中的"出席"和"参与"转化成名词后，位置也发生改变，紧跟在动词后面充当宾语，符合英语思维，同时简化宾语结构，变从句为短语，更加简洁易懂。第二例是无主句，译者没有简单通过添加 We 来显化主语，而是巧妙地将"最不发达国家、内陆发展中国家、小岛屿发展中国家和中等收入国家"作为主语，将"关注"变为"需要"的宾语，使用 deserve the attention to do something 结构完成翻译，英译效果同样简洁易懂。再如：

原文 两国政府同意在互相<u>尊重</u>主权和领土完整、互不<u>侵犯</u>、互不<u>干涉</u>内政、平等<u>互利</u>、和平<u>共处</u>的原则基础上发展两国友好关系。

译文 The two Governments agree to develop friendly relations between the two countries on the basis of the principles of mutual <u>respect</u> for sovereignty and territorial integrity, mutual non-<u>aggression</u>, non-<u>interference</u> in each other's internal affairs, equality, mutual <u>benefit</u> and peaceful <u>coexistence</u>.

在这个例子中，汉语原文连续使用了 6 个动词，它们分别是"尊重""侵犯""干涉""互利""共处"和"发展"，这种连续使用动词的现象充分体现了汉语的动态性，如果译者在翻译过程中没有考虑到英语的句式特点和语言特征而在译文中全部保留这些动词，译文要么就像中文一样变成流水句，要么就不符合英语语法要求。因此翻译时必须考虑到汉英的动静差别，保留汉语中的一个动词作为英语的谓语动词，而其他动词可以转译为相应的名词。"侵犯""干涉""共处"的英文分别为 aggress、interfere 和 coexist，通过词性转换分别译成名词 aggression、interference 和 coexistence，削减了原文的动作性，符合英语喜静的特征。而 respect 和 benefit 本身就是兼类词，既可作动词又可作名词，且意思大体一致，因此翻译时可直接利用其名词词性。

英语中还有一类特殊的派生名词，它们是由动词加后缀 -er、-or 而来，用以表示某种身份和职业。但这类名词并不只是用作这一种含义，也可以用来表达较强的动作意义。比如"He was a regular visitor."中的 visitor 一词并不是强调主语的身份，而侧重于其中所隐含的动作意味，由于 visitor 是一个名词，它使得英文原文的动态性减弱，但在翻译成中文时我们可以将之译为"他经常来"。反其道而行之，在汉译英时，我们可以将汉语的动词翻译成这种带 -er 或 -or 后缀的名词。

原文 我们一致认为论坛机制日益高效，引领国际对非合作。

译文 We recognize that the FOCAC mechanism is increasingly efficient and has become a leading player in international cooperation with Africa.

在上面这个句子中，"引领"这个动词在英语译文中被译作名词短语 a leading player，由于 player 是一个名词，尽管此处不是用来表达某种职业或身份，而是隐含了动作意味，但由于它采用的是名词形式，使得译文更符合英文喜静的特征。

2 汉语动词转译为英语形容词

英语中常用形容词来表示动作意义是英语喜静的另一表现。英语形容词有极强的动作表现力，既可以用来描述某种短暂性或持续性状态，也可以展现某一特定时刻的动作。因此，在汉英翻译时，可以根据语境需求将动词转为形容词，同样可以传达动词意义。比如本章范例中"更好应对儿童、残疾人、老年人等弱势群体诉求"译为"to be more responsive to all the needs of those in vulnerable situations such as, children, persons with disabilities and older persons"。"应对"在原文是动词，在目标语中译为 responsive，变为形容词，但并未影响原意的表达，等效再现了"应对"的动词意义。再如下例：

原文 成员国认为，恐怖主义，恐怖主义和极端主义思想通过互联网等方式传播，境外恐怖分子回流，大规模杀伤性武器扩散，军备竞赛风险，破坏国际安全体系的地区和局部冲突持续，非法贩运麻醉药品，有组织犯罪，贩卖人口，信息通信领域犯罪，发展不均衡，粮食市场波动，气候变化，饮用水短缺和疫病蔓延等安全挑战和威胁日益加剧并跨越国界，要求国际社会高度重视，并开展紧密协调和建设性协作。

| 译文 | The Member States believe that <u>increasing</u> challenges and security threats that are <u>becoming cross-border</u> in their nature such as terrorism, the spread of terrorist and extremist ideology, including on the internet, <u>returning</u> foreign terrorist fighters, proliferation of the weapons of mass destruction, the risk of an arms race, <u>unsettled</u> regional and local conflicts undermining the international security system, illicit drug trafficking, organised crime, human trafficking, cybercrime, development imbalances, food market instability, climate change, lack of potable water and the spread of infectious diseases require special attention, close coordination and constructive cooperation of the entire international community. |

上文中的动词"回流""持续"被译为形容词 returning 和 unsettled，动词短语"日益加剧"被译为形容词 increasing，动宾短语"跨越国界"被译为系表结构，恰当地为受众描述一个矛盾冲突日趋严重、问题层出不穷的世界格局。

此外，用形容词比较级来表示由于某种变化而造成结果差异，动态性更强，有强调结果是由于变化或发展导致的意味，但在中文中我们常用"深化""强化""增加""减缓"等动词表示这种变化和发展，译成英语时，可以用 deeper、stronger、more、less 等形容词比较级来表示相应的变化结果。

| 原文 | 我们一致欢迎中非<u>加强</u>在联合国安理会层面相关事务中的沟通协调，通过中国与安理会非洲非常任理事国会晤、磋商等机制，密切在涉非和平安全事务中的协作，维护共同利益。欢迎中方同非盟和平安全理事会在会议、磋商等机制下<u>加强</u>合作，维护共同利益。 |

| 译文 | We welcome <u>closer</u> communication and coordination between China and Africa in the UN Security Council. We will enhance coordination and cooperation on affairs related to African peace and security to uphold our common interests through the meetings and consultations between China and Africa's non-permanent members of the Security Council. We welcome <u>closer</u> cooperation between China and the African Union Peace and Security Council (AUPSC) through meetings and consultations, as it serves our common interests. |

在此例外交公告的英译中，动词"加强"均被译成形容词 closer，用以修饰之后由动词派生出的名词，减少动词的使用频率，保持英语的静态特征。

除此之外，汉语中有些动词用来描述知觉或者情感等心理状态，这类动词在汉译英的过程中往往可以转换成英语形容词，通常多以"Be+形容词"的结构来表达。

原文 成员国指出，<u>不允许</u>以打击恐怖主义和极端主义为借口干涉别国内政，或利用恐怖主义、极端主义和激进组织谋取私利。

译文 They note that interfering in other countries' domestic affairs under the pretext of fighting terrorism and extremism as well as using terrorist, extremist and radical groups to achieve one's own mercenary ends <u>is unacceptable</u>.

在原文中，动词"不允许"表达的正是主语的一种主观意愿，通过词性转换译成 is unacceptable，恰当地表达了主语的心理状态，同时又保证了译文更符合英语的行文习惯。

原文 成员国注意到乌兹别克斯坦提出的关于制定《联合国青年权利公约》草案的倡议，并<u>愿</u>就此保持协调。

译文 The Member States praise the initiative of the Republic of Uzbekistan on preparing a UN Convention on Youth Rights, and <u>are set</u> to pursue coordinated activities on this issue.

在这个例子中，原文中用动词"愿（意）"描述主语的一种心理倾向，译文通过词性转换译作 are set。这种转换不但表达出主语有此倾向，还暗含已经为此倾向做出响应的状态。

3 汉语动词转译为英语介词

据统计汉语里的介词就 30 个左右，而英语里介词的数量远远多于汉语，美国语言学家 Curme 认为有 286 个[1]，介词就像语言润滑剂一样对英语必不可少，英语也因此被称为介词的语言。像 from（来自）、toward（朝向）、across（穿过）、into（进入）、through（通过）、along（沿着）、off（脱离）、against（针对）等介词同时包含强烈的动作意味，因此在汉译英时，可以将汉语的动词译作英语的介词或者介词短语。

原文 <u>围绕</u>"合作共赢，携手构建更加紧密的中非命运共同体"主题，<u>致力于推

---

1 Curme, G. O. 1931. *Syntax*. Boston: D. C. Heath and Company.

进中非合作论坛建设，深化中非全面战略合作伙伴关系，协商一致通过《关于构建更加紧密的中非命运共同体的北京宣言》。

译文 Under the theme "China and Africa: Toward an Even Stronger Community with a Shared Future Through Win-Win Cooperation" and committed to the development of FOCAC and to deepening China-Africa comprehensive strategic and cooperative partnership, we adopted by consensus the Beijing Declaration—Toward an Even Stronger China-Africa Community with a Shared Future.

在这个例子中，原文有大量动词或动词短语，动词或动词短语频频连用，光主题名称"合作共赢，携手构建更加紧密的中非命运共同体"中就有四个动词，与英语中动词较少的现象有很大差异，增加了翻译的难度。如果在译文中保留原文动词的词性，必然会增加译文的句子数量，大量短句的存在会使译文变得琐碎杂乱，为了解决这一难题可以求助介词。

首先，原文"围绕……主题"表达"以……为主题的情况下"之意，这一句式被译成 under the theme…，动词"围绕"被译成了介词 under，under 具有"在……情况下"的意思，与"围绕……主题"的意义契合；其次，主题名称"合作共赢，携手构建更加紧密的中非命运共同体"中的"合作共赢"和"携手构建"可以理解为"合作以共赢，携手去构建"，是汉语常见的连动结构，但是译文没有保留其中任何一个动词，前者被转换成介词 + 名词词组 Through Win-Win Cooperation，而后者被替换成带有强烈动作意味的介词 toward，让英文标题更确切、简练、醒目。

原文 （中方）为非洲发展提供不附加政治条件的各类帮助和支持。

译文 China will, as always, offer assistance and support to Africa's development with no political strings attached.

在这个例子中，译文正是通过介词 with 后接宾语以及宾语补足语的方式进行了状态描写，用静态的方式体现了原文的动态意味。

汉语是动态性语言，英语是静态性语言，外交公告汉英翻译中常将汉语的动词转换成英语中的名词、形容词和介词的典型情况。当然，偶尔也可反其道而行之，将汉语的名词、形容词或介词译成英语动词，此外其他词类之间也常相互转换。

五 中国关键词加油站

1 丝路精神 spirit of the Silk Road

古丝绸之路绵亘万里，延续千年，不仅是商业通道，更重要的是它所承载的丝路精神。古丝绸之路作为人文社会的交往平台，多民族、多种族、多宗教、多文化在此交汇融合，在长期交往过程中，各国之间积淀形成了以和平合作、开放包容、互学互鉴、互利共赢为核心的丝路精神。这一精神，也是现代国际社会交往的最基本原则之一。

2 21世纪海上丝绸之路 the 21st Century Maritime Silk Road

自秦汉时期开通以来，海上丝绸之路一直是东西方经济文化交流融通的重要桥梁。东南亚地区是海上丝绸之路的重要枢纽和组成部分。在中国与东盟建立战略伙伴关系10周年之际，为了进一步加强双方的海上合作，发展双方的海洋合作伙伴关系，构建更加紧密的命运共同体，2013年10月3日，习近平主席在印度尼西亚国会发表演讲时提出，共同建设21世纪海上丝绸之路。21世纪海上丝绸之路的战略合作伙伴并不仅限于东盟，而是以点带线，以线带面，串起联通东盟、南亚、西亚、北非、欧洲等各大经济板块的市场链，发展面向南海、太平洋和印度洋的战略合作经济带。

3 "五通" five-pronged approach，"三同" community of shared interests, responsibility and future

2013年9月7日，习近平主席在哈萨克斯坦纳扎尔巴耶夫大学发表演讲，首次提出加强"政策沟通、道路联通、贸易畅通、货币流通、民心相通"，共同建设"丝绸之路经济带"的战略倡议。2015年3月28日，中国政府在博鳌亚洲论坛2015年年会期间正式发布《推动共建丝绸之路经济带和21世纪海上丝绸之路的愿景与行动》，提出要以"政策沟通、设施联通、贸易畅通、资金融通、民心相通"（简称"五通"）为主要内容，打造"一带一路"沿线国家政治互信、经济融合、文化互容的利益共同体、责任共同体和命运共同体。在"一带一路"建设全面推进过程中，"五通"

既相互独立，在不同时间阶段各有重点，也是统一整体，需要相互促进，不可分割。

4 绿色丝绸之路 Silk Road to green development

环境问题是人类社会面临的共同问题。2016年6月22日，习近平主席在乌兹别克斯坦最高会议立法院发表演讲时指出，要着力深化环保合作，践行绿色发展理念，加大生态环境保护力度，携手打造绿色丝绸之路。此前中国公布的《推动共建丝绸之路经济带和21世纪海上丝绸之路的愿景与行动》也明确提出，强化基础设施绿色低碳化建设和运营管理，在建设中充分考虑气候变化影响，在投资贸易中突出生态文明理念，加强生态环境、生物多样性和应对气候变化合作，共建绿色丝绸之路。绿色丝绸之路体现了可持续发展的理念，它要求在"一带一路"建设中秉承绿色和环保理念，正确处理经济增长和环境保护的关系，充分考虑沿线国家的生态承载能力，共建一个良好的生态环境。"一带一路"建设已将生态环保、防沙治沙、清洁能源等列为重点发展产业，绿色丝绸之路面临发展良机。

5 智力丝绸之路 Silk Road to innovation

推进"一带一路"战略，人才是关键。2016年6月20日，习近平主席在华沙出席丝路国际论坛时提出，智力先行，强化智库的支撑引领作用。加强对"一带一路"建设方案和路径的研究，在规划对接、政策协调、机制设计上做好政府的参谋和助手，在理念传播、政策解读、民意通达上做好桥梁和纽带。两天后的6月22日，他在乌兹别克斯坦最高会议立法院发表演讲时明确提出，中方倡议成立"一带一路"职业技术合作联盟，培养培训各类专业人才，携手打造智力丝绸之路。在"一带一路"建设推进过程中，会面临很多新问题、新挑战，需要越来越多的智力和人才支持，需要各方相互学习、取长补短，共同提出解决方案。当前，"一带一路"沿线国家人才短缺的问题不同程度地存在，智力丝绸之路的主要目标是推进沿线国家人才培养和智力交流。

6 健康丝绸之路 Silk Road to health cooperation

推进全球卫生事业，是落实2030年可持续发展议程的重要组成部分。2016年6月22日，习近平主席在乌兹别克斯坦最高会议立法院发表演讲时提议，着力深化医疗卫生合作，加强在传染病疫情通报、疾病防控、医疗救援、传统医药领域互利合作，携手打造健康丝绸之路。2017年1月18日，中国政府与世界卫生组织签署了双方关于"一带一路"卫生领域合作的谅解备忘录。健康丝绸之路的主要目标是提高"一带一路"沿线国家整体的健康卫生水平。主要措施包括：沿线国家加强在卫生体制政策、卫生领域相关国际标准和规范的磋商和沟通，加强重点传染病防控合作，加强人员培训，推动更多中国生产的医药产品进入国际市场，使质优价廉的中国医药产品造福"一带一路"国家人民，等等。

7 和平丝绸之路 Silk Road to peace

"一带一路"沿线，尤其是丝绸之路经济带沿线，面临较为严重的恐怖主义、分裂主义和极端主义威胁，部分国家之间的关系较为紧张，时常伴有局部冲突，也有部分国家内部政局不稳。因此，破解地区动荡局势，维护地区和平稳定，对于"一带一路"建设至关重要。2016年6月22日，习近平主席在乌兹别克斯坦最高会议立法院发表演讲时提出，着力深化安保合作，践行共同、综合、合作、可持续的亚洲安全观，推动构建具有亚洲特色的安全治理模式，携手打造和平丝绸之路。和平丝绸之路包含两个基本内涵：一是"一带一路"建设必须在相对和平的环境里进行；二是"一带一路"建设能促进地区和平稳定。以发展促和平促安全，这是中国提出的思路，也是被实践证明很有成效的办法。

8 多边贸易体制 multilateral trading system

以世贸组织为核心的多边贸易体制是国际贸易的基石，为推动全球贸易发展、建设开放型世界经济发挥了中流砥柱作用。世贸组织成员贸易总额占全球的98%，它作为世界经济体系的三大支柱之一，对全球贸易投资自由化便利化起着非常关键的作用。加入世界贸易组织以来，中国始终坚定支持多边贸易体制，全面参与世贸组织各项工作，坚决反对单边主义和保护主义，维护多边贸易体制的权威性和有效性，不断为完善全球经济治理贡献中国智慧、中国方案，成为多边贸易体制的积极参与者、坚定维护者和重要贡献者。为积极推进贸易投资自由化便利化，中国多次发挥弥合分歧、凝聚共识的关键作用。中国始终倡导通过加强合作、平等对话和协商谈判来解决国际贸易中的问题，为多边贸易体制的稳定和全球贸易的健康发展注入了正能量。

9 金砖国家新工业革命伙伴关系 BRICS partnership on new industrial revolution

金砖国家包括中国、俄罗斯、印度、巴西、南非5个国家。2006年9月，巴西、俄罗斯、印度和中国四国外长在联合国大会期间举行首次会晤，将一个经济概念转化为具体行动，此后每年依例举行。由于四国英文首字母组成的BRIC一词，其发音与英文的"砖（Brick）"十分相似，故被称为"金砖四国"。为应对金融危机，2009年6月，"金砖四国"领导人在俄罗斯举行首次正式会晤。金砖国家间的合作机制正式启动。2010年12月，南非正式加入金砖国家后，这一合作机制由最初的"金砖四国"变为"金砖五国"（现在用BRICS）。近年来，金砖国家合作机制不断完善，已经形成以领导人会晤为引领，以安全事务高级代表会议、外长会晤等为支撑，在广泛领域开展务实合作的多层次架构。金砖国家共同利益不断增加，合作基础不断扩大，合作势头不断上升，在重大国际事务中的沟通和协调不断加强，成为带动世界经济增长、完善全球经济治理、推动国际关系民主化的重要力量。

10 中国—中亚—西亚经济走廊 China-Central Asia-West Asia Economic Corridor

中国—中亚—西亚经济走廊东起中国，向西至阿拉伯半岛，是中国与中亚和西亚各国之间形成的一个经济合作区域，大致与古丝绸之路范围相吻合。走廊从新疆出发，穿越中亚地区，抵达波斯湾、地中海沿岸和阿拉伯半岛，主要涉及中亚五国（哈萨克斯坦、吉尔吉斯斯坦、塔吉克斯坦、乌兹别克斯坦、土库曼斯坦）和西亚的伊朗、沙特阿拉伯、土耳其等17个国家和地区，是丝绸之路经济带的重要组成部分。尽管中亚、西亚地区资源丰富，但制约经济社会发展的因素很多，其中基础设施建设落后、缺乏资金技术等问题较为突出。通过中国-中亚-西亚经济走廊建设，打通该地区对外经贸合作和资金流动通道，有利于促进相关国家经济社会发展。

六 外交公报翻译练习

1. 请将下列外交公报译成英语，注意术语、措辞及准确性。

1）外长们强调，上合组织成立15年来，秉持"互信、互利、平等、协商、尊重多样文明、谋求共同发展"的"上海精神"，已成为当代国际关系体系中富有影响力的参与者之一。各方重申，将共同巩固上合组织在国际舞台上遵循的原则，即在解决地区和国际重大问题的过程中坚持不结盟、不对抗，不针对其他国家和国际组织。

2）外长们重申，根据上合组织宪章及其他文件规定，制定和落实相关措施，共同打击各种形式的恐怖主义、分裂主义、极端主义，打击非法生产和贩运毒品、跨境有组织犯罪、现代信息技术犯罪、非法移民、贩卖人口、非法贩卖武器弹药和爆炸物、防止扩散大规模杀伤性武器及其运载工具，仍是本组织合作的优先任务之一。

2. 请仔细阅读下面外交公报的原文和译文，画出其中使用了词性转换译法的部分，并说明是怎样转换的。

1）

原文 双方回顾了近年来中国与加勒比国家关系所取得的重要进展，同意继续努力深化中加相互尊重、平等互利、共同发展的全面合作伙伴关系。

译文 The two sides reviewed the progress made in the relations between China and the Caribbean countries in recent years and jointly agreed to intensify efforts in order to deepen their comprehensive cooperation and partnership based on the principles of mutual respect and equality, as well as mutual benefit and common development.

2）

原文 外长们强调叙利亚问题只能通过政治和外交途径解决。外长们重申支持日内瓦和谈，发挥联合国斡旋主渠道作用，落实好安理会第2254号决议要求。外长们欢迎阿斯塔纳担保国在改善叙利亚局势方面做出的努力及2019年2月在索契举行的阿斯塔纳担保国第四次三方会议有关成果。外长们希望尽快启动宪法委员会工作，通过"叙人主导、叙人所有"的包容性政治进程，找到兼顾各方合法关切的政治解决方案，推动政治解决叙冲突，维护叙主权、独立和领土完整。

译文 The Ministers stressed that a political and diplomatic solution is the only reliable way to solve the Syrian issue. They reaffirmed support for the Geneva peace talks, the role of the UN as the main channel of mediation and the implementation of UNSC Resolution 2254. The Ministers welcomed the efforts of the Astana guarantors for improvement of the situation in Syria and the results of the fourth trilateral meeting in Sochi in February 2019. The Ministers hoped to see that the Constitutional Committee starts its work as early as possible, and that a political solution that accommodates the legitimate concerns of all parties could be found through an inclusive "Syrian-led and Syrian-owned" political process, with a view to seeking a political settlement of the Syrian conflict and safeguarding Syria's sovereignty, independence and territorial integrity.

3. 请将下面外交公报翻译成英语，画线部分请用词性转换法完成。

外长们欢迎2018年以来朝鲜半岛形势发生的重要积极变化，欢迎朝鲜就无核化所<u>作出的承诺</u>。外长们欢迎朝美<u>开展对话协商</u>，欢迎朝韩<u>改善关系</u>。外长们重申应通过和平与外交手段解决半岛问题，<u>希望</u>有关各方共同推动半岛问题政治解决进程<u>不断取得进展</u>，早日实现半岛无核化和持久和平。

第五章

外交宣言翻译

一　外交宣言的概念及其文体特点

"宣言"一词在词典中有两种解释，一是用作名词，是"（国家、政党或团体）对重大问题公开发表意见以进行宣传号召的文告"；二是用作动词，表"宣告；声明"[1]。由此可见"外交宣言"（diplomatic declaration/statement）就是某一国家、政党或团体发布其政治纲领、政治主张，或对重大政治问题向国内外公众发表其意见的文告，用以公开宣告和声明自己的态度和立场。

外交宣言和其他宣言一样，至少包括标题和正文两个部分。受众可以从标题获知发表宣言的主体和事由。《亚洲相互协作与信任措施会议第五次外长会议关于通过对话促进亚洲和平、安全、稳定和可持续发展的宣言》是一个典型的外交宣言标题，从中可以获知发布宣言的主体是亚洲相互协作与信任措施会议，该宣言的事由是第五次外长会议的召开。此外，通过标题可知该宣言主体的主旨是"通过对话促进亚洲和平、安全、稳定和可持续发展"。有些外交宣言标题下还包括时间，用括号将宣言签署的具体时间标注，以显示宣言的生效时间。

外交宣言的正文一般有导语和主体两个部分。导语交代发布宣言的主体，以及宣言所秉承的原则和依据。主体部分是宣言的主要内容，一般书写成带有序号的条文，有的宣言在外交国际事务中还承担着条约的义务。如果发布宣言的主体是两个或两个以上的国家、政党或团体，那么该宣言就是"共同宣言"或"联合宣言"；如果发布宣言的主体是某一会议的参与者，主要公布在该会议上达成的一致意见，那么该宣言就是"会议宣言"。

1　中国社会科学研究院语言研究所．2016．现代汉语词典（第七版）．北京：商务出版社．

二 外交宣言汉英对照举隅

中非合作论坛约翰内斯堡峰会宣言
Declaration of the Johannesburg Summit of the Forum on China-Africa Cooperation

我们，中华人民共和国和50个非洲国家（名单见附件）的国家元首、政府首脑、代表团团长和非洲联盟委员会主席，于2015年12月4日至5日在南非约翰内斯堡举行以"中非携手并进：合作共赢、共同发展"为主题的中非合作论坛峰会，旨在巩固中非人民的团结与合作。

11亿非洲人民和13亿中国人民紧密团结，共同开启新的时代，抓住未来发展机遇，为维护世界和平稳定和促进中非发展作出贡献。

中国和非洲同属发展中世界，在正在和将要发生深刻复杂变化的世界中，中非面对共同的发展挑战，拥有广泛的共同利益。我们必须继续加强现

We, the Heads of State, Government and Delegations of the People's Republic of China and 50 African countries (listed in the schedule annexed hereto), and the Chairperson of the African Union Commission, convened in Johannesburg, South Africa on the 4th and 5th of December 2015 for the Summit of the Forum on China-Africa Cooperation (FOCAC) under the theme "China-Africa Progressing Together: Win-Win Cooperation for Common Development", to consolidate solidarity and cooperation among the peoples of China and Africa.

Coming together as Africa, with a population of 1.1 billion people, and China, with 1.3 billion people, we are committed to ushering in a new blueprint to realize opportunities for future mutual development, and to contribute to promoting world peace, stability and the development of Africa and China.

Both African countries and China are developing countries facing common challenges of development and sharing broad common interests in a world that is undergoing and will continue to undergo profound and complex changes.

有集体对话，巩固传统友谊，深化战略合作，提升务实合作机制建设。双方同意将中非新型战略伙伴关系提升为全面战略合作伙伴关系，推动中非友好互利合作实现跨越式发展。

我们高兴地看到，中非合作论坛成立15年来取得了互利成果。我们高度评价论坛北京峰会及历届部长级会议制定和实施的重大后续行动。

中非合作内涵不断丰富，合作领域持续扩大，合作主体更加多元。论坛已经成为中非团结合作的响亮品牌和引领国际对非合作的样板。我们欢迎并赞赏论坛深化同非洲联盟及其所属机构、区域经济体和非洲开发银行的系统性联系。

我们认为，中非关系在过去15年维护了双方人民的共同利益，推动了双方繁荣发展

Therefore, it is incumbent on us to continue to strengthen the current platform for collective dialogue, consolidate Africa-China traditional friendship, deepen strategic collaboration and enhance the mechanism of practical cooperation between China and Africa. Both sides agree to upgrade the new type of strategic partnership to comprehensive strategic and cooperative partnership and promote a comprehensive upgrading of the China-Africa friendly and mutually beneficial cooperation.

We are pleased to observe that FOCAC has achieved mutually beneficial results during the past 15 years since its establishment. We highly commend the major follow-up actions initiated and implemented by the Beijing Summit and the Ministerial Conferences of FOCAC in this regard.

China-Africa cooperation has been constantly enriched, covering broader areas with more diversified participants and FOCAC has become a resounding brand for China-Africa solidarity and cooperation, and a model for leading international cooperation in Africa. In this regard, we further welcome with appreciation the efforts that FOCAC has made to deepen structured ties with regional bodies such as the African Union and its structures, Regional Economic Communities and the African Development Bank.

We believe that China-Africa relations promote the common interests of both our peoples and continue the trend of prosperous

的势头。

在联合国成立70周年之际,我们认为,维护第二次世界大战成果和国际公平正义对维护世界和平、稳定与繁荣至关重要。我们承诺坚决反对歪曲第二次世界大战成果的任何企图。我们在铭记战争灾难的同时,强调构建和平与发展的未来是共同的责任。

我们认为,全球化让世界相互依存和关联空前加深,多样化在不同层面演进,各国利益相互交织,人类越来越成为一个你中有我、我中有你的命运共同体。

我们强调维护《联合国宪章》的宗旨、原则和联合国在国际事务中的权威和领导地位。我们致力于在国际组织和多边机制内就共同关心的地区和国际事务加强合作、协调和支持,共同促进国际关系民主化、法治化和合理化,推动国际秩序朝着更加公正合理的方向发展,建立持久和平和共同繁荣的和谐世界。

我们认为国际形势正在发

growth evident over the last 15 years.

With the United Nations (UN) marking its 70th anniversary, we believe that to safeguard the results of the world victory in the World War II, international equity and justice is vital to maintaining world peace, stability and prosperity. We express our commitment to resolutely reject any attempts to misrepresent the results of World War II. While remembering the scourge of wars, we highlight that it is our common duty to build a future of peace and development.

We believe that, with the development of a world characterised by inter-dependence and connectivity under globalisation, and diversification at various levels, the interests of countries have become inextricably linked, with a growing sense of common destiny.

We underscore upholding the purposes and principles of the Charter of the UN, as well as its authority as the leading institution in international affairs. We are committed to strengthening cooperation, coordination and support between the two sides in international organizations and multilateral mechanisms on regional and international issues of common interest, jointly advancing democracy and the rule of law in international relations, advocating for an equitable and just international order, in order to build a harmonious world of durable peace and common prosperity.

We believe that in the midst of complex and

生深刻复杂的变化，需要采取更多行动确保一个公正、公平、具有代表性、更符合世界政治现实的国际治理体系，维护世界和平、稳定和繁荣。

我们致力于坚持多边主义原则，反对干涉别国内政，反对在国际事务中滥用武力或以武力相威胁。我们支持构建以合作共赢为核心的新型国际关系，促进世界更加公平、公正、合理地发展，维护和促进发展中国家的正当权益。

我们主张维护联合国在国际事务中的核心地位和作用，重申有必要对联合国进行改革，重申应解决非洲国家遭受的历史不公，优先增加非洲国家在联合国安理会和其他机构的代表性。

我们强调，非洲作为重要、强大、具有活力和影响力的国际力量和伙伴，积极、平等参与全球事务至关重要。我们赞赏非洲联盟在解决、预防和管控冲突中发挥的关键作用，积极评价非洲国家、非洲联盟和区域经济体自主解决地

profound global changes, more needs to be done to ensure an international system of governance that is just, equitable, representative and better suited to the political realities of the world in order to maintain peace, stability and prosperity.

Therefore, we are committed to the principles of multilateralism, while opposing interference in the internal affairs of countries and the use or threat of force in international affairs. In this regard, we stand for the establishment of a just international order with win-win cooperation at its core to promote a more equitable, fair and reasonable development and to safeguard and enhance the legitimate rights and interests of the developing countries.

We stand for upholding the UN's core position and role in international affairs, and reaffirm the need for reform of the UN. In this regard, we reaffirm that the historical injustices endured by African countries should be undone, and priority should be given to increasing the representation of African countries in the UN Security Council (UNSC) and other agencies.

We furthermore underscore the significance of Africa as an important, strong, resilient and influential global player and partner, through being an active and equal participant in global affairs. In this regard, we recognise the critical role of the African Union in conflict resolution, prevention and management and commend the efforts of African countries, the African Union and

区冲突和维护地区和平与稳定的努力。我们强调联合国和非洲联盟根据联合国宪章第八章特别是联合国安理会第1809和2033号决议进行合作的重要性。我们重申危机和争端必须通过政治手段和平解决，倡导共同、综合、合作、可持续的安全观。

我们对《2030年可持续发展议程》获得通过表示欢迎，这是一个具有广泛性、变革性的综合发展计划。发达国家兑现其对《2030年可持续发展议程》特别是与17项可持续发展目标相关的承诺至关重要，并应继续兑现其所作官方发展援助承诺，确保议程得到全面落实。

我们呼吁国际社会加大对发展问题关注并展示政治诚意，优先支持解决发展中国家、特别是非洲最不发达国家实现自主可持续发展所面临的困难和挑战。我们敦促发达国家切实兑现对发展中国家特别是非洲国家的援助承诺。我们认为，南北发展失衡是阻碍世界经济强劲复苏和可持续增长的重要原因。

Regional Economic Communities to independently resolve regional conflicts and maintain regional peace and stability. We emphasize the significance of cooperation between the UN and the AU in accordance with Chapter 8 of the UN Charter and particularly UNSC Resolutions 1809 and 2033. We reiterate that crises and disputes must be resolved peacefully through political means and advocate the doctrine of common, comprehensive, cooperative and sustainable security.

We welcome the adoption of the 2030 Agenda for Sustainable Development as a universal, transformative and integrated development plan. It remains important for the developed countries to honor commitments made in respect of the 2030 Agenda, in particular those relating to Goal 17, as well as continuing to meet their current commitments to ensure the full implementation of the Agenda.

In this regard, we also call on the international community to pay greater attention to the issues of development, show political sincerity and give priority to supporting the resolution of difficulties and challenges faced by developing countries, especially the least developed countries in Africa to independently achieve sustainable development. We urge developed countries to honor their commitments to provide aid to developing countries, African countries in particular, as we believe that the North-South imbalance in development is an

我们支持加强南南合作,坚信中非合作是南南合作的典范。中国致力于支持非洲实施《2063年议程》及其第一个十年规划和"非洲发展新伙伴计划",认为上述规划对非洲谋求和平、稳定、一体化、增长和发展十分必要。

我们反对任何形式的贸易保护主义,赞成推进世界贸易组织多哈回合谈判,维护和发展开放型世界经济。我们欢迎将于2015年12月15日至18日在肯尼亚内罗毕、也是首次在非洲举办的世贸组织第十届部长级会议,期待内罗毕会议取得成功,为发展中国家和最不发达国家的发展带来实质性和有意义的成果。

我们主张对现有国际金融体系进行必要改革,致力于建设更为公平公正、包容有序的国际金融体系,切实增加发展中国家特别是中国和非洲国家在国际金融机构和国际货币体系中的代表性和发言权,加强国际金融机构的发展和减贫职

important factor hindering the strong recovery and sustained growth of the world economy.

We support strengthened South-South cooperation and are convinced that China-Africa cooperation is a model manifestation of this. In this regard, China is committed to supporting Africa's efforts to implement Agenda 2063, its First 10-Year Implementation Plan and NEPAD and believes that they are essential to Africa's pursuit of peace, stability, integration, growth and development.

We oppose trade protectionism in all its forms and are in favour of advancing the World Trade Organization (WTO) Doha Development Round negotiations and safeguarding and developing an open world economy. We further welcome the first hosting of the 10th WTO Ministerial Conference in Africa, taking place from 15 to 18 December 2015 in Nairobi, Kenya, and stress the importance of a successful meeting in Nairobi that brings tangible results and meaningful outcomes on the developmental agenda for Developing and Least Developed Countries.

We stand for necessary reform of the existing international financial system, and the establishment of a fair, just, inclusive and orderly international financial system. Efforts should be made to truly increase the voice and representation of developing countries particularly China and African countries in the international financial institutions and the international monetary

责，努力缩小南北差距。我们欢迎成立金砖国家新开发银行，该银行总部设在上海并在南非设立非洲区域中心，该中心将重点为非洲发展尤其是基础设施和可持续发展项目提供支持。

我们愿本着公平、共同但有区别的责任、各自能力原则，支持《联合国气候变化框架公约》第21次缔约方会议达成议定书、其他法律文书或具有法律效力的议定成果，为全球应对气候变化提供有效的解决方案，为发展中国家提供实施所需要的资源。我们进一步确认平衡减缓和适应行动的重要性。适应行动同样是一项全球性的责任。我们进一步确认，实现公约最终目标需要加强多边、法律架构，并需要抓紧、持续落实对公约的现有承诺，包括使《京都议定书》第二承诺期多哈修正案生效。我们认为气候变化加重了非洲现存挑战，并给非洲国家预算和实现可持续发展的努力带来额外负担。非方赞赏中国倡议设

system, and strengthen the mandate of the international financial institutions in development and poverty eradication, in an effort to narrow the North-South gap. In this regard, we welcome the establishment of the BRICS New Development Bank, with its headquarters in Shanghai and the African Regional Centre in South Africa, with a focus on supporting development in Africa, in particular on infrastructure and sustainable development projects.

We will, in keeping with the principles of equity and "common but differentiated responsibilities and respective capabilities", support the 21st Conference of Parties to the United Nations Framework Convention on Climate Change to adopt a protocol, another legal instrument or an agreed outcome with legal force under the Convention, which provides an effective solution to the global response to climate change with means of implementation required by developing countries. We further affirm the importance of addressing mitigation and adaptation in a balanced manner. Adaptation is equally a global responsibility. We further affirm that fulfilling the ultimate objective of the Convention will require strengthening the multilateral, rules-based regime and the urgent and sustained implementation of existing commitments under the Convention, including the entry into force of the Doha Amendment on the 2nd Commitment Period of the Kyoto

立气候变化南南合作基金，支持非洲国家应对气候变化、干旱和荒漠化。

我们致力于走和平发展道路，为世界和平、稳定和经济增长作出贡献，认为中国的经济结构调整和进步将助推非洲工业化和现代化进程。

非洲赞赏中国第一个向埃博拉疫区国家提供紧急支援，发挥引领作用并作出贡献。

我们重申坚持一个中国立场，双方将继续支持彼此维护国家主权、安全与发展利益，推进国家统一大业和区域一体化进程的努力。

我们支持非洲在维护地区和平稳定、实现经济更快增长和联合自强等方面卓有成效的努力。中国相信，非洲是世界政治、经济和文化的重要一极。

Protocol. We acknowledge that climate change is exacerbating existing challenges in Africa and is placing additional burdens on national budgets and efforts of African States to achieve sustainable development. In this regard, the African side recognizes China's initiative in capitalising the China South-South Cooperation Fund to support African Countries combat climate change, drought and desertification.

We are committed to the path of peaceful development and its contribution to world peace, stability and economic growth, and are of the view that China's economic restructuring and progress will help Africa advance its own industrialization and modernization processes.

The African side acknowledges and appreciates the leading efforts and contribution made by China as the first responder to deliver Ebola Virus Disease emergency support to the affected countries.

We reaffirm our commitment to the One China policy. Both sides will continue to support each other's efforts to safeguard national sovereignty, security and development interests and to promote the causes of national reunification and regional integration respectively.

We support Africa's effective endeavours to safeguard and maintain regional peace and stability, aimed at achieving higher economic growth rates and promoting integration and self-reliance. China believes that Africa is a significant

我们认为,中非发展战略互补,体现了互利、平等、开放、包容和负责任的特点,为发展中国家之间的团结、互相支持和互相尊重展示了可能和机遇。中非双方将探索和充分利用各自比较优势,促进和提升互利合作。

我们郑重宣示,中非将本着真实亲诚的理念和正确义利观,致力于建立和发展政治上平等互信、经济上合作共赢、文明上交流互鉴、安全上守望相助、国际事务中团结协作的全面战略合作伙伴关系,并为此:

(1)坚持平等相待,增进团结互信。加强中国与非洲各国政府间各层级对话与合作;尊重彼此核心利益,照顾彼此合理关切和诉求,在重大战略上凝聚共识。加强司法、执法和立法领域交流合作,加强同

force of politics, economy and culture in the world.

We believe that China and Africa's development strategies, are complementary and characterised by mutual benefit, equality, openness, inclusiveness, accountability, and that they demonstrate the possibilities and opportunities of solidarity, mutual support and respect among the developing countries. Therefore, both sides shall explore and fully utilize their comparative strengths to promote and further improve this mutually beneficial cooperation.

We solemnly declare that, adhering to the principles of sincerity, practical results, affinity and good faith and the values of friendship, justice and shared interests, both China and Africa are committed to building and developing comprehensive strategic and cooperative partnership featuring political equality and mutual trust, economic cooperation for win-win results, exchanges and mutual learning between Chinese and African civilizations, mutual assistance in security affairs and solidarity and cooperation in international affairs. To this end, we will:

(1) Remain committed to treating each other as equals and enhancing solidarity and mutual trust. Increase, improve and strengthen dialogue and cooperation between the governments of the two sides at all levels; respect each other's core interests, accommodate each other's legitimate concerns and aspirations, cement consensus on

非洲国家、非洲联盟及其所属机构、区域经济体、非洲开发银行的合作，推动区域一体化进程，维护非洲和平稳定，促进非洲经济社会发展。

（2）坚持弘义融利，促进共同发展。积极开展产业对接和产能合作，共同推动非洲工业化和农业现代化进程。重点加强铁路、公路、区域航空、电力、供水、信息通信、机场、港口等基础设施项目合作和人力资源开发合作等能力建设，优先推进农业和粮食安全、加工制造业、能源资源、海洋经济、旅游、投资、贸易、金融、技术转移等领域互利合作。认识到深化资源深加工合作与提高技术和智力能力同等重要。建立工业园、科技园区、经济特区以及培训工程、技术和管理人员的工程中心，加强工业生产领域合作，提高附加值。积极探讨中方建设"丝绸之路经济带"和"21世纪海上丝绸之路"倡议与非洲经济一体化和实现可持续发

key strategies; promote exchanges and cooperation in the judicial, law enforcement and legislative fields; strengthen China's cooperation with the African countries, the African Union and its structures, the Regional Economic Communities and the African Development Bank to advance the regional integration agenda, to safeguard peace and stability in Africa and to promote the socio-economic development of Africa.

(2) Adhere to the principle of upholding justice and promoting common interests and common development. Actively pursue cooperation between our industries and develop industrial capacity, and jointly promote the process of industrialization and agricultural modernization in Africa; focus on strengthening cooperation in infrastructure projects including, but not limited to, railways, highways, regional aviation, power, water supply, information and communication, airport and ports, as well as human resource development cooperation and capacity building; give priority to promoting mutually beneficial cooperation in agriculture and food security, processing and manufacturing, energy resources, maritime economy, tourism, investment, trade, finance, technology transfer and other fields. We underscore the importance of intensifying cooperation in projects related to beneficiation at source, while enhancing technical and intellectual capacities; enhance collaboration in the development of industrial production

展的对接，为促进共同发展、实现共同梦想寻找更多机遇。

（3）坚持互学互鉴，共谋和谐繁荣。加强发展经验交流，深化发展援助、医疗和公共卫生、教育、减贫、科技合作与知识分享、生态环境保护等领域合作。认识到依靠技术和创新促进非洲经济增长的重要性，特别是在采掘业、医药、信息技术、化学、石油化工、自然资源开采和加工等领域。加强双方民间和文化交流与合作，尤其是密切文化与艺术、教育、体育、旅游、新闻与媒体、学者与智库、青年、妇女、工会、残疾人等领域交流，深化双方人民的相互了解和友谊。

capabilities and value addition by establishing industrial parks and clusters, technology parks, special economic zones (SEZs) and engineering centers providing training for engineering and technical personnel and managers; actively explore the linkages between China's initiatives of building the Silk Road Economic Belt and 21st Century Maritime Silk Road and Africa's economic integration and sustainable development agenda, and seek more opportunities to promote common development and realize our common dreams.

(3) Promote mutual learning and seek harmonious progress through mutual efforts. Share experience for development, deepen cooperation in various fields such as development assistance, medical care and public health, education, poverty eradication, science and technology and knowledge sharing, and ecological and environmental protection; recognize the importance of developing technology and innovation in advancing the economic growth of African countries in areas such as the mining and extractive industry, pharmaceuticals, information technology, and chemicals and petrochemicals, both in the area of exploration and extraction of natural resources and in their processing; strengthen people-to-people and cultural exchanges and cooperation between the two parties and, in particular, enhance exchanges in culture and art, education, sports, tourism, press and media, and between academia, think tanks,

the youth, women, trade unions and persons with disabilities, with a view to deepening the understanding and friendship between the peoples of China and Africa.

（4）坚持互帮互助，维护和平安全。坚持通过对话协商和平解决争端，支持非洲以非洲方式解决非洲问题。落实"中非和平安全合作伙伴倡议"，支持非洲集体安全机制建设，共同应对粮食安全、能源安全、网络安全、气候变化、保护生物多样性、重大传染性疾病和跨国犯罪等非传统安全问题和全球性挑战。恐怖主义是人类及其和平、宽容价值观的全球性威胁。我们强烈谴责一切形式的恐怖主义，致力于采取协调、有效措施合作打击这一公害。

(4) Continue to support each other on security matters and maintain peace and security. We remain committed to seeking the peaceful settlement of disputes through dialogue and consultation, and China supports Africa in its efforts to solve African problems through African solutions; implement the Initiative on China-Africa Cooperative Partnership for Peace and Security, support the building of the collective security mechanism in Africa, and jointly manage non-traditional security issues and global challenges such as, but not limited to, food security, energy security, cyber security, climate change, biodiversity conservation, major communicable diseases and transnational crimes. We firmly condemn terrorism in all its forms and we commit to combining our efforts in a coordinated and more efficient way to fight against this scourge which constitutes a global threat for humanity and its values of peace and tolerance.

（5）坚持协调协作，维护共同利益。在联合国、国际金融机构等多边组织机构中，就共同关心的地区和国际问题加强协调和协作，坚决维护中非和发展中国家的共同利益。非洲国家支持中国主办2016年

(5) Unswervingly coordinate and cooperate with each other and safeguard our common interests. In the United Nations, international financial institutions and other multilateral organizations, we will strengthen coordination and cooperation on regional and international issues of common interests, and firmly safeguard

二十国集团峰会，赞赏中国致力于进一步加强二十国集团同非洲国家合作。我们赞赏和欢迎国际社会，特别是发达国家为非洲和平、发展与繁荣作出积极努力和贡献。

我们对最近三个月在南非举行的第二届中非部长级卫生合作发展会议、第五届中非企业家大会取得的成果表示欢迎。

我们对双方参加中非合作论坛第六届部长级会议的部长们的不懈努力和出色工作表示赞赏。根据本《宣言》精神，我们通过了《中非合作论坛—约翰内斯堡行动计划（2016—2018年）》，并将致力于推进落实，确保成功实施。

我们衷心感谢南非共和国总统雅各布·盖德莱伊莱基萨·祖马和中华人民共和国主席习近平共同主持2015年中非合作论坛约翰内斯堡峰会。

the common interests of China, Africa and other developing countries. African countries support China's hosting of the G20 Summit in 2016 and laud China's commitment to promote further cooperation between the G20 and African countries. In this regard, we appreciate and welcome the international community, especially developed countries, making active efforts and contributing to the peace, development and prosperity of Africa.

We welcome the outcomes of the 2nd Ministerial Forum of China-Africa Health Development and the 5th China-Africa Business Forum held in South Africa at various times over the last three months.

We commend the Ministers participating in the 6th Ministerial Conference of the Forum on China-Africa Cooperation for their dedicated efforts and outstanding work. In this regard, we have, in the spirit of this Declaration, adopted the Johannesburg Action Plan (2016-2018) of the Forum on China-Africa Cooperation. We commit ourselves to implementing the Johannesburg Action Plan and will work to ensure its successful implementation.

We express our profound gratitude to H.E. President Jacob Gedleyihlekisa Zuma of the Republic of South Africa, and H.E. President Xi Jinping of the People's Republic of China, for co-chairing the 2015 Johannesburg Summit of the Forum on China-Africa Cooperation (FOCAC).

我们衷心感谢南非共和国政府和人民在 2015 年中非合作论坛约翰内斯堡峰会期间给予各方的热情接待和便利。	We further express our profound gratitude to the Government and the People of the Republic of South Africa for their kind hospitality and excellent facilities for the duration of the 2015 Johannesburg Summit of the Forum on China-Africa Cooperation.
中非合作论坛第七届部长级会议将于 2018 年在中华人民共和国召开。	The 7th Ministerial Conference of FOCAC will be held in the People's Republic of China in 2018.

三 外交宣言的翻译原则与难点

外交宣言的主要内容是表达主体的态度、立场和意见,因此用语不能含混模糊、模棱两可,而应措辞明确,态度明朗。外交宣言公布的是重要纲领、主张和意见,带有一定的政治倾向,因此非常严肃认真,无论语言还是行文都必须小心谨慎。外交宣言常用于公开昭示发布主体的立场和主见,体现一定的情感色彩,因此具有鼓动性和号召力,表现主体的力量、意志和决心。

外交宣言翻译首先要遵循的原则是忠实再现。一方面,在内容上尽可能全面真实地向受众反馈、传达宣言主体的观点和意见。全面是指内容不能有任何遗漏,真实是指译者不能以主观推测替代客观内容,更不能有任何歪曲和谬误。比如上面的宣言中有这样一句话,"我们必须继续加强现有集体对话……"译者将其译为 "Therefore, it is incumbent on us to continue to strengthen the current platform for collective dialogue...",仔细对照不难发现,译文中添加了原文中没有的 "platform (平台)"一词,这种添加并非译者随意为之,也非翻译谬误。有学者指出,在 2000 年之前"中非关系稳步发展,但缺乏统一的机制化合作平台,在国际社会普遍加强对非合作而中非双方又均有强烈合作意愿的大背景下,中非合作论坛的成立为中国与非洲之间搭建起规范化的政策对话和沟通平台。"[1] 因此这里的 platform 就是指中非合作论坛,译者通过增加该词使得"加强集体对话"的内在含义更为明确,准确再

---

[1] 唐丽霞,赵文杰,李晓云. 2020. 中非合作论坛框架下中非农业合作的新发展与新挑战. 西亚非洲,(5):3-20.

现了宣言主体要巩固中非合作论坛的意思。另一方面，忠实再现也指对宣言主体语气、态度的传达，即赞赏还之以赞赏，反对还之以反对，高雅还之以高雅，庄重还之以庄重。比如"我们认为，中非关系在过去 15 年维护了双方人民的共同利益，推动了双方繁荣发展的势头。"译为"We believe that China-Africa relations promote the common interests of both our peoples and continue the trend of prosperous growth evident over the last 15 years.", 原文对于中非关系在过去 15 年的积极作用表示高度认可。为了突显宣言主体的褒奖态度，译者在译文中加入了 evident 一词。其次，在翻译外交宣言时也要有受众意识，需要考虑译语的规范及目标读者的文化背景、知识水平、阅读习惯等，尽可能为译文读者着想。外交宣言主要目的是为读者提供信息，译文应确保受众迅速捕捉信息，了解宣言主体的意思。

王平新认为，翻译外交文本要达到"政治等效"的目标无法实现，也就是既要求翻译必须忠实反映源语和说话者的政治思想和政治语境，又要求翻译做到使双方得到的政治含义信息等值是不太可能[1]。但翻译外交宣言还是需要注意措辞选择的准确性，而把握好敏感话题的措辞分寸也是外交宣言翻译的难点之一。译者要有正确的立场和敏锐的政治性才能彰显宣言主体的立场、观点和态度。此外，译者还要把握措辞分寸，避免冒犯他人，引发不必要的争端。比如"反对达赖在国际窜访"翻译为 Dalai Lama visit, Dalai Lama visit trip, 还是 Dalai Lama visit tour 都是缺乏政治敏感性的表现，没有体现我方的立场和观点。有学者认为"'窜访'是一个具有中国特色的新造词，在英语中无法找到一个意义上完全对等的词"，"有必要采取造词译法"，"将 tout 和 visit 组合成一个新单词 tout visit, 是比较贴切的译法"[2], 译文 tout 是"四处兜售、贩卖、沿街叫卖、吹嘘、刺探、拉选票"的贬义，与"窜"字所包含的情感意义吻合。

四 外交宣言的英译技巧

1 外交宣言标题的翻译技巧

外交宣言标题一般采用"宣言主体 + 发布地点 + 宣言"等结构。2017 年 9 月 4

---

1 王平新. 2016. "政治等效"翻译：臆想还是现实？中国翻译，（1）：91-95.
2 杨明星，李志丹. 2015. "政治等效"视野下"窜访"译法探究. 中国翻译，（5）：88-92.

日，金砖国家领导人在厦门国际会议中心举行第九次会晤后发表会议宣言。宣言标题为《金砖国家领导人厦门宣言》。译者保留原标题的格式，将其译为 BRICS Leaders Xiamen Declaration。发表该宣言的主体是金砖国家，包括巴西（Brazil）、俄罗斯（Russia）、印度（India）、中国（China）和南非（South Africa），这五个国家代表着世界新兴市场。"金砖国家"从 21 世纪初至今，逐步形成了一个多层次的合作架构，领导人会晤是其主要机制，辅之以安全事务高级代表会议、外长会议、常驻多边组织使节会议等，并以各国在智库、工商、银行等诸多领域的合作为支撑。BRICS 一词由五个成员国名称的英文首字母缩略构成，该词与英语单词 Bricks（砖）的发音相似，因此译为"金砖国家"。正是由于 BRICS 这一主体称谓比较简短，译者才能在译文中保留"宣言主体 + 发布地点 + 宣言"结构。

《中非合作论坛约翰内斯堡峰会宣言》与《金砖国家领导人厦门宣言》两个中文标题结构基本相同，采用的是"宣言主体 + 发布地点 + 宣言"结构。但是前者由于宣言主体（中非合作论坛）的英文名称比较长，如果按照原文的结构来翻译，译文标题会出现头重脚轻的问题。为了保持句子结构平衡，译者有必要作相应调整，可以采用"Declaration of+ 发布地点 + 宣言主体"的结构，因此该宣言标题被译为 Declaration of the Johannesburg Summit of the Forum on China-Africa Cooperation。

还有一种宣言标题包含宣言的主题，或用副标题的形式表达宣言主体的倡议、主张、观点等。2016 年 4 月 28 日，亚洲相互协作与信任措施会议（Conference on Interaction and Confidence Building Measures in Asia，CICA），简称亚信会议或亚信，在北京召开了第五次外长会议。这是一个有关安全问题的多边论坛，其宗旨是在亚洲国家之间讨论加强合作、增加信任的措施，峰会和外长会议均为每四年举行一次，两会交错举行，间隔两年。会议发表了《亚洲相互协作与信任措施会议第五次外长会议关于通过对话促进亚洲和平、安全、稳定和可持续发展的宣言》。这一宣言标题采用了"宣言主体 +主张 + 宣言"的结构，宣言主体是"亚信会议第五次外长会议"，宣言主张是"通过对话促进亚洲和平、安全、稳定和可持续发展"。为避免标题过于冗长难懂，译者采用了"主标题 + 副标题"的方式译为：Declaration of the Fifth Meeting of the Ministers of Foreign Affairs of the Conference on Interaction and Confidence Building Measures in Asia: Promoting Peace, Security, Stability and Sustainable Development in Asia Through Dialogue，其中主标题包括"亚信会议第五次外长会议"，而副标题则是该宣言的主张，这种处理方法让标题更为简洁易懂。2018 年 9 月 3 日至 4 日在中国举行了中非合作论坛北京峰会，会议发表了《关于构建更加紧密的中非命运共同体的北京宣言》。这一宣言标题中没有宣言主体，由"主

张 + 发布地点 + 宣言"组成，译者同样采用"主标题 + 副标题"的方式译为"Beijing Declaration—Toward an Even Stronger China-Africa Community with a Shared Future"，将主张部分作为副标题。此外，还有一种情况值得关注，即原文宣言标题由宣言主体 + 宣言构成，翻译时除了再现原文标题结构，还要增加宣言的主题、地点等，使标题内涵更为鲜明。比如，2017年11月11日，亚太经合组织第二十五次领导人非正式会议在越南岘港举办，之后发表了《亚太经合组织第二十五次领导人非正式会议宣言》。从原文标题来看，该宣言并未包含发布的地点和主体的主张，只由宣言主体 + 宣言构成。译文不但再现宣言主体 The 25th APEC Economic Leaders' Meeting，而且附加以下内容"Da Nang Declaration: Creating New Dynamism, Fostering a Shared Future"，包括会议地点岘港及会议主题。由此可见，宣言标题的构成存在一定灵活性，翻译时需弄清结构，结合上下文，选择最佳处理方式，恰切传达源语信息。

2 外交宣言正文翻译技巧

思维方式"是语言生成和发展的深层机制"，"语言是思维的主要工具，是思维方式的构成要素。思维以一定的方式体现出来，表现于某种语言形式之中。思维方式的差异，正是造成语言差异的一个重要原因"[1]。东西方民族在思维上有很大的区别，因此语言差异也是巨大的。这种差异在句子层面上来看尤为明显，译者应对这样的差异既要有宏观的认识，又要有具体的方法，分清信息的主次，把握信息的整体与部分，必要时整合或者拆分信息。

1）信息的主次处理

汉语复句和英语复合句一样，也有主次之别，因此进行汉译英时，首先要分清句子的逻辑关系，然后再确定主次。比如，两个句子之间是因果关系时，"果"应当是信息的重点，而"因"相对而言就是次要信息。

原文 我们强调环境合作对金砖国家可持续发展和人民福祉的重要性，同意在预防空气和水污染、废弃物管理、保护生物多样性等领域采取具体行动，推进成果导向型合作。

译文 Stressing the importance of environmental cooperation to sustainable

---

[1] 连淑能. 2010. 英汉对比研究增订本. 北京：高等教育出版社，第283页.

development of our countries and the well-being of our peoples, we agree to take concrete actions to advance result-oriented cooperation in such areas as prevention of air and water pollution, waste management and biodiversity conservation.

汉语重"意合"(paratactic)，语义的连贯依靠读者的逻辑推理，而英语重"形合"(hypotactic)，语义的连贯必须借助外在的有形手段。因此，在进行汉英翻译时，需要将汉语里隐含的逻辑关系，在英语中用一定的有形手段加以明示。上述例子隐含了一种因果关系，即：(因为)"我们强调环境合作对金砖国家可持续发展和人民福祉的重要性"，(所以)同意采取行动、推进合作。原文表示结果的部分译成英语时，就变成了主句，而表示原因的部分被译成了非谓语动词短语。另外，在表示结果的主句中，译者又通过推理得出以下逻辑关系："采取具体行动"的目的在于"推进合作"，而"预防空气和水污染""废弃物管理""保护生物多样性"则是需要采取行动的领域。译者通过调整原文的语序、使用表目的 to 结构以及增加 such as 等清晰表达了原文的逻辑关系。对于这种能明确理出其偏正关系的汉语句子，译者应当首先理清主次。一般而言，在汉语中表达推断、结论、结果、本质等意味的句子常占主要地位，可英译为主句或者谓语部分，而表示原因、条件、时间、地点、方式、方法、状态等非本质内容可英译为从句、非谓语动词短语或是介词短语。

原文 基于共同历史遭遇、发展任务和政治诉求，中非人民同呼吸、共命运，结下深厚友谊。一致承诺，加强集体对话，增进传统友谊，深化务实合作，携手打造更加紧密的中非命运共同体。

译文 Sharing weal and woe, the Chinese and African peoples have forged a deep friendship rooted in our similar historical experiences, development tasks and political aspirations. We agree to strengthen collective dialogue, enhance traditional friendship, deepen practical cooperation, and work together toward an even stronger China-Africa community with a shared future.

原句第一句可以这样理解：由于中非人民有"共同历史遭遇、发展任务和政治诉求"，所以中非人民才能"同呼吸、共命运，结下深厚友谊"。前后两部分之间存在因果逻辑。"果"是信息的重点，故译者将其译成英语的主句，译文为"the Chinese and African peoples have forged a deep friendship"，而表示原因的"共同历史遭遇、发展任务和政治诉求"则被译作过去分词短语，用以修饰 friendship，"同呼吸、共命运"译为 sharing weal and woe，以现在分词短语形式充当方式状语。通过分析信息的主次，译者对原文的结构进行了一定调整，但是信息的主次却没有改变。

原文 我们强调加强贸易投资合作有助于释放金砖国家经济潜力，同意完善并扩展贸易投资合作机制和范围，以加强金砖国家经济互补性和多样性。

译文 Stressing the role of enhanced trade and investment cooperation in unleashing the potential of BRICS economies, we agree to improve and broaden trade and investment cooperation mechanism and scope, with a view to enhancing BRICS economic complementarity and diversification in BRICS countries.

在这个例子中，原文的结构是"强调……，同意……，以（达到）……"，按照原文结构，译者应将原文最后一部分，也就是表达目的的部分作为信息重点。然而译文可见，译者将"同意完善并扩展贸易投资合作机制和范围"，亦即原文的第二部分，作为主句或信息重点。这似乎违反了上文提到的信息主次的原则。其实不然，影响信息主次的因素也不仅限于逻辑关系，还应考虑句子所在的语境。除了上下文语言语境，还有文本之外的社会历史语境等。此例出自《金砖国家领导人厦门宣言》，宣言的主题是"我们致力于本着未来共同发展的愿景，在金砖国家合作已有进展的基础上更进一步"。由此可见，"金砖国家之间的进一步合作"是该宣言主要强调的信息，因此"完善并扩展贸易投资合作机制和范围"应是此例的信息重点，译成主句"we agree to improve and broaden trade and investment cooperation mechanism and scope"是合理化选择。另外两个句子则分别用分词短语和介词短语译为主句的状语部分，恰切烘托出该例表达的重点。

2）信息的分合处理技巧

（1）分译

汉语之美在于言简意赅，有时简短的话语包含了大量的信息，为了将这些信息完整地传达，可以将原文译成两句或更多的句子。有时原文是长句，为了让译文变得更为易懂、通顺、条理清晰，也可以将汉语的长句分译成多个句子。

原文 ①我们尊重各自选择的发展道路，理解和支持彼此利益。②我们一直坚持平等团结，坚持开放包容，建设开放型世界经济，深化同新兴市场和发展中国家的合作。③我们坚持互利合作，谋求共同发展，不断深化金砖务实合作，造福世界。

译文 ① We have shown respect for the development paths of our respective choices, and rendered understanding and support to each other's interests. ② We have upheld equality and solidarity. ③ We have also embraced openness and inclusiveness, dedicated to forging an open world economy. ④ We have furthered our cooperation with emerging markets and developing countries (EMDCs). ⑤ We have worked together for mutually beneficial outcomes and common development, constantly deepening BRICS practical cooperation which benefits the world at large.

这个例子中的汉语原文有三个句子，但是译文中却有五个句子，通过对比我们可以看到原文的第一、第三个句子和译文的第一、第五个句子基本上是对应的，译者将汉语原文中的第二个句子拆分成三个句子。"我们一直坚持平等团结，坚持开放包容，建设开放型世界经济，深化同新兴市场和发展中国家的合作"，这个句子的结构是"我们坚持……，坚持……，建设……，深化合作"。前一个"坚持"是金砖国家合作的基础，不容动摇。后一个"坚持"是在此基础上的进一步发展，只有坚持"平等团结"，才能实现"开放包容"，从而达到建设开放型世界经济的目标。另外，金砖国家在前期已经和新兴市场以及发展中国家有了一定的合作，宣言主张进一步加深这种合作。因此译者将这三层意思，用不同的句子表达出来，让译文的逻辑更为清晰。此外，译文中的五个句子都用了完成时，且均以 we have 的结构出现，展示出金砖国家为世界和平和经济发展所作出的种种努力。

原文 ①在境外组织和支持一国政变，是干涉别国内政的行为，威胁到国家主权和政治独立，②与联合国宗旨和原则相悖，也违反了《联合国宪章》，将导致威胁国际和平与安全的形势。

译文 ① Organisation and support of externally-based coups, as form of interference in the internal affairs of states, poses a threat to the sovereignty and political independence of states; ② and is contrary to the purposes and principles of the United Nations, violates the UN Charter, and also leads to the creation of situations which can threaten international peace and security.

汉语原文如果用表示判断或小结的从句结尾，也可使用分译法。比如在这个例子中，尽管只在第二个小句用了判断词"是"，但之后的所有小句都可以看作是判断句。比如第三句可以改为"（是）威胁到国家主权和政治独立（的）"，第四句则是，"（是）与联合国宗旨和原则相悖（的）"，加上"是……的"的判断结构，就将原文表示判断或总结意味变得更为明晰。原文的主题是从两个层面谈论"在境外组织和支持一国政变"这一行为的性质,由国家层面到国际层面,性质越来越严重,因此译文也分成两个层面来论述这种行为的性质和后果。

> **原文** ①我们高度赞赏中华人民共和国自 2014 年 5 月担任亚信主席国以来所做工作,②认为中方在推进亚信发展进程、机制化建设、制定和落实各领域信任措施方面发挥了重要作用。

> **译文** ① We highly commend the work carried out by the People's Republic of China since it assumed CICA Chairmanship in May 2014. ② We recognise the important role the People's Republic of China has played advancing the CICA process, promoting CICA institution building, and adopting and implementing CBMs.

原文是一个长句,包含两层意义,首先表达了对中国任亚信主席国以来所做工作的赞赏,其次具体说明中国作为主席国在哪些领域发挥了重要作用。句子结构是从一般到具体,译文也是按照从一般到具体的结构处理为两个层次,一是"We highly commend the work",二是"We recognize the important role",这样一来译文逻辑关系更清晰。

> **原文** ①成员国积极并有针对性地打击国际恐怖主义、分裂主义、极端主义,跨国有组织犯罪,非法贩运麻醉药品、精神药物及其前体,非法贩运武器弹药和爆炸物,非法移民,应对生物信息安全威胁,②支持进一步完善上述领域合作的法律基础。

> **译文** ① The Member States are actively and persistently countering international terrorism, separatism and extremism, transnational organised crime, illegal trade in narcotic drugs, psychotropic substances and their precursors, as well as weapons, munitions and explosives, threats to biological and information security and illegal migration. ② They advocate further improvement of the legal and regulatory framework for cooperation in these areas.

这个例子的结构与上一个例子相反,上一个例子是从一般到具体,而这个例子是从具体到一般。原文首先表明上海合作组织在打击"国际恐怖主义、分裂主义、极端主义,跨国有组织犯罪,非法贩运麻醉或药品,非法贩运武器弹药和爆炸物,非法移民,应对生物信息安全威胁"等具体领域达成了合作意向,随后发出要制定更有利于合作、更为完善的法律法规制度的倡议。译文也是从具体到一般，并且在译文中将原文的一个句子拆分成两个句子。第一个句子说明具体的合作领域，第二个句子涵盖为具体合作制定法律法规的意愿，逻辑更为清晰明了。因此，当汉语长句中含有从一般到具体或从具体到一般的过渡，英译时可分译。

> **原文** ①我们致力于推动实现充分、高效、高质量就业和同工同酬，②确保民众获得银行、保险和金融服务，③提高民众金融素养和融资能力，④促进社会所有成员，⑤特别是妇女、青年、残疾人和其他弱势群体的收入持续稳步增长，使其能够分享全球机遇。

> **译文** ① We commit to advance progress towards achieving full, productive and quality employment and equal pay for equal work; ② ensure access to banking, insurance and financial services, and increase financial literacy and capability of all to access finance; ③ and progressively achieve and sustain income growth for all members of society, especially women, and youth, persons with disabilities and other vulnerable groups, and enable them to seize global opportunities.

不仅中文言简意赅的句式特点使得汉译英时需要经常采用分译法，原文的行文逻辑更是译者采取分译法的重要原因。上面这个例子的背景是指APEC已经批准了《APEC促进经济、金融和社会包容行动议程》。在此背景下，APEC同意将以此行动议程来指导其下一步的工作，而例子中涉及的就是APEC（我们）下一步要开展的主要工作内容。原文有五个小句，但每个小句的逻辑主语一致，主要围绕涉及的下一步工作——展开。这些工作包括三个方面：一是就业和酬劳；二是银行、保险和金融服务；三是社会成员的收入增长。从行文逻辑上来看，译文也必须符合原文的逻辑，因此译文可以这三个方面的工作内容作为依据，将原文分译为三个句子。原文的②③小句说的是同一个方面，故合并一起，④⑤小句涉及的也是同一方面，也合并为一句，使得译文层次更分明，逻辑更清晰，信息更明确。尽管在处理小句时，译者合并了一些句子，但从逻辑结构上来看，分译法的应用比较突出。由此可见，处理围绕同一主题的若干小句构成的长句时，译者首先应当理顺小句之间的逻辑关系，以原文主题为纲，将其中的逻辑关系一一表达出来。

（2）合译

通常来说，从句子长度来看，英语句子普遍长于汉语句子，且句子中状语和定语的位置相对比较自由，使得英语长句比汉语的句子更为包容，拥有较大的信息容纳量。在汉译英时，有时可把两个或两个以上的汉语句子译成一个英语句子。

> **原文** ①同时，我们也注意到世界经济中的不确定性和下行风险依然存在，③强调有必要警惕防范内顾政策和倾向。②这种政策和倾向正在对世界经济增长前景和市场信心带来负面影响。

> **译文** ① Noting the uncertainties and downside risks that persist, ③ we emphasize the need to be vigilant in guarding against inward-looking policies and tendencies ② that are weighing on global growth prospects and market confidence.

原文指出世界经济中存在不确定性和下行风险，由于这种状况的存在我们必须要警惕内顾政策和倾向，接着又警告了这种政策和倾向正在对世界经济带来的负面影响。②句的主语"这种政策和倾向"和前一句的宾语"内顾政策和倾向"同指。因此译者采用合译法，将原文标号③的句子当作主句，而原文标号②的句子译为定语从句，原文标号①的句子处理为译文的状语，这样一来使得译文条理清晰，层次分明，也更符合英语表达的特征。

> **原文** ①我们希望有关各方忠实、充分执行全面协议及安理会第2231号决议。②这将有助于该地区国家加强互信。

> **译文** ① We hope that all relevant parties will fully implement JCPOA and the UN Security Council Resolution 2231 in good faith, ② which will contribute to enhancing mutual trust among regional countries.

汉语原文有两个句子。第一个句子是一个兼语句，所谓兼语句是指一个句子里有两个动词，前一个动词的宾语是后一个动词的主语，而第一个句子中第二个动词"执行"的宾语是"全面协议及安理会第2231号决议"。第二句一开头的指示代词"这"应当是指"有关各方忠实、充分执行全面协议及安理会第2231号决议"，因此可以将第二个句子处理为定语从句，使得译文的逻辑关系清楚明白。这个例子与上一个例子类似，也就是当后一个部分以前一个句子的结尾开头时，往往可以采用合译法。

> **原文** ①我们忆及金砖国家灾害管理部长会圣彼得堡和《乌代布尔宣言》，②以及建立金砖国家灾害风险管理联合工作组的决定，③强调在金砖国家应急服务方面携手合作非常重要。④我们着眼于通过灾害风险管理最佳实践信息交流和自然、人为灾害预报预警及有效应对等领域的合作，⑤减少灾害风险，构建更加安全的未来。

> 译文　① Recalling the Saint-Petersburg and Udaipur Declarations of BRICS Ministers for Disaster management and the decision to establish a BRICS Joint Taskforce on Disaster Risk Management, ② we underline the importance of consistent joint work of emergency services of BRICS countries aimed at building a safer future by reducing existing disaster risks, ③ including exchange of information on best practices concerning disaster risk management and cooperation in the field of forecasting and early warning for effective response to natural and human induced disasters.

《圣彼得堡宣言》和《乌代布尔宣言》是2016年4月19日至20日在圣彼得堡和2016年8月22日在乌代布尔举行的两次金砖国家灾害管理部长会议的成果。原文的第一句回忆了金砖国家在灾害风险管理和应对合作方面的成果，并强调合作的必要性。第二句则说明合作的领域及其意义。无论第一句还是第二句，都是围绕灾害风险管理和应对合作这个主题展开，因此紧紧抓住这个主题，译文将原文两个句子合译为一句。在下面这个例子中，原文的多个句子围绕同一个话题展开，我们同样可以采用合译法。

> 原文　①我们热烈欢迎东盟共同体于2015年12月31日成立。②它包括政治安全共同体、经济共同体和社会文化共同体三大支柱，③旨在建立具有政治凝聚力、经济一体化和承担社会责任的共同体。

> 译文　① We warmly welcome the establishment on 31 December 2015 of the ASEAN Community comprising of three pillars, ② namely the ASEAN Political-Security Community, ③ ASEAN Economic Community and ASEAN Socio-Cultural Community, ④ aiming at building a politically cohesive, economically integrated and socially responsible community.

这个例子的原文包含了三个层次，首先是祝贺东盟共同体的成立，其次是说明该组织的构成，最后是该组织的目标，三个层次都是围绕东盟共同体展开。在译文中这三个层次被融合在一起，原文的第一个句子为译文的主句，第二个句子译为同位语，第三个句子译作状语。

另外，如果汉语原文的句子里有明显的关联词，译文可以在关联词处合译。即使原文没有使用关联词，但是句子之间存在某种逻辑关系时，我们可以在译文中加上关联词，合并句子，使逻辑关系更明确。

原文 ①我们敦促发达国家切实兑现对发展中国家特别是非洲国家的援助承诺。②我们认为,南北发展失衡是阻碍世界经济强劲复苏和可持续增长的重要原因。

译文 ① We urge developed countries to honor their commitments to provide aid to developing countries, African countries in particular, ② as we believe that the North-South imbalance in development is an important factor hindering the strong recovery and sustained growth of the world economy.

汉语原文的两个句子之间隐藏着因果关系。因为"南北发展失衡是阻碍世界经济强劲复苏和可持续增长的重要原因",所以"我们敦促发达国家切实兑现对发展中国家特别是非洲国家的援助承诺"。译文通过表示因果关系的连接词 as 将表示原因的第二个句子处理为从句,将两个句子连接起来,同时还明示出句子之间的因果关系。

3 外交宣言附件翻译技巧

除了标题和正文之外,有些外交宣言还有附件部分。附件可能是公文、图标、名单等,它能起到补充和完善宣言正文内容的作用,与正文有同等的效力。在翻译附件时,要保留如附件编号等格式;要注意文件名是否已经有现成的译文,如果已经有获得官方认可的译文,就应直接引用;文件名的翻译要做到言简意赅。

五 中国关键词加油站

1 中非合作论坛 Forum on China-Africa Cooperation

为进一步加强中国与非洲国家的友好合作,共同应对经济全球化挑战,谋求共同发展,在中非双方共同倡议下,"中非合作论坛——北京 2000 年部长级会议"于 2000 年 10 月在京召开,标志着中非合作论坛正式成立。该论坛的宗旨是平等互利、平等磋商、增进了解、扩大共识、加强友谊、促进合作。成员包括中国和与中国建交的 53 个非洲国家以及非洲联盟委员会。中非合作论坛部长级会议每 3 年举行一届。

2 中拉命运共同体 China-LatAm community with a shared future

2014年7月，习近平在巴西利亚与拉美和加勒比国家领导人举行会晤，决定建立平等互利、共同发展的中拉全面合作伙伴关系，共同宣布成立中拉命运共同体。

2016年11月，习近平在秘鲁国会发表演讲，再次从打造中拉命运共同体出发，提出高举和平发展合作旗帜、推动发展战略对接、推进合作换挡加速、实现合作成果共享四点建议，充分体现了中国一贯倡导的人类命运共同体理念，为共创中拉关系美好未来指明了前进方向。

中拉命运共同体的建设遵循共商共建共享的原则，坚持双边合作与多边平台建设并行推进，支撑起全面合作的大厦，符合时代潮流，也符合中拉两大地区人民的根本利益。中拉命运共同体不仅是利益共同体，还是责任共同体，更是紧密的发展伙伴关系，开拓了南南合作实现新发展的崭新思路。

3 《联合国宪章》 Charter of the United Nations

联合国的基本大法，它既确立了联合国的宗旨、原则和组织机构设置，又规定了成员国的责任、权利和义务，以及处理国际关系、维护世界和平与安全的基本原则和方法。《联合国宪章》除序言和结语外，共分19章111条，国际法院规约是《联合国宪章》的组成部分。《联合国宪章》于1945年6月26日在旧金山会议上签署，于1945年10月24日正式生效。

4 多边主义 multilateralism

约翰·罗杰将多边主义定义为"依据普遍行为的原则，协调三个或三个以上国家的制度形式"。除了这种从制度层面界定外，多边主义还表现为国家行为体之间的行为方式，以及对国际普遍的行为准则和规制的重视和遵守。多边主义在本质上是一种"多元、平等、互利、合作"的国际关系准则。作为一种着眼于发展国家行为体之间良性互动的社会性安排，协调与合作是多边主义的基本特征。多边主义主要包括多边机制与多边外交两个层面，其形态表现为全球多边主义、地区多边主义、跨地区多边主义、同盟多边主义、大国多边主义以及货币多边主义、贸易多边主义等，现已运用到政治、经济、文化、军事、环境等各个领域。

5 单边主义 unilateralism

单边主义是指举足轻重的特定大国，不考虑大多数国家和民众的愿望，单独或带头退出或挑战已制订或商议好了的维护国际性、地区性、集体性和平、发展、进步的规则和制度，并对全局或局部的和平、发展、进步有破坏性的影响和后果的行为与倾向。

世贸组织改革必须坚持反对保护主义和单边主义的方向，必须有助于推进世界范围的贸易自由化、投资便利化进程，必须坚持非歧视的原则，必须充分发扬民主。

2019年6月27日至29日，中国国家主席习近平应邀赴日本大阪出席二十国集团（G20）领导人第十四次峰会。习近平主席接连出席20多场活动，高举多边主义旗帜，倡导伙伴合作精神，践行互利共赢理念，阐释共同发展主张。在各方共同努力下，G20大阪峰会发出支持多边主义的主流声音，为国际形势发展注入稳定性和正能量。

6 经济全球化观 economic globalization

2017年1月17日，习近平在世界经济论坛2017年年会开幕式上发表主旨演讲，畅论要坚定不移地推进经济全球化，引导好经济全球化走向，打造富有活力的增长模式、开放共赢的合作模式、公正合理的治理模式、平衡普惠的发展模式，牢固树立人类命运共同体意识，共同促进全球发展。

此次演讲深刻诠释了经济全球化的客观必然性，同时不回避全球化进程中的结构性难题；明确阐述了经济全球化不仅符合中国自身利益，也符合世界各国的共同利益。他指出，经济全球化是社会生产力发展的客观要求和科技进步的必然结果，既为世界经济增长提供强劲动力，又是一把"双刃剑"，面对存在的不足应该积极引导其走向；要主动作为、适度管理，更多发挥经济全球化正面效应；要顺应大势、结合国情，正确选择融入经济全球化的路径和节奏；要讲求效率、注重公平，共享经济全球化带来的好处。中国的发展是世界的机遇，中国是经济全球化的受益者，更是贡献者。中国经济快速增长，为全球经济稳定和增长提供持续强大的推动。中国人民欢迎各国人民搭乘中国发展的"快车""便车"。上述观点构成了经济全球化观的主要内容。它厘清了人们对全球化效应的认识，坚定了各国对全球化前景的信心，有力引领了全球化发展的正确方向；同时也为世界认识中国发展模式、把握中国发展理念提供了全面视角，提振了各方对中国道路的信心，拉近了中国同世界的距离。

7 贸易保护主义 trade protectionism

贸易保护主义是一种为了保护本国制造业免受国外竞争压力而对进口产品设定极高关税、限定进口配额或其他减少进口额的经济政策。它与自由贸易模式正好相反，后者使进口产品免除关税，让外国的产品可以与国内市场接轨，而不使它们负担国内制造厂商背负的重税。贸易保护主义经常被人们与重商主义和进口替代联系起来。重商主义认为保持一个可观的贸易顺差对一个国家是很有利的。在对外贸易中实行限制进口以保护本国商品在国内市场免受外国商品竞争，并向本国商品提供各种优惠以增强其国际竞争力的主张和政策。在限制进口方面，主要是采取关税壁垒和非关税壁垒两种措施。前者主要是通过征收高额进口关税阻止外国商品的大量进口；后者则包括采取进口许可证制、进口配额制等一系列非关税措施来限制外国商品自由进口。这些措施也是经济不发达国家保护民族工业、发展国民经济的一项重要手段。对发达国家来说则是调整国际收支、纠正贸易逆差的一个重要工具。在自由竞争资本主义时期，较晚发展的资本主义国家，常常推行贸易保护主义政策。发达国家则多提倡自由贸易，贸易保护主义只是用作对付危机的临时措施。到了垄断阶段，垄断资本主义国家推行的贸易保护主义，已不仅仅是抵制外国商品进口的手段，更成为对外扩张、争夺世界市场的手段。

8 贸易壁垒 trade barrier

贸易壁垒又称贸易障碍。对国外国间商品劳务交换所设置的人为限制，主要是指一国对外国商品劳务进口所实行的各种限制措施。一般分关税壁垒和非关税壁垒两类。就广义而言，凡使正常贸易受到阻碍，市场竞争机制作用受到干扰的各种人为措施，均属贸易壁垒的范畴。如进口税或起同等作用的其他捐税；商品流通的各种数量限制；在生产者之间、购买者之间或使用者之间实行的各种歧视措施或做法（特别是关于价格或交易条件和运费方面）；国家给予的各种补贴或强加的各种特殊负担；以及为划分市场范围或谋取额外利润而实行的各种限制性做法等等。关税及贸易总协定所推行的关税自由化、商品贸易自由化与劳务贸易壁垒，尽管在关税方面取得较大进展，在其他方面却收效甚微。某种形式的贸易壁垒削弱了，其他形式的贸易壁垒却加强了，各种新的贸易壁垒反而层出不穷。随着WTO等国际间贸易组织成员的不断增加以及各地区组织的建立，如北美自由贸易区等，对这两类组织的非成员国关税壁垒还在起着作用。但值得注意的是，国际上非关税壁垒的作用正在上升，或有上升的趋势。一些发达国家利用其自身的技术优势对来自其他国家产品的认证要求，极大地阻碍了欠发达和发展中国家制成品的出口；而只能出些资源性的初级产品。加剧了南北间的经济及贸易发展差距。另外，发达国家，以及一些次发达甚至发展中国家越来越多地采用的反倾销手段，也是非关税壁垒之一。就我国而言，配额，许可证制度也属于后者。

9 可持续发展战略 strategy for sustainable development

中国是人口众多、资源相对不足的国家。改革开放以来，中共中央、国务院高度重视中国的可持续发展，1994年3月，国务院通过《中国21世纪议程》，确定实施可持续发展战略。2003年初，国务院颁布《中国21世纪初可持续发展行动纲要》，明确未来10年到20年的可持续发展目标、重点和保障措施。中共十五大、十六大、十七大、十八大，都对可持续发展战略提出新要求。可持续发展战略事关中华民族的长远发展，事关子孙后代福祉，具有全局性、根本性、长期性。中共十九大报告将可持续发展战略确定为决胜全面建成小康社会需要坚定实施的七大战略之一。可持续发展是基于社会、经济、人口、资源、环境相互协调和共同发展的理论和战略，主要包括生态可持续发展、经济可持续发展和社会可持续发展，要求坚持不懈地全面推进经济社会与人口、资源和生态环境相协调，不断提高中国的综合国力和竞争力。其以保护自然资源环境为基础，以激励经济发展为条件，以改善和提高人类生活质量为目标，以既能相对满足当代人的需求，又不能对后代的发展构成危害为宗旨。实施可持续发展战略的指导思想是坚持以人为本，主线是人与自然相和谐，核心是经济发展，根本出发点是提高人民群众生活质量，突破口是科技和体制创新。中共十九大报告赋予可持续发展战略新的时代内涵，首次提出建设"富强民主文明和谐美丽"的社会主义现代化强国目标，生态文明建设上升为新时代中国特色社会主义的重要组成部分。

10 上海精神 the Shanghai Spirit

2001年6月，中、俄、哈、吉、塔、乌等六国在上海宣布成立永久性政府间国际组织——上海合作组织。在成员国相互协作过程中逐步形成了以"互信、互利、平等、协商、尊重多样文明、谋求联合发展"为基本内容的"上海精神"，成为本地区国家积累的宝贵精神财富。多年来，上海合作组织保持强劲发展势头，成为促进地区安全稳定和发展繁荣的重要建设性力量,根本原因在于始终遵循"上海精神"、不断加强团结互信。"上海精神"表达了各成员国人民的共同愿望,顺应了和平与发展的时代主流,已成为上海合作组织的核心价值。

六 外交宣言翻译练习

1. 翻译下列外交宣言标题。

1)《上海合作组织成员国元首理事会青岛宣言》
2)《金砖国家领导人第十次会晤约翰内斯堡宣言》
3)《金砖国家领导人第十一次会晤巴西利亚宣言》
4)《二十国集团领导人布宜诺斯艾利斯峰会宣言:为公平与可持续发展凝聚共识》
5)《澜沧江—湄公河合作首次领导人会议三亚宣言——打造面向和平与繁荣的澜湄国家命运共同体》

2. 分析下列句子的逻辑关系和信息主次,并根据分析翻译成英文。

1)我们继续致力于促进体面劳动、职业培训和技能开发,帮助劳动者学习新技能,改善各种就业形式的劳动条件,并认识到包括数字平台工作在内的劳动领域社会对话的重要性。重点关注基于各国不同法律和国情,促进劳动正规化并加强社会保障体系及其可转移性,从而打造包容、公平、可持续的未来工作。

2)国际贸易和投资是增长、生产力、创新、创造就业与发展的重要引擎。我们认识到多边贸易体制为此做出的贡献。因此,我们支持对世贸组织进行必要改革,以使其更好发挥作用。我们将在下一次峰会上审议进展情况。

3)考虑到各方在中东和平进程问题上的不同立场,我们对此保持关切并呼吁相关各方切实履行联合国所有相关决议,通过重启和谈,在该地区实现全面、持续和公正的和平、安全与稳定。我们并呼吁根据联合国相关决议和国际公认有关该问题的法律基础,通过制定能够确保两国和平、安全相处并完全保障本地区其他国家和平、安全、主权、领土完整和政治独立的两国方案,实现建立巴勒斯坦国。

4)叙利亚危机已进入第六年,该国近半数的人口,约1200万的成年男女和儿童流离失所,其中近500万人在埃及、伊拉克、约旦、黎巴嫩和土耳其等周边邻国获得栖身之所。

5)我们一致认为,六国山水相连,人文相通,传统睦邻友好深厚,安全与发展利益紧密攸关。

3．用合 / 分译法将下列句子翻译成英文，并思考为何该句子要采用合 / 分译法。

1）我们，巴西联邦共和国、俄罗斯联邦、印度共和国、中华人民共和国、南非共和国领导人于 2019 年 11 月 14 日在巴西利亚举行金砖国家领导人第十一次会晤。本次会晤主题是"金砖国家：经济增长打造创新未来"。

2）我们认为，违反《联合国宪章》及国际法，针对一国的主权、领土完整和政治独立直接或间接使用或威胁使用武力，剥夺外国占领下人民的自决权（行使此项权利须依照《联合国宪章》和国际法），以及干涉他国内政和奉行进攻性的战略方针等都对地区及国际和平构成威胁。

3）我们感谢中国主办本次亚信外长会议，商定于 2020 年举行亚信第六次外长会议，欢迎中方经与下任主席国协调，于 2018 年举办亚信第五次峰会。

4）成员国决心扩大并深化相互协作，消除上合组织地区安全和稳定威胁，指出《上合组织反极端主义公约》现已生效，强调 2019 年 4 月 29 日在比什凯克举行的上合组织成员国国防部长会议和 5 月 14 日至 15 日在比什凯克举行的上合组织成员国安全会议秘书会议取得积极成果。

第六章

白皮书翻译

一 白皮书的概念及其文体特点

白皮书是指某个国家的政府或其他职能部门公开发表的关于政治、经济、军事、国情、外交等重大问题的正式文件或报告书,由于这些文件或报告是以白色封面装帧,所以被称为白皮书。每个国家对外公布重要文件都会有其各自惯用的封皮颜色,比如英国惯用蓝皮,西班牙惯用红皮,法国惯用黄皮,意大利惯用绿皮等。白皮和蓝皮使用的频率最高,特别是白皮书已经成为某些国家官宣文书的代名词。

白皮书篇幅可长可短,长可达一本书(whitebook),短仅限于一篇文章(whitepaper)。白皮书可以是在某种特定社会历史条件下应对某一具体问题而发表的单独文件。比如1991年11月1日,国务院新闻办公室向世界公布了中华人民共和国的第一份白皮书。这份名为《中国的人权状况》的白皮书,以政府文件的形式正面肯定了人权在中国政治发展中的地位,有力回击了西方国家对中国人权政策的诟病。白皮书也可按照规律时间发布,从而形成白皮书系列,比如从1998年开始,我国每两年发布一篇关于国防的白皮书,形成中国国防系列白皮书。1987年,中国政府首次推出《中国外交》白皮书,之后每年出版一册,全面分析年度国际形势的演变动向,总结中国外交工作取得的成果,权威解读中国外交政策与实践,被称为了解世界和中国外交的"百科全书"。

从文本特点上来说,白皮书主要包括以下三个特征。首先,作为一种官宣文件,白皮书明确表达了政府在重大问题上的观点、立场和政治主张,不允许任何模棱两可的表达,具有明确的政治性;其次,白皮书是由行使国家行政权力的职能部门拟定和颁发的,白皮书包含清楚的事实、精确的数据,并且通过摆事实、讲道理的方式阐明我方的观点和立场,语言果断、坚决,具有难以辩驳的权威性;最后,白皮书的文字简练概括、语言措辞精准,不带文学色彩,也不需要冗余修饰,具有显而易读的简洁性。

二 白皮书汉英对照举隅

新疆的文化保护与发展

中华人民共和国国务院新闻办公室

2018年11月

目录

前言

一、新疆各民族文化是中华文化的组成部分

二、各民族语言文字广泛使用

三、宗教文化受到尊重和保护

四、文化遗产保护和传承取得成就

五、文化事业和文化产业不断发展

六、对外文化交流日趋活跃

结束语

前言

中国是统一的多民族国家。在5000多年文明发展史中，中华各民族共同创造了悠久历史、灿烂文化。新疆自古以来就是多民族迁徙聚居生活的地方，也是多种文化交流交融的舞台。

在历史长河中，新疆各民

Cultural Protection and Development in Xinjiang

The State Council Information Office of the People's Republic of China

November 2018

Contents

Preamble

Ⅰ. Xinjiang Ethnic Cultures Are Part of the Chinese Culture

Ⅱ. The Spoken and Written Languages of Ethnic Groups Are Widely Used

Ⅲ. Respecting and Protecting Religious Culture

Ⅳ. Protecting and Carrying Forward Cultural Heritage

Ⅴ. Constant Development of Cultural Undertakings and the Cultural Industry

Ⅵ. Active Cultural Exchanges with Other Countries

Conclusion

Preamble

China is a unified multi-ethnic country. In the course of a civilization that dates back more than 5,000 years, the various ethnic groups of China have created a long history and a splendid culture. Since ancient times many ethnic groups have made their way to Xinjiang, and it has become their home and a place for cultural integration.

Various ethnic cultures of Xinjiang have their

族文化扎根中华文明沃土，既推动了各民族文化发展，也丰富了中华文化内涵。

中华人民共和国成立后，中国政府高度重视新疆各民族优秀传统文化的挖掘、传承与保护，坚持创造性转化、创新性发展，鼓励各民族相互学习语言文字，促进各民族交往交流交融，尊重各民族宗教信仰自由，推动文化事业和文化产业发展，推进各民族文化现代化，加强对外文化交流，在不同文化交流互鉴中，增强文化自信。

一、新疆各民族文化是中华文化的组成部分

新疆历来是多民族聚居、多种文化并存地区。各民族文化长期交流交融，在中华文明沃土中枝繁叶茂，是中华文化的组成部分。

各民族文化是中华文化不可分割的一部分。自古以来，

roots in the fertile soil of Chinese civilization, advancing their own cultural development while enriching the overall culture of China.

Since the People's Republic of China was founded in 1949, the Chinese government has attached great importance to documenting and protecting the excellent traditional ethnic cultures in Xinjiang, and ensuring that they are passed on to succeeding generations. It has promoted creative transformation and innovative development, encouraging these ethnic groups to learn spoken and written languages from each other, promoted communication and integration, respected their freedom of religious belief, and worked to develop their cultural undertakings and industries. The government has worked to modernize ethnic cultures, to strengthen cultural exchanges with foreign countries, and to enhance each group's cultural confidence while engaging in exchanges with and mutual learning from others.

I. Xinjiang Ethnic Cultures Are Part of the Chinese Culture

Since ancient times, Xinjiang has been home to various ethnic groups, where different ethnic cultures coexist. Through many years of communication and integration, these cultures thrive in the fertile soil of China's civilization and are part of the Chinese culture.

Ethnic cultures make up an inseparable part of the Chinese culture. Since ancient times, China

中华文化因环境多样性而呈现丰富多元形态。各民族文化在中华大地上交流交融，形成气象恢宏的中华文化。各民族文化都是中华民族共有精神财富，为中华文化的发展与进步做出了贡献。

早在先秦时期，新疆就与中原地区展开了密切交流，考古证实，新疆出土的彩陶就受到黄河中游地区仰韶文化的影响，在河南安阳的商代妇好墓中，陪葬了大量新疆和田玉制成的器物。西汉统一新疆地区后，汉语成为西域官府文书中的通用语之一。中原的农业生产技术、礼仪制度、汉文书籍、音乐舞蹈等在西域广泛传播。西域的乐器与音乐传入中原，对中原音乐产生重大影响。中华文化宝库中，就包括维吾尔族十二木卡姆艺术、哈萨克族阿依特斯艺术、柯尔克孜族史诗《玛纳斯》、蒙古族卫拉特史诗《江格尔》等各民族的优秀文化作品。

has been multicultural as a result of the diversity of its environment. Different ethnic cultures have communicated and integrated with each other, constituting a legacy shared by the Chinese nation that has brought into being a splendid Chinese culture.

As early as in the pre-Qin period (c. 2100-221 BC), Xinjiang was in close contact with the Central Plains. Archaeological excavations demonstrate that painted pottery-ware unearthed in Xinjiang shows the influence of the Yangshao Culture in the middle reaches of the Yellow River, while many articles made from Xinjiang's Hetian jade were unearthed in the Shang-dynasty (c.1600 BC-1046 BC) Tomb of Fu Hao in Anyang, Henan in central China. After the Western Han (206 BC-AD 25) united Xinjiang, Chinese became one of the official languages used in government documents of the Western Regions where Xinjiang is located. Agricultural production techniques, the system of etiquette, Chinese-language books, music, and dances of the Central Plains spread widely in the Western Regions. Musical instruments and music from the Western Regions were introduced to the Central Plains and exerted a great influence on local music. The treasure house of Chinese culture boasts elements of the Uygur Muqam, the Kazak Aytes art, the Kirgiz epic *Manas*, the Jangar epic of the *Oirat Mongols*, and many other great cultural works of various ethnic groups.

新疆地区历来多种文化并存。中国的历史演进，决定了各民族在分布上交错杂居、经济上相互依存、文化上兼收并蓄的基本特征。新疆独特的自然地理环境造就了绿洲农耕与草原游牧文化的相得益彰，不同生产生活方式的族群交流互补、迁徙汇聚，开创了多种文化并存的生动局面。

新疆地区陆续发现大约20种语言文字。时至今日，汉藏语系、阿尔泰语系、印欧语系诸语言仍在新疆存在。生活中各民族语言兼用是新疆文化的传统特征。新疆各民族在交往交流交融中，不同语言的互借互用成为普遍现象。新疆克孜尔千佛洞、柏孜克里克石窟、北庭故城等融合了汉、回鹘、吐蕃以及新疆古代居民的多种文化元素，是古代中国文化艺术的典范。

历史上新疆是中华文明向西开放的门户和中介。丝绸之路的畅通开启了东西方文化交

Different cultures have long coexisted in Xinjiang. China's historical evolution has determined that various ethnic groups live together. They are economically interdependent and embrace each other's cultures. The unique natural environment and geographical conditions in Xinjiang resulted in the development of refined oasis farming and grassland nomadism, and migrating ethnic groups with different lifestyles and working practices communicated with, complemented and integrated with each other, creating a dynamic coexistence of different cultures.

Around 20 different spoken and written languages have been identified in Xinjiang. The Sino-Tibetan, Altaic, and Indo-European languages still exist in Xinjiang today, and a traditional feature of Xinjiang culture is that different languages are used in daily life. It was common for different ethnic groups to borrow from and use each other's languages. The Kizil Thousand-Buddha Caves, Bezkilik Grottoes, Beiting Ancient City Site, and some other Xinjiang sites that integrate multiple cultural factors from the Han, Huihu (an ancient name for modern Uygur), Tubo (an ancient name for modern Tibetan) and other ancient residents of Xinjiang are typical of the culture and art of ancient China.

Historically Xinjiang was the gateway and medium through which the Chinese civilization opened to the West. The Silk Road opened a new

流交融的新篇章。丝绸之路繁盛时期，中国的造纸术、桑蚕丝织等先进技术通过新疆西传，对世界文明产生了深远影响。佛教、摩尼教、景教沿着丝绸之路传播到新疆，和当时的原始宗教一起在当地流传。在漫长的历史演进中，新疆多种宗教并存的情况从未发生改变。新疆的文化景观始终是多种文化并存、多元文化交流。

各民族文化长期交流交融。中华文化是凝聚各民族的精神纽带。在长期的生产生活中，各民族文化交流交融始终贯穿于中华文化形成、发展的全过程。受中原文化影响，新疆地区的蚕桑技术与丝绸织造取得了相当成就；最初形成于漠北时期的回鹘文化，深受我国北方游牧文化、中原文化以及佛教、摩尼教等影响。在各个历史发展阶段，各民族互学互鉴，涌现出一批政治家、文学家、艺术家、史学家、农学家、翻译家等，助推新疆各民族文化在中华文化怀抱中进一

chapter in cultural exchanges and integration between East and West. China's papermaking, sericulture, silk weaving, and other advanced technologies spread to the West via Xinjiang during the glory days of the Silk Road, exerting a far-reaching impact on world civilizations. Buddhism, Manichaeism and Nestorianism were introduced into Xinjiang through the Silk Road, and practiced together with primitive local religions. During Xinjiang's long historical evolution, it has always been a place where many religions have coexisted. The cultural landscape of Xinjiang has long been characterized by coexistence and communication between different cultures.

There is a long history of different ethnic cultures communicating and integrating with each other. The Chinese culture is a bond that unites various ethnic groups, while in the course of daily life and work, the communication between and integration of different ethnic cultures has helped to form and develop the Chinese culture. Influenced by the culture of the Central Plains, Xinjiang learned and rapidly developed sericulture and silk weaving. The Huihu culture that originated in the Mobei (the area north of the vast deserts on the Mongolian Plateau) regime was deeply influenced by the nomadic culture of northern China, Central Plains culture, Buddhism and Manichaeism. In different stages of history, various ethnic groups learned from

步发展。中华人民共和国成立后,在中国共产党领导下,新疆各民族文化进入新的繁荣发展时期,《我们的祖国是花园》《我们新疆好地方》等经典歌曲传唱大江南北;《冰山上的来客》《库尔班大叔上北京》等优秀电影在全国家喻户晓,成为各民族共同创造、共同享有的精神财富。

新疆各民族成员共居、共学、共事、共乐,在语言、饮食、服饰、音乐、舞蹈、绘画、建筑等社会生活和文化艺术各方面相互影响、吸收融合,"你中有我,我中有你"始终是各民族文化的共同特点。

二、各民族语言文字广泛使用

语言文字是文化的重要载体和鲜明标志。新疆是多语言、多文字地区,学习使用国家通用语言文字,是繁荣发展新疆各民族文化的历史经验。中国政府大力推广和规范

each other, resulting in the emergence of a number of statesmen, writers, artists, historians, agronomists, and translators who made further contribution to the development of the ethnic cultures of Xinjiang in the embrace of the Chinese culture. After the People's Republic of China was founded in 1949, and under the leadership of the Communist Party of China (CPC), the ethnic cultures of Xinjiang entered a new period of prosperity and development. *Our Motherland Is a Garden*, *Xinjiang, a Good Place* and other classic songs are heard around the country; *Visitors on the Icy Mountain*, *Uncle Kurban Visits Beijing* and other quality films have become widely known. They are elements of a cultural wealth that has been created by and is shared by all ethnic groups.

The ethnic groups of Xinjiang live together, study together, work together, and share happiness. They influence, assimilate and integrate with each other in language, diet, costume, music, dance, painting, architecture and other aspects of social life, culture and art. A common feature of these ethnic cultures is that all are interrelated.

II. The Spoken and Written Languages of Ethnic Groups Are Widely Used

Language, in both spoken and written forms, is an important carrier and a distinct symbol of culture. Xinjiang is a multilingual region, and historical experience shows that learning and using the commonly used standard Chinese as a spoken and written language has helped

使用国家通用语言文字，依法保障各民族使用和发展本民族语言文字的自由，提倡和鼓励各民族相互学习语言文字，不断促进各民族语言相通、心灵相通。

依法推广国家通用语言文字。学习和使用国家通用语言文字，有利于促进各民族交往交流交融，推动各民族发展进步。1982年，"国家推广全国通用的普通话"写入《中华人民共和国宪法》。2001年1月1日《中华人民共和国国家通用语言文字法》正式施行，进一步明确了普通话和规范汉字作为国家通用语言文字的法定地位。2015年修订的《中华人民共和国教育法》规定"国家通用语言文字为学校及其他教育机构的基本教育教学语言文字""民族自治地方以少数民族学生为主的学校及其他教育机构，从实际出发，使用国家通用语言文字和本民族或者当地民族通用的语言文字实施双语教育"。2015年修订的《新疆维吾尔自治区语言文字工作

develop Xinjiang's ethnic cultures. The Chinese government works hard to promote the use of the standard Chinese language, protects by law ethnic people's freedom to use and develop their own languages, and advocates and encourages ethnic groups to learn spoken and written languages from each other, so as to promote language communication and ethnic unity among all Chinese people.

Promote standard Chinese by law. Learning and using standard Chinese helps different ethnic groups to communicate, develop and progress. When the Constitution of the People's Republic of China was revised in 1982, the sentence "The state promotes the nationwide use of Putonghua (common speech based on Beijing pronunciation)" was added. On January 1, 2001, the Law of the People's Republic of China on the Standard Spoken and Written Chinese Language took effect, clarifying the legitimate status of Putonghua and standardized Chinese characters as the standard Chinese language. The Educational Law of the People's Republic of China (Revised in 2015) provides: "The standard spoken and written Chinese language shall be the basic language used by schools and other educational institutions in education and teaching. Schools and other educational institutions dominated by ethnic minority students in ethnic autonomous areas shall, according to the actual circumstances, use the standard spoken and written Chinese language

条例》规定"大力推广国家通用语言文字"。各民族成员为适应经济社会发展及交往日渐频繁的需要,积极主动学习和使用国家通用语言文字。

加强国家通用语言文字教育教学工作。响应国家号召,20世纪50年代开始,新疆在中小学对少数民族学生开设汉语文课程。1984年,新疆提出在少数民族学校加强汉语教学工作,实现"民汉兼通"的目标。目前,新疆在学前和中小学全面普及国家通用语言文字教学、加授本民族语言文字的双语教育,确保到2020年少数民族学生基本掌握和使用国家通用语言文字。

以多种形式开展国家通用语言文字培训工作。2013年启动"国家通用语言培训项目",在少数民族人口集中的县(市)面向参加职业培训或创业培训

and the spoken and written languages of their respective ethnicities or the spoken and written language commonly used by the local ethnicities to implement bilingual education." Regulations on the Work Concerning Spoken and Written Languages of Xinjiang Uygur Autonomous Region, revised in 2015, state the need to "promote the standard spoken and written Chinese language". Ethnic people are enthusiastic about learning and using standard Chinese to adapt to economic and social development and increased communication.

We should strengthen education and teaching of standard Chinese. In the 1950s, in response to the call of the state, Xinjiang began Chinese courses for ethnic minority students at elementary and secondary schools. In 1984, Xinjiang proposed to strengthen Chinese teaching at ethnic minority schools to achieve the goal that students "master both standard Chinese and their own ethnic languages". Currently, students at preschool institutions and elementary and secondary schools in Xinjiang have universal access to bilingual education, including teaching of standard Chinese and ethnic minority languages, ensuring that by 2020 all ethnic minority students will be able to master and use standard Chinese.

We should carry out various forms of training on the standard spoken and written Chinese language. In 2013, the "training program on the standard spoken and written Chinese language" was launched, a special program for ethnic

的少数民族青年开展国家通用语言文字专项培训。2017年启动实施国家通用语言文字普及攻坚工程。

科学保护各民族语言文字。《中华人民共和国宪法》和《中华人民共和国民族区域自治法》均明确规定，各民族都有使用和发展自己的语言文字的自由。目前，新疆各民族主要使用10种语言和文字，少数民族语言文字在司法、行政、教育、新闻出版、广播电视、互联网、社会公共事务等领域得到广泛使用。全国人民代表大会、中国人民政治协商会议召开的重要会议，提供维吾尔、哈萨克、蒙古等少数民族语言文字的文稿和同声传译。新疆本级和各自治州、自治县机关执行公务时，同时使用国家通用语言文字、实行区域自治的民族的语言文字。各民族成员有权使用本民族语言文字进行选举或诉讼。以少数民族学生为主的学校及其他教育机构，在课程设置和各类招生考试中均重视少数民族语言文字的学习和使用。每年一度

minority youths participating in vocational or business training in counties or cities where people of ethnic minorities live in concentrated communities. In 2017, a program aimed to popularize standard Chinese by the year 2020 was launched.

Protect spoken and written ethnic minority languages in a scientific way. The Constitution of the People's Republic of China and the Law on Regional Ethnic Autonomy both clearly prescribe that all ethnic groups have the freedom to use and develop their own spoken and written languages. Currently, 10 spoken and written languages are used among the various ethnic groups of Xinjiang. Ethnic minority languages are extensively used in such areas as judicature, administration, education, press and publishing, radio and television, internet, and public affairs. At important meetings such as those of the National People's Congress and the Chinese People's Political Consultative Conference documentation and simultaneous interpretation in Uygur, Kazak, Mongolian or other ethnic minority languages are provided. When performing official duties, Party and government organs of Xinjiang and lower-level autonomous prefectures and counties use at the same time standard Chinese and the languages of those ethnic minorities that exercise regional autonomy. All ethnic minorities have the right to use their own spoken and written languages in elections and judicial matters. Schools and other

的普通高等学校招生全国统一考试，新疆使用汉、维吾尔、哈萨克、柯尔克孜、蒙古5种文字试卷。

为保护中国丰富的语言资源，中国政府自2015年起组织实施中国语言资源保护工程，收集记录汉语方言、少数民族语言和口头语言文化的实态语料。该工程作为目前世界上规模最大的语言资源保护项目，已实现全国范围覆盖，其中在新疆开展包括30多个少数民族语言调查点、10个汉语方言调查点、6个濒危语言调查点和2个语言文化调查点的田野调查。截至目前，已完成新疆规划调查点超过80%的调查任务，并形成一批标志性成果。

多语言、多文种的新闻出版和广播电视是新疆的一大特色。新疆使用汉、维吾尔、哈萨克、柯尔克孜、蒙古、锡伯6种语言文字出版报纸、图书、音像制品和电子出版物。新疆电视台有汉、维吾尔、哈萨克、柯尔克孜4种语言电视节

educational institutions where ethnic minority students are the majority highlight the study and use of ethnic minority languages in setting their curricula and in various entrance examinations. Xinjiang uses Chinese, Uygur, Kazak, Kirgiz and Mongolian languages for the annual national higher education entrance examination.

In 2015 the Chinese government organized and launched a program to protect the rich language resources of China, collecting and recording physical forms of linguistic data such as Chinese dialects, spoken and written languages of ethnic minorities, and oral language cultures. The largest of its kind in the world, this program has covered the whole country. Field surveys have been conducted in Xinjiang, covering more than 30 survey locations of ethnic minority languages, 10 locations of Chinese dialects, six locations of endangered languages, and two locations of language cultures. To date more than 80 percent of survey tasks in these locations have been completed, and some symbolic successes have been achieved.

Multilingual press and publication and radio and television are a major feature of Xinjiang. Xinjiang publishes newspapers, books, audio and video products, and e-publications in six spoken and written languages—Chinese, Uygur, Kazak, Kirgiz, Mongolian and Xibe. Xinjiang TV broadcasts in Chinese, Uygur, Kazak, and Kirgiz. Xinjiang People's Broadcasting Station broadcasts

目，新疆人民广播电台有汉、维吾尔、哈萨克、柯尔克孜、蒙古5种语言广播节目，《新疆日报》用汉、维吾尔、哈萨克、蒙古4种文字出版。

为使各民族成员共享信息化时代的成果，中国政府制定了蒙古、藏、维吾尔、哈萨克、柯尔克孜等文字编码字符集、键盘、字模的国家标准，研究开发出多种少数民族文字排版系统、智能语音翻译系统，支持少数民族语言文字网站和新兴传播载体有序发展，不断提升少数民族语言文字信息化处理和社会应用能力。新疆设立民族语言文字工作委员会和各级民族语言文字研究机构，负责各民族语言文字的科学研究，推动各民族语言文字的规范化、标准化、信息化。鼓励各民族互相学习语言文字。

中国政府鼓励民族自治地方各民族互相学习语言文字，既要求少数民族学习国家通用语言文字，也鼓励少数民族地区的汉族居民学习少数民族语言文字，尤其重视基层公务

in Chinese, Uygur, Kazak, Kirgiz, and Mongolian. *Xinjiang Daily* is printed in Chinese, Uygur, Kazak and Mongolian.

To enable ethnic minorities to share the achievements of the information age, the Chinese government has set national specifications of coded character set, keyboard, and type matrix for Mongolian, Tibetan, Uygur, Kazak, Kirgiz, and some other languages. It has studied and developed different typesetting systems and intelligent voice translation systems for several written ethnic minority languages. The government supports the orderly development of websites and emerging media in spoken and written ethnic minority languages, and works to improve information processing and application capabilities in ethnic minority languages. Xinjiang has set up the Ethnic Language Work Committee and ethnic minority language research institutes at different levels, which are responsible for scientific research into ethnic minority languages, and which work to make them more standardized and apply them in IT.

Encourage ethnic groups to learn spoken and written languages from each other. The Chinese government encourages different ethnic groups in ethnic autonomous areas to learn languages from each other, urging ethnic minorities to learn standard Chinese while encouraging Han

员、新录用公职人员、公共服务行业从业人员的双语学习，并提供学习条件。新疆专门开办了汉族干部学习少数民族语言培训班。20世纪50年代以来，国家在新疆高校开设中国少数民族语言文学（维吾尔语言、哈萨克语言方向）专业，这些专业的学生毕业后大多从事行政、教育、少数民族语言文字研究工作。多年来，新疆各民族相互学习语言文字蔚然成风，掌握双语、多语的人员越来越多，推动了各民族交往交流交融。

三、宗教文化受到尊重和保护

新疆历来是多种宗教并存地区，宗教文化丰富多样，是中国传统文化的组成部分。中国政府保障公民宗教信仰自由权利，尊重和保护宗教文化。

多种宗教文化交融共存。新疆历来是多种宗教传播的重要地区，是宗教文化的汇聚之地。新疆最初流行原始宗教、

residents to learn ethnic minority languages. It emphasizes that grassroots civil servants, newly recruited civil servants, and employees in the public service sector should know two or more languages and provides facilities for their learning. Xinjiang conducts special training courses for Han officials to learn ethnic minority languages. Since the 1950s, the state has offered majors in ethnic minority languages and literature (Uygur and Kazak) at colleges and universities in Xinjiang; most graduates of these majors work in the fields of administration, education, and research on ethnic minority languages. For many years, it has been a common practice that different ethnic groups of Xinjiang learn languages from each other. More and more people are becoming bilingual or multilingual, which promotes communication and integration among all the ethnic groups.

Ⅲ. Respecting and Protecting Religious Culture

Since antiquity Xinjiang has seen the coexistence of a variety of religions, whose rich cultures have become part of traditional Chinese culture. China's government is committed to protecting its citizens' freedom of religious belief while respecting and protecting religious cultures.

Many religious cultures blend and coexist. Xinjiang has long been a region where multiple religions are practiced and their cultures have met and blended. Primitive religion and Shamanism

萨满教。公元前4世纪起，随着祆教、佛教等相继传入，逐步形成多种宗教并存的格局。后来，道教、摩尼教、景教、伊斯兰教等先后传入，多种宗教并存的格局不断发展演变。一教或两教为主、多教并存是新疆宗教格局的历史特点。多种宗教文化长期交融共存，互相借鉴，并在适应中国社会发展过程中调整变化。目前，新疆有伊斯兰教、佛教、基督教、天主教、道教等。萨满教和祆教的元素遗留至今，并且以生活习俗的形式表现出来。佛教文化影响深远，在喀什、哈密、伊犁等地，仍可见到佛龛、莲花图案、莲花宝座等遗存。

宗教典籍文献依法出版发行。国家以多种语言文字翻译出版发行伊斯兰教、佛教、基督教等宗教典籍文献，满足各族信教公民的多样化需求。新疆已翻译出版发行汉、维吾尔、哈萨克、柯尔克孜等多种文字的《古兰经》《布哈里圣训实录精华》等宗教经典书籍，编辑发行汉、维吾尔两种文字的《卧尔兹演讲集》系列。开

were practiced in Xinjiang before Zoroastrianism, Buddhism and other faiths were introduced into the region from the 4th century BC onward. Gradually there came into being a network of coexisting religions. This network further evolved with the introduction of Taoism, Manichaeism, Nestorianism, and Islam. A coexistence of multiple religions, with one or two predominant, was a basic characteristic of Xinjiang's religious history. During their lengthy coexistence and interaction, the religious cultures in the region learned from one another and adapted to China's social development. At present, the major religions in Xinjiang are Islam, Buddhism, Protestant and Catholic Christianity, and Taoism. Certain Shamanistic and Zoroastrian elements can still be observed in local customs today. The remains of Buddha niches, lotus patterns, and lotus seat sculptures in Kashgar, Hami, and Ili testify to the once widespread influence of Buddhism in the region.

Religious texts are published and distributed in accordance with the law. The state has translated, published and distributed Islamic, Buddhist, Protestant, and other religious texts to meet the diverse demandof religious believers. *The Koran* and *Irshad al-Sari li Sharh Sahih al-Bukhari* have been published in Chinese, Uygur, Kazak and Kirgiz languages. *The New Collection of al-Wa'z Speeches* series have been compiled and published in both Chinese and Uygur languages. A website available in both Chinese

办汉、维吾尔两种语言文字的新疆穆斯林网站。整理出版《金光明经卷二》《弥勒会见记》等宗教古籍文献。在专营宗教书刊的销售点，可以购买《古兰经》《圣经》《金光明经》等各种宗教典籍。

宗教文化遗产得到有效保护。目前，新疆有喀什艾提尕尔清真寺、昭苏圣佑庙、克孜尔千佛洞等109处宗教文化古迹被列入全国重点文物保护单位和自治区级文物保护单位。其中，全国重点文物保护单位46处，自治区级文物保护单位63处。中央政府拨专款对列入国家和新疆文物保护单位的克孜尔千佛洞、柏孜克里克石窟、喀什艾提尕尔清真寺等进行修缮。新疆出资维修吐鲁番苏公塔、昭苏圣佑庙、乌鲁木齐红庙子道观等28处宗教建筑（场所）。涉及宗教的非物质文化遗产也得到了保护和传承。

坚持宗教中国化方向。同所在社会相适应是宗教生存发展的规律。在中华文化兼容并

and Uygur languages was set up for Xinjiang's Muslim community. Ancient religious books, including *Volume II of the Golden Light Sutra* (Suvarnaprabhasa Sutra) and *Maitrisimit Nom Bitig*, have been published. Important scriptures such as the *Koran*, Bible, and *Golden Light Sutra* are available at stores specializing in selling religious publications.

Religious heritages are effectively protected. A total of 109 religious sites in Xinjiang, including Id Kah Mosque in Kashgar, Shengyou Lamasery in Zhaosu, and the Kizil Thousand-Buddha Caves have been designated as major cultural heritage sites under the protection of the autonomous region and the state. Among the 109 sites, 46 are key cultural heritage sites under the protection of the state and 63 are under the protection of the autonomous region. The central government has allocated special funds to renovate cultural heritage protection sites at the state and autonomous-region levels, including the Kizil Thousand-Buddha Caves, Bezkilik Grottoes, and Id KahMosque. Xinjiang has funded the repair of 28 religious venues, including the Emin Minaret in Turpan, Shengyou Lamasery in Zhaosu, and Red Temple (Taoist) in Urumqi. Elements of intangible cultural heritage relating to religion are also effectively protected and passed on.

Religions adapt to China's realities. Adapting to local society is essential for the survival and development of any religion. With influence

蓄、求同存异、和而不同思想影响下，佛教等外来宗教都经历了中国化、本土化过程。佛教传入新疆后，主动适应社会发展、融入主流文化，对新疆历史和文化产生了深远影响。伊斯兰教传入新疆后沿着中国化方向发展，经过长期与当地传统信仰和文化融合，逐渐成为中华文化的一部分，并表现出地域特征和民族特色。天主教的独立自主、自办教会，基督教的自传、自治、自养等，都为实现宗教中国化做出了积极努力。新疆坚持宗教中国化的历史传统，积极引导宗教与社会主义社会相适应，支持宗教界深入挖掘教义教规中有利于社会和谐、时代发展、健康文明的内容，对教义教规做出符合当代中国发展进步、符合中华优秀传统文化的阐释，引导各种宗教坚持中国化方向。

四、文化遗产保护和传承取得成就

新疆文化遗产丰富。中央

from such Chinese cultural traditions as being inclusive, seeking common ground while reserving differences, and pursuing harmony without uniformity, Buddhism and other foreign religions have all directed their efforts to localization after entering China. After Buddhism was introduced into Xinjiang, it has exerted a far-reaching influence on Xinjiang's history and culture through proactive adaptation to local social norms and integration into the mainstream culture. Through extended fusion with local faiths and traditions, Islam gradually became part of Chinese culture and developed distinct regional and local ethnic features. The Catholic Church's principles of independence and self-management of its religious affairs, and Protestantism's compliance with the principles of self-propagation, self-governance, and self-support facilitated their adaptation to conditions in China. Xinjiang upholds the tradition of religious localization and provides guidance to religions on adaptation to China's socialist system. Religious circles in Xinjiang are encouraged to promote social harmony and development as well as cultural progress with the aid of religious doctrines and rules, and elaborate on the doctrines and rules that contribute to China's development and conform to China's traditions.

Ⅳ. Protecting and Carrying Forward Cultural Heritage

Xinjiang is a region rich in cultural heritage.

政府和新疆地方政府不断加强法制建设，推进文化遗产保护工作。《中华人民共和国文物保护法》和《中华人民共和国非物质文化遗产法》等法律法规对保护新疆各民族丰富多彩的文化遗产提供了重要法治保障。

文物保护成果丰硕。目前，新疆有各级文物保护机构189个，文物保护网络基本建成。全面完成全国不可移动文物普查3次，可移动文物普查1次，文化遗产家底进一步摸清。截至2017年，新疆文物点9542处，其中世界文化遗产6处、全国重点文物保护单位113处、自治区级文物保护单位558处。文化文物系统现有博物馆93个（包括自治区博物馆和吐鲁番地区博物馆2个国家一级博物馆），馆藏文物45万件/套。

新疆历史文化名城名镇名村街区保护取得显著成效。确立国家级历史文化名城5座、历史文化名镇3个、历史文化名村4个、历史文化街区2个、中国传统村落17个、中国少数民族特色村寨22个。多年

The central government and the local government of Xinjiang have made a continuous effort to strengthen the legal system for the protection of the region's cultural heritage. The Law of the People's Republic of China on the Protection of Cultural Relics and the Law of the People's Republic of China on Intangible Cultural Heritage provide important legal protection for the diverse cultural heritage of all ethnic groups in Xinjiang.

Protection of cultural heritage yields results. Xinjiang has formed a cultural heritage protection network comprising 189 institutions at all levels. The region has completed three surveys on fixed national cultural relics and one on movable national cultural relics, forming a comprehensive database. By the end of 2017 Xinjiang had 9,542 cultural heritage sites, of which six were World Heritage sites, 113 were key national sites, and 558 were at the autonomous-region level. Xinjiang's cultural heritage system contains 93 public museums, including two national first-grade museums—the Xinjiang Uygur Autonomous Region Museum and the Turpan Museum, with a collection of 450,000 items.

Xinjiang has made great headway in protecting its historical and cultural cities, towns, villages and localities. The region now has five cities, three towns, four villages, and two localities that have been recognized as state-level historical and cultural divisions, as well as 17 traditional Chinese villages and 22 ethnic-minority villages

来，中国政府对高昌故城遗址、北庭故城遗址、惠远新老古城遗址等一大批文物古迹进行修缮保护，抢救性保护修复3000余件珍贵文物。

考古发掘成果中外瞩目。截至2017年，新疆民丰尼雅遗址、尉犁营盘墓地、若羌小河墓地、库车友谊路晋十六国砖室墓、巴里坤东黑沟遗址、吉木乃通天洞遗址等8项考古发掘项目先后被列入当年全国十大考古新发现，出土了"五星出东方利中国"锦护臂、"王侯合昏千秋万岁宜子孙"锦被等国宝级文物。

古籍保护力度加大。成立了新疆维吾尔自治区古籍整理出版规划领导小组及办公室、古籍保护中心、古籍修复中心，建立少数民族古籍特藏书库。2011年，新疆古籍保护中心启动第一次古籍普查工作，对重点、珍贵古籍的基本内

with cultural significance. Over the years, the Chinese government has supported the repair and conservation of many cultural heritage sites, such as the Gaochang Ancient City Ruins, Beiting Ancient City Ruins, and new and old Huiyuan Ancient City, while rescuing and restoring more than 3,000 rare cultural relics.

Archeological findings attract wide attention. By the end of 2017 eight archeological programs, including the Niya Ruins in Minfeng County, Yingpan Cemetery in Yuli County, Xiaohe Cemetery in Ruoqiang County, 3rd-4th century brick graves in Kucha County, Dongheigou Ruins in Barkol County, and the Tongtiandong Cave in Jeminay County, had been listed among the National Top 10 Archeological Discoveries of the Year. The arm protector with the inscriptions of "Five stars appear in the East, sign of Chinese victory over the Qiang" and the silk quilt with inscriptions of "Marriages between princes and dukes bring prosperity to their posterity" unearthed from the Niya Ruins are national treasures.

Protection of ancient books has been strengthened. Xinjiang has set up a leading group and office in charge of the classification and publishing of the autonomous region's ancient books, an ancient books preservation center, an ancient books restoration center, and a repository for ancient books and special collections of ethnic minorities. In 2011 the region's Ancient Books

容、破损情况和保存状况登记造册。之后又数次开展普查。截至2017年，完成古籍整理普查14980种。已收藏的古代典籍文献包括汉文字（汉文字、西夏文和契丹文等）、阿拉美文字（佉卢文、帕赫列维文、摩尼文和回鹘文等10多种）和婆罗米文字（梵文、焉耆-龟兹文、于阗文、吐蕃文等）三大系统，共19种语言、28种文字，内容涵盖政治、经济、社会、宗教、天文、数学、医学、艺术等领域。古籍整理数字化建设日益加强。

中国政府支持新疆以汉文和维吾尔文翻译、整理、出版了濒于失传的《福乐智慧》和《突厥语大词典》等古籍。组织古籍专家开展学术研究、提供咨询服务，邀请国内外古籍保护工作者、研究者和管理者交流研讨。2011年，国家文化部和新疆维吾尔自治区人民政府共同主办"西域遗珍——新疆历史文献暨古籍保护成果展"，其中孤本古籍超过半数，

Preservation Center started its first survey of ancient books, registering important and rare volumes and recording their content, physical condition, and preservation requirements. This was the first of several such surveys. By the end of 2017 the center had examined 14,980 books. Ancient books in its collection are written in 19 languages and 28 scripts, and fall into three language families: the Chinese language family (Chinese, Tangut, and Khitan scripts), the Aramaic family (more than 10 scripts, including the Kharosthi, Pahlavi, Manichaean, and Huihu scripts), and the Brahmi family (Sanskrit, Tocharian, Khotanese, and Tubo scripts). These books cover a wide range of subjects, including politics, the economy, society, religions, astronomy, mathematics, medicine, and the arts. Digitalization of ancient books and related work are further strengthened.

The Chinese government has supported the translation, editing and publishing into Chinese and Uygur languages of Kutadgu Bilig (*Wisdom of Fortune and Joy*) and *A Comprehensive Turki Dictionary*, two works of the Karahan Kingdom period in the 11th century. The government has also organized experts in ancient books to carry out research and provide expertise in this field, and helped to arrange exchanges between Chinese and foreign professionals, researchers, and administrators engaged in the preservation of ancient books. In 2011 the Ministry of Culture

受到社会各界称赞。

非物质文化遗产得到有效保护。按照"保护为主、抢救第一、合理利用、传承发展"的原则，加强政策立法。2008年，新疆出台《新疆维吾尔自治区非物质文化遗产保护条例》；2010年，《新疆维吾尔自治区维吾尔木卡姆艺术保护条例》颁布实施。新疆出台一系列非物质文化遗产保护制度，为科学、系统地抢救保护非物质文化遗产提供了制度保障。

中国政府1951年、1954年两次抢救性录制维吾尔十二木卡姆。20世纪60年代开始，投入大量资金和人力，整理出版了包括柯尔克孜族史诗《玛纳斯》、蒙古族史诗《江格尔》

and the local government of Xinjiang co-hosted an exhibition, titled "Recovered Treasures from the Western Regions: Progress in Preserving Xinjiang's Historical Literature and Ancient Books". More than half of the ancient books displayed at the exhibition were the only copies extant. This achievement was acclaimed by the widest range of interested parties.

Intangible cultural heritage is effectively protected. Under the guiding principle of giving priority to both preservation and restoration, and pursuing sound utilization and development, the policy and legislation for protecting intangible cultural heritage have been strengthened. In 2008 the Regulations of the Xinjiang Uygur Autonomous Region on the Protection of Intangible Cultural Heritage were enacted. In 2010 the Regulations of the Xinjiang Uygur Autonomous Region on the Protection of Uygur Muqam Arts were promulgated and put into force. In addition, Xinjiang has introduced a number of rules for protecting its intangible cultural heritage, which provide institutional guarantees for rescuing and preserving this heritage in a coordinated and systematic manner.

In 1951 and 1954 the central government made recordings of the music of the Twelve Muqams to rescue the Muqam arts. Since the 1960s, firm funding and manpower support from the government has enabled the publication of works of folk literature, including the *Kirgiz epic*

等多种民间口头文学作品。编纂出版《中国民族民间舞蹈集成·新疆卷》《中国民间歌曲集成·新疆卷》《中国民间故事集成·新疆卷》等涵盖各民族音乐、舞蹈、戏曲等门类的十大艺术集成志书。

"中华文脉——新疆非物质文化遗产保护记录工程"持续实施。截至2017年,新疆完成23位国家级代表性传承人抢救性记录工作,运用文字、图片、音像等多种记录手段,对非物质文化遗产项目实施了抢救性保护;创建了维吾尔族乐器、地毯和艾德莱斯绸织造3个非物质文化遗产项目国家级生产性保护示范基地;命名91个自治区级非物质文化遗产保护传承基地。

新疆维吾尔木卡姆艺术、柯尔克孜史诗《玛纳斯》、维吾尔族麦西热甫分别列入联合国教科文组织"人类非物质文化遗产代表作名录"和"急需保护的非物质文化遗产名录"。入选国家级、自治区级非物质文化遗产代表性名录的项目分

Manas and *Mongolian epic Jangar*. *The Collection of Chinese Ethnic and Folk Dances (Xinjiang Volume)*, *Collection of Chinese Folk Songs (Xinjiang Volume)*, and *Collection of Chinese Folk Tales (Xinjiang Volume)* have been compiled and published to introduce the folk music, dances, drama and other arts of the region.

The program for protecting and preserving Xinjiang's intangible cultural heritage as part of the initiative to promote Chinese cultural traditions is well under way. By the end of 2017, to rescue and preserve its intangible cultural heritage, Xinjiang had completed the recording of intangible cultural items presented by 23 state-level representative trustees in the form of written texts, images, audios and videos. Furthermore, the region had established three state-level demonstration bases that produce Uygur musical instruments, carpets and Etles silk for the preservation of these intangible cultural items. In addition, the region had set up 91 autonomous-region level bases for preserving and handing down its intangible cultural heritage.

Uygur Muqam of Xinjiang and the Kirgiz epic *Manas* were registered on the "UNESCO Representative List of the Intangible Cultural Heritage of Humanity", and Uygur Meshrep on the "List of Intangible Cultural Heritage in Need of Urgent Safeguarding". Xinjiang has 83 items on the national representative list of intangible cultural heritage and 294 items on the

别有 83 项、294 项，国家级、自治区级非物质文化遗产代表性传承人分别有 112 位、403 位。

民俗文化得到尊重与传承。新疆坚持尊重差异、包容多样、相互欣赏，充分尊重和保护各种民俗文化，实现多元文化和谐共处，各民族优秀传统文化得到有效保护和传承。在春节、清明节、端午节、中秋节以及肉孜节、古尔邦节等传统节日，各族人民都能享受法定假期。每逢节日，新疆各地民众用音乐、歌舞、传统体育竞技等文化活动来庆祝。汉族的"元宵灯会"、维吾尔族的"麦西热甫"、哈萨克族的"阿依特斯"、柯尔克孜族的"库姆孜弹唱会"、蒙古族的"那达慕大会"、回族的"花儿会"等民俗活动广泛开展，受到各族民众的欢迎。新疆提倡各民族相互尊重风俗习惯，倡导各民族在衣食住行、婚丧嫁娶、礼仪风俗等方面崇尚科学、文明、健康的风尚。

五、文化事业和文化产业不断发展

文化发展的核心是满足人

autonomous-region list, as well as 112 state-level representative trustees and 403 autonomous-region representative trustees of its intangible cultural heritage.

Folk cultures are respected and preserved. Xinjiang embraces cultural diversity and inclusiveness, and upholds mutual learning among cultures. The region fully respects and protects folk cultures, thus realizing the harmonious coexistence of different cultures and enabling the effective protection and preservation of the best traditions of all ethnic groups. All people in Xinjiang have the right to observe their own statutory festivals such as the Spring Festival, Qingming Festival, Dragon Boat Festival, Mid-Autumn Festival, Ramadan, and Corban. They celebrate the festivals in many forms, such as playing music, dancing, and holding traditional sports events. Among popular folk festivals are the Han people's Lantern Festival, the Uygur's Meshrep, the Kazak's Aytes, the Kirgiz's Kobuz Ballad Singing Fair, the Mongolian Nadam Fair, and the Hui people's Hua'er Folk Song Festival. The local government promotes mutual respect for folkways among all ethnic groups while encouraging appropriate and healthy lifestyles, wedding and funeral practices, and customs and rituals.

V. Constant Development of Cultural Undertakings and the Cultural Industry

The core of cultural development is to satisfy

的精神文化需求。中国政府支持新疆努力提高公共文化服务水平，促进文学艺术创作和新闻出版繁荣进步，增强文化产业实力，保障公民文化权利，丰富各族人民精神文化生活。《中华人民共和国公共文化服务保障法》《中华人民共和国公共图书馆法》《中华人民共和国电影产业促进法》等法律法规为保障新疆各族人民基本文化需求，提供公共文化服务，促进文化产业发展提供了重要法治保障。

公共文化服务水平日益提高。1955年，新疆有1个公共图书馆、各类体育场地425个。在中央政府大力支持下，近年来，新疆实施"县级文化馆、图书馆修缮工程""文化信息资源共享工程""乡镇综合文化站工程"等一系列文化基础工程。截至2017年，新疆有公共图书馆112个、博物馆和纪念馆173个、美术馆57个、文化馆119个、文化站和文化室12158个，有各级各类广播电视台（站）302个，广

people's cultural and intellectual needs. The Chinese government has given steady support to Xinjiang in its efforts to improve the quality of public cultural services, promote progress in literary and artistic creation and the press and publishing, strengthen the cultural industry, protect citizens' cultural rights, and enrich the cultural life of all ethnic groups. The Law of the People's Republic of China on Protection of Public Cultural Service, Law of the People's Republic of China on Public Libraries, and Law of the People's Republic of China on the Promotion of the Film Industry among others have served as important legal guarantee to protect the basic cultural needs of all ethnic groups in Xinjiang, provide them with public cultural services and promote the development of its cultural industry.

The quality of public cultural services is improving. In 1955, there were only 425 sports venues and one public library in Xinjiang. With the massive support of the central government, successive cultural projects have been launched in Xinjiang such as "conservation and renovation project of county-level cultural centers and libraries", "cultural information sharing project" and "township cultural centers project". By the end of 2017, Xinjiang had 112 public libraries, 173 museums and memorial halls, 57 art galleries, 119 cultural centers, 12,158 cultural stations, 302 radio and television stations (covering 97.1 percent and 97.4 percent of the population, respectively), and

播和电视人口覆盖率分别达到97.1%和97.4%，有体育场地29600个，形成了相对完整的各级公共文化服务体系。

新疆积极推进城乡公共文化服务均等化。文化馆、图书馆、博物馆、乡镇（街道）文化站等公共文化设施免费向社会开放。基本实现户户通广播电视。农村电影放映实现行政村全覆盖。财政安排资金支持为贫困乡村提供戏曲等多种形式的文艺演出。广泛开展全民阅读活动，农家书屋工程覆盖所有行政村。截至2017年，共举办13届自治区运动会、8届少数民族传统体育运动会、5届老年人运动会、6届残疾人运动会。村级"农牧民体育健身工程"实现全覆盖。新颖多样的健身器材在边远乡村普及，丰富有趣的体育比赛和健身活动深受各族群众欢迎。

文学艺术创作和新闻出版持续繁荣。新疆文学艺术佳作纷呈，生动展现了中华文化魅力。小说《天山深处的"大兵"》、诗集《神山》、散文集《在新疆》、文学评论集《西

29,600 sports venues, representing a comparatively complete public cultural service system at all levels.

Xinjiang has made efforts to ensure equal access to public cultural services for both urban and rural residents. Public cultural facilities such as cultural centers, libraries, museums and cultural stations are open to the public for free. The radio and television network covers almost every household. Movie projection is available in all administrative villages. Theatrical performances of various types are given in impoverished villages with the support of government funds. A reading campaign is encouraged by ensuring full coverage of rural libraries over all administrative villages. By the end of 2017, 13 sports meetings, eight traditional ethnic minority sports meetings, five games for senior citizens and six games for disabled people had been held in Xinjiang. Fitness projects for farmers and herdsmen cover all villages. Gym equipment of all sorts is available even in remote villages. Rich and interesting sports events and fitness activities are popular with people of all ethnic groups.

Literary, artistic creation, press and publishing are booming. A variety of brilliant works of literature and art created in Xinjiang demonstrate the glamour of Chinese culture. The following have all won national prizes such as the Best Works Award, Lu Xun Literary Prize, China

部：偏远省份的文学写作》、油画作品《来自高原的祈福——5·19国家记忆》、摄影作品《风雪人生》、话剧《大巴扎》、舞剧《阳光下的舞步》《戈壁青春》、歌舞剧《情暖天山》、音乐剧《冰山上的来客》、音乐杂技剧《你好，阿凡提》、歌曲《屯垦爹娘》、广播剧《马兰谣》和电影《大河》《鲜花》《真爱》《生死罗布泊》《塔克拉玛干的鼓声》等一批文学艺术作品获得精神文明建设"五个一工程"奖、鲁迅文学奖、中国电影华表奖等国家级奖项，杂技《生命之旅》《抖杠——担当》等获得国际杂技节金奖。

2006年，成立新疆广播影视译制中心，相继在11个地、州和伊宁市、莎车县、库车县、于田县建立电视译制部。目前，少数民族语言影视剧年译制量达6200集左右。中华

Movie Awards, and the first prize in International Acrobatic Festival:

- *Soldiers from the Snow Mountain* (novel),
- *Holy Mountain* (poetry anthology),
- *In Xinjiang* (collection of prose writings),
- *Western China: Literary Writing in Remote Provinces* (collection of literary review),
- *Praying on Plateau, Chinese Mourning Day on May 19th* (oil painting),
- *Braving the Storm* (photography),
- *Grand Bazaar* (drama),
- *Dance Steps in the Sun* and *Young Blood in Gobi Desert* (dance drama),
- *A Uygur Mother and Visitors on the Icy Mountain* (musical),
- *Hello, Advanti* (musical and acrobatic drama),
- *My Parents Stationing and Reclaiming Wasteland in Xinjiang* (song),
- *A Nuclear Scientist's Story in the Desert* (radio play),
- *The Great River, Flower, Genuine Love, Life and Death in Lop Nor, Taklimakan's Drumbeat* (movie).
- *Travel of Life* (acrobatic show),
- *Somersault on Balance Beam* (acrobatic show).

In 2006, Xinjiang Radio, Film and Television Translation and Production Center was set up, establishing branches in 11 prefectures, Yining City, Shache, Kucha and Yutian counties. Currently, about 6,200 episodes of translated ethnic film and television programs are being produced every

人民共和国成立前,新疆仅有2种报纸。截至2017年,新疆共有报纸126种,期刊223种,每年出版图书、音像制品和电子出版物约1万种。

文化、体育和民族医药产业实力逐步增强。目前,新疆有文化企业1万余家,已形成门类较为齐全的文化产业发展体系,涵盖新闻出版发行、广播影视、演艺、文化娱乐、游戏、文化旅游、工艺美术、艺术品、动漫、文化会展、创意设计、数字文化服务等领域。截至2017年,有国家级文化产业示范基地6家,自治区级文化产业示范基地109家,获得国家认定的动漫企业11家,建成各类文化产业园区20家;有国家5A级景区12家,导游17000人。文化及旅游产业增加值逐年增长。

成立一批职业体育俱乐部,体育竞赛与表演市场日趋活跃。环塔克拉玛干汽车摩托车越野拉力赛、中国篮球职业联赛新疆区比赛保持较高市场化运作水平。以中国国际露营大会、国际沙漠越野挑战赛、环艾丁湖摩托车赛、环赛里木

year. There were only two newspapers in Xinjiang before the founding of the People's Republic of China. But by the end of 2017, Xinjiang had 126 newspapers, 223 periodicals, and publishes around 10,000 titles of books, audio and video products and electronic publications every year.

Strength in cultural, sports and ethnic medicine industries is growing. At present, Xinjiang has over 10,000 cultural companies covering press, publishing and distribution, radio, film and television, performances, entertainment, games, cultural tourism, arts and crafts, artwork, animation, cultural exhibitions, innovation design and digital cultural services. By the end of 2017, there were six model bases for cultural industries at national level, 109 at autonomous region level, 11 government-approved animation companies, 20 cultural industry parks, 12 national 5A tourist attractions and 17,000 tourist guides. The added value of the cultural and tourist industries is growing every year.

A group of professional sports clubs have been set up, with sports competitions and sports show flourishing. The Taklimakan Rally is a commercial success and China Basketball Association (CBA) in Xinjiang is doing well. The sports leisure market is maturing as demonstrated by the success of the China International Camping Congress, International Desert Cross

湖公路自行车赛等为代表的体育休闲市场日趋成熟。赛马、冰雪运动、航空体育产业发展潜力巨大。

新疆已形成中华医药（含民族药）、医疗机构制剂、食品（含保健食品）、医疗器械和药用包装材料等门类较为齐全的医药健康产业体系。其中维吾尔医药、哈萨克医药、蒙医药等少数民族传统医药历史悠久，是中华文化瑰宝，许多药材被纳入国家标准和国家相关标准化研究项目。新疆民族医药销售产值占制药行业销售总产值比重逐年提高；民族医药企业的产品在不断开拓国内市场的同时，还销往周边国家和地区，进入国际市场。

网络文化蓬勃发展。随着互联网在中国的不断发展，近年来，互联网越来越成为新疆各族人民学习、工作、生活的新空间，获取公共服务的新平台。截至2017年，新疆备案网站11520家，固定宽带用户达569.9万户，移动互联网用户达1855.8万户。微信公众平台"最后一公里"用户遍及全国所有省、自治区、直辖市

Rally, Aydingkol Motorcycle Rally, and Sayram Bicycle Rally. Huge potential is also apparent in horseracing, winter sports and aviation sports.

Xinjiang has formed a complete industrial system of medicine and health covering Chinese medicine (including ethnic medicine), hospital-made preparations, foods (including health foods), medical equipment, and packaging for medicines. Among ethnic medicines, many Uygur medicines, Kazak medicines, and Mongolian medicines—boasting a long history and regarded as cultural treasures—have been categorized under national standards or included in national standardization research projects. The sales of ethnic medicines in Xinjiang's pharmaceutical industry are increasing year by year, and ethnic medicine companies are expanding sales not only in domestic markets, but also in neighboring countries and regions as an effort to enter the international markets.

Internet culture develops rapidly. The rapid development of the internet in China has made it the new space for people of all ethnic groups in Xinjiang to study, work and live, and a new platform to access public services. By the end of 2017, Xinjiang had 11,520 registered websites, 5.7 million fixed broadband subscribers, and 18.56 million mobile internet users. The subscribers on the official WeChat platform "Last Kilometer" extend across all provinces, autonomous regions, municipalities directly under the central

和几十个国家、地区。先后实施争做中国好网民、艾德莱斯网络引领、网络融情等工程，开展"网络中国节""我是一颗石榴籽""艾德莱斯出天山"等系列网络文化活动30余项，示范带动新疆各地开展各类网络文化活动7000余项。2017年，新疆本地消费者网购零售额达569.1亿元，比上年增长29.8%。蓬勃发展的网络文化引领了向上向善的社会风尚。

六、对外文化交流日趋活跃

新疆是中华文明向西开放的重要门户，在东西方文明交流互鉴中发挥了重要作用。在中央政府支持下，新疆已形成全方位、多层次的对外文化交流格局。

以多种形式参与国际文化交流与合作。中国新疆国际民族舞蹈节、中国－亚欧博览会"中外文化展示周"和"出版博览会"等成为具有一定国际影响力的文化交流品牌。2009年以来，举办了7届"中国·新疆国际青少年艺术节"，邀请中亚四国及俄罗斯、蒙古、巴基斯坦、印度、马来西亚、泰

government and dozens of countries and regions. Over 30 internet cultural projects such as "making a good netizen", "Etles Silk from Tianshan to the World" and "video programs on ethnic solidarity" launched more than 7,000 online cultural activities across Xinjiang. In 2017, online retail sales to Xinjiang consumers reached 56.91 billion yuan, an increase of 29.8 percent over 2016. The prosperity of Xinjiang's internet culture helps to foster healthy social morals.

Ⅵ. Active Cultural Exchanges with Other Countries

Xinjiang has been an important gateway for China's civilization to open to the West, and has played a significant role in cultural communication and mutual learning between East and West. Supported by the central government, Xinjiang has created a framework of cultural exchanges with other countries in all sectors and at all levels.

Xinjiang participates in international cultural exchanges and cooperation in various forms. Xinjiang International Ethnic Dance Festival, Chinese and Foreign Culture Week of China-Eurasia Expo, and Publishing Expo have become branded cultural exchange projects of considerable international influence. Since 2009, Xinjiang has held seven China International Youth Arts festivals, inviting more than 2,330 young people representing 119 art troupes from Turkmenistan,

国、韩国、阿塞拜疆等12个国家及国内共119个文艺团体的2330余名青少年来新疆演出交流。2012年至2017年，新疆连续举办7期"丝绸之路经济带相关国家媒体负责人研修班"，邀请了25个国家的100多家媒体负责人来新疆研修、交流、考察。

近年来，新疆积极推进"丝绸之路经济带"核心区建设，加强与沿线国家的人文科技交流。2016年，举办第五届中国—亚欧博览会科技合作论坛，30多个国家和国际组织的154名嘉宾受邀参加。建成12个国家级国际科技合作基地，与30多个国家和地区以及10个国际组织和研究机构开展了国际科技合作与交流，涉及农业、资源环境、农产品加工、天文、煤化工、生物医药、能源等领域。

稳步实施"留学中国计划"，逐步扩大丝绸之路经济带沿线国家优秀留学生奖学金资助规模。新疆高校积极开展国际交流与合作，留学生教育规模逐年增加、质量不断

Kazakhstan, Uzbekistan, and Kyrgyzstan of Central Asia and Russia, Mongolia, Pakistan, India, Malaysia, Thailand, the Republic of Korea and Azerbaijan. From 2012 to 2017, Xinjiang has held seven seminars for directors of media from countries along the Silk Road Economic Belt, inviting directors of more than 100 media from 25 countries to Xinjiang on study, communication and visits.

In recent years, Xinjiang has been active in building the core area along the Silk Road Economic Belt, strengthening cultural and scientific and technological exchanges with countries along the Belt. In 2016, it hosted the scientific and technological cooperation forum of the Fifth China-Eurasia Expo, inviting 154 guests from more than 30 countries and international organizations. Xinjiang has built 12 state-level bases for international sci-tech cooperation, launching cooperation and exchanges with more than 30 countries and regions and 10 international organizations and research institutes in such fields as agriculture, resources and the environment, processing of agricultural products, astronomy, coal chemicals, bio-medicine, and energy.

It has steadily implemented the "Study-in-China" initiative, gradually increasing scholarships for outstanding students from countries along the Silk Road Economic Belt. Institutions of higher learning in Xinjiang engage in active international exchanges and cooperation, and their foreign

提升。从 1985 年开始，截至 2017 年，新疆高校接收外国留学生达 5 万人次。

新疆积极发挥包括维吾尔医药、哈萨克医药在内的中华医学特色优势，筹建中外联合中医机构，开展中医民族医药国际医疗服务体系建设项目，吸引了越来越多的周边国家患者前来就医。2015 年至 2017 年，乌鲁木齐市有 5 家医院开展国际医疗服务，累计接诊外籍患者 1.7 万人次。新疆举办一系列高水平体育赛事，吸引大批国际优秀运动员和体育爱好者积极参与。

积极对外展示新疆各民族文化风采。从上世纪末开始，"中国新疆古代丝绸之路文物展""丝路奥秘——新疆文物大展"等新疆文物精品展览陆续在日本、美国、德国、韩国等国家举行。一批非物质文化遗产项目赴联合国总部、英国、日本、法国及新疆周边国家进行表演展示。近年来，"感知中国——中国西部文化行·新疆篇""中国新疆文化交流团""中国新疆文化周"分别在美国、加拿大、德国、法

students are growing in number and their teaching quality is much improved. From 1985 to 2017, colleges and universities of Xinjiang enrolled 50,000 foreign students.

With its particular strength in traditional Chinese medicine (TCM), including Uygur and Kazak medicine, Xinjiang plans to establish Chinese-foreign institutions of traditional Chinese medicine and worked to establish a system of international medical services for TCM including ethnic minority medicine, attracting more and more patients from neighboring countries. From 2015 to 2017, five hospitals in Urumqi began to offer international medical services, accepting 17,000 foreign patients in total. Xinjiang has held a series of high-level sports events, attracting numerous international athletes and sports fans.

Xinjiang presents different ethnic cultures to foreign countries. Since the late 20th century, quality exhibitions of Xinjiang cultural relics, such as the "Exhibition of Ancient Silk Road Cultural Relics of Xinjiang" and "Secrets of the Silk Road—Exhibition of Xinjiang Cultural Relics", have been held in Japan, the United States, Germany, the Republic of Korea, and some other countries. Some of Xinjiang's intangible cultural heritage items have been presented in performances or exhibitions in the UN headquarters, the United Kingdom, Japan, France, and in those countries adjacent to Xinjiang. In recent years, cultural communication events such as "Experiencing

国、意大利、西班牙、澳大利亚、新西兰、俄罗斯、哈萨克斯坦、格鲁吉亚、埃及、土耳其、伊朗、沙特、巴基斯坦、阿富汗、马来西亚、文莱、老挝等国举办多种文化交流活动。新疆多次组团代表中国参加国际伊塞克湖运动会，加强了与上海合作组织成员国之间的体育交流与合作。

结束语

中华文化是中国各族人民共同创造、传承和发展的，是民族团结和国家统一的精神纽带。事实证明，新疆各民族文化是中华文化的组成部分，中华文化始终是新疆各民族的情感依托、心灵归宿和精神家园，也是新疆各民族文化发展的动力源泉。

中共中央总书记、国家主席、中央军委主席习近平指出："中国共产党从成立之日起，既是中国先进文化的积极引领者和践行者，又是中华优秀传统文化的忠实传承者和弘扬者。当代中国共产党人和中国人民应该而且一定能够担负

Xinjiang—Cultural Exploration of Xinjiang, West China", "Xinjiang Cultural Exchange Forum", and "Xinjiang Culture Week" have been held in the United States, Canada, Germany, France, Italy, Spain, Australia, New Zealand, Russia, Kazakhstan, Georgia, Egypt, Turkey, Iran, Saudi Arabia, Pakistan, Afghanistan, Malaysia, Brunei, and Laos. Xinjiang has also sent several delegations on behalf of China to attend the World Nomad Games on the shores of Lake Issyk-Kul, strengthening sports exchanges and cooperation with other member states of the Shanghai Cooperation Organization.

Conclusion

The Chinese culture was created, carried forward and developed by all ethnic groups of China, and is a bond of ethnic unity and national unification. Facts have proven that ethnic cultures of Xinjiang are components of the Chinese culture, which is always the emotional attachment and spiritual home for all ethnic people in Xinjiang, as well as the dynamic source for the development of ethnic cultures.

Xi Jinping, general secretary of the CPC Central Committee, Chinese president and chairman of the Central Military Commission, pointed out: "Since its founding, the Communist Party of China has actively guided and promoted China's advanced culture while keeping China's fine traditional culture alive and strong. Today, we Chinese Communists and the Chinese people

起新的文化使命，在实践创造中进行文化创造，在历史进步中实现文化进步！"今天，在以习近平同志为核心的党中央坚强领导下，中华民族已经走进新时代，踏上新征程，在文化交流交融的舞台上，新疆各族人民应该而且一定能够担负起自己新的文化使命，在文化创造中铸就新繁荣，在文化进步中取得新发展！

should and can shoulder our new cultural mission, make cultural creations through practice, and promote cultural advancement along with the progress of history." Today, under the strong leadership of the CPC Central Committee with Xi Jinping as the core, the Chinese nation has marched into a new era and onto a new journey. On the stage of cultural exchanges and integration, people of all ethnic groups in Xinjiang should and can shoulder their new cultural mission to create a new boom in cultural creations and make new developments along with cultural progress.

三 白皮书的翻译原则与难点

白皮书是政府对外发布的有关政治、经济、外交等重大问题的官方文件，在措辞选择、立场表达、政策主张、行文规范、术语使用等方面都极为严谨，尤其涉及国防军控等高度敏感领域时，更是慎之又慎，既要引发国际社会对中国的广泛关注，也要引导各国对中国领土主权、治国理政、人权问题、环境治理、宗教问题等的正确认识，进而加深国际社会对中国的理解，提升中国的国际地位。

白皮书的翻译需要译者以求真求实作为首要原则从事翻译活动，白皮书有时可能会遇到看似简单，却有着复杂内涵的问题，译者遇到疑问时一定要用求真求实的精神彻底查明问题，结合上下文以及其他语境理解句子、短语和词汇的真实含义，坚决杜绝翻译错误。李长栓通过教学发现《一个中国的原则与台湾问题白皮书》的官方英译本有不少错误，造成这些错误的原因是多方面的，其中最主要的原因就是译者对原文中存在的问题不求甚解，指出"翻译或检验译文正误时，不能仅仅满足于字字对应，应当问自己：这句话到底要人们怎么做？如果实际执行起来是不可能的，一定是翻译出了问题。"[1] 译者还要把自己想象成读者，以读者身份去阅读译文，弄清

---

[1] 李长栓. 2001.《一个中国的原则与台湾问题白皮书》英语译文值得推敲. 中国翻译，（5）：62-64.

是否有难懂的部分，是否有佶屈聱牙的部分，如果有，那么应该尽可能改善，恪守通顺原则。最后，译者在翻译时应当遵循讲政治的原则。比如"充分考虑到台湾的政治现实，为了照顾台湾当局关于平等谈判地位的要求"中的"要求"一词，官方译文用的是 request，那么对于强势的台湾当局使用一个含有示弱含义的 request 是否合适？这说明译者并没有理解台湾当局在提出要求时的强势态度，缺乏政治敏锐性，如果要把这种蛮横之意表达出来的话，把 request 改成 demand 更好。

白皮书翻译的一大难点在于精准到位，翻译的质量直接关系到国际社会对我国情况了解的实效。白皮书涉及领域广泛，目的在于赢得国际社会对我国各领域发展的认识和关注，以及对我国颁布的国内国际政策的理解。各个领域的专属用语讲究准确到位，遵循国际表达习惯，翻译时同样要精准传达专属用语，注重国际接受度，确保内涵和分寸恰当，按照通用的翻译原则增强译文的认同度。其次，白皮书翻译必须精准措辞，正确传达中国立场，尤其涉及领土主权和民族尊严等重大问题时，必须斟酌选词。对于汉语的同一表达，虽然经常会在英语中找到多种近似表达，但需根据原文语境以及使用方法甄别不同，恰切选择。如不严谨对待，一字之差都会造成误导，引发误解。最后，白皮书翻译也会遇到生动形象表达的问题，虽不可能逐字对等，但常可通过直译展现中国语言风格，准确再现原文的异域特色。当然，处理形象化语言时，做到绝对的严丝合缝或者完美再现不太可能。多数情况下，如不能保留形式，可选择准确传达原意，或者形式上灵活微调，以达读者接受和认可的目的。

四 白皮书的英译技巧

1 专有名词的翻译技巧

白皮书内容涉及政治、经济、历史、文化等领域，译者会遇到大量专有名词，有些专有名词还带有明显的中国特色，这些专有名词的翻译是外交翻译的重点和难点之一。中国历史悠久、地域广大，民族组成复杂，地名翻译具有一定的挑战。

> **原文** 截至 2017 年，新疆民丰尼雅遗址、尉犁营盘墓地、若羌小河墓地、库车友谊路晋十六国砖室墓、巴里坤东黑沟遗址、吉木乃通天洞遗址等 8 项考古发掘项目先后被列入当年全国十大考古新发现。

> **译文** By the end of 2017 eight archeological programs, including the Niya Ruins in Minfeng County, Yingpan Cemetery in Yuli County, Xiaohe Cemetery in Ruoqiang County, 3rd-4th century brick graves in Kucha County, Dongheigou Ruins in Barkol County, and the Tongtiandong Cave in Jeminay County, had been listed among the National Top 10 Archeological Discoveries of the Year.

这个例子不但包括汉语地名，还包括来自维吾尔语等少数民族语言的地名。首先来看汉语地名的翻译。1977 年，中国向联合国第三届地名标准化会议提交了名为 *Rules for Spelling Chinese Place Names with Chinese Phonetic Alphabet* 的中国地名拼写方案，该方案获得会议批准，从而成为中国地名翻译的国际标准。方案第二条写道："拼写汉族地名，专名和通名分开，但是在拼写城镇和乡村名时不需要分开"，比如"台湾海峡"中的台湾是专名，海峡是通名，因此拼写时要分开，译成 Taiwan Haixia，而拼写"周口店""王村"时不需要分开，分别拼成 Zhoukoudian 和 Wangcun。例子中的"民丰、尼雅、尉犁、小河、若羌"等汉语地名对大多数中国人而言都是首次听说，因此根据名从主人的原则，按照新疆当地人民的实际发音翻译即可。"民丰尼雅遗址"是指位于新疆民丰县尼雅乡的精绝国遗址，"民丰县"属于由专名+通名（县）构成，分专名和通名拼写，因此译为 Minfeng County。其中通用名"县"这个行政单位在英语中有对应的翻译 county，但也可按汉语拼音译为 Xian。此处译者采用的是专名用汉语拼音音译而通名意译的方法。

新疆是少数民族聚居地区，少数民族使用的语言种类较多，主要包括维吾尔语、哈萨克语、蒙古语、柯尔克孜语、吐火罗语、突厥语等。在处理由少数民族语言命名的地名时需要遵照一定的规范。1976 年国务院颁布的《少数民族语地名汉语拼音字母音译转写法》是处理少数民族语地名翻译的主要依据，另外本地颁发的规范文件以及具有权威性的地名词典等也是参考依据。"巴里坤"全称是"巴里坤哈萨克自治县"，其中主要的少数民族语言为哈萨克语，根据"名从主人"的原则，"巴里坤"沿用本地的发音和拼写方法译作 Barkol，而不是采用汉语拼音 Balikun；同样"吉木乃"这个带有少数民族特色的名字采用当地维语的拼读方法译作 Jeminay。上文中"库车县"被译作 Kucha 值得商榷，因为库车一名来自古龟兹语，遵从龟兹语的发音和拼写方法，译为 Kuqa 更好。

人名的翻译也是按照汉语拼音方案的规则。翻译中国人名时姓在前，名在后，姓名之间要空格，并且首字母都要大写，如果名是两个字，这两个字连在一起拼写，不需要空格也不需要连字符。

> **原文** 1708年，琉球学者、紫金大夫程顺则所著《指南广义》记载，姑米山为"琉球西南界上之镇山"。

> **译文** In 1708, Cheng Shunze (TeiJunsoku), a noted scholar and the Grand Master with the Purple-Golden Ribbon (ZiJin Da Fu) of Ryukyu, recorded in his book *A General Guide* (Zhi Nan Guang Yi) that "Gumi Mountain is the mountain guarding the southwest border of Ryukyu".

程顺则是人名，按照拼音规则音译为 Cheng Shunze，其后括号内附带了这个名字的旧译 TeiJunsoku，该译法采用的是威妥玛式拼音法。该拼音法是清末至1958年汉语拼音方案形成前，中国和国际上惯用的中文拼音方案，被普遍用于拼写中国人名和地名。程顺则作为具有一定知名度的学者，其名的旧译已经为人所知，因此采用新规则拼写其名时，译者将旧译附带其后，方便读者在阅读相关文献时能将两个译名统一，而不至于将新旧译认作两个人的名字。其次，译者在翻译中国特有的官衔、职位、称号时采用的是意译在前，增补音译的方法。程顺则上奏琉球王设立琉球最早的学校和儒学传播中心"明伦堂"并出任"紫金大夫"，监督学生学习的同时也处理与朝廷的往来事务。因此"大夫"是指有学识的学者，而"紫金"就是学者的等级，这里意译为 the Grand Master with the Purple-Golden Ribbon，其后附带拼音 ZiJin Da Fu，减少回译到中文时产生错误的可能性。出于同样的考虑，这种增补方法也用在了古籍名的翻译上，比如上文中的《指南广义》先被意译为 *A General Guide*，然后再补充拼音 Zhi Nan Guang Yi。

2 措辞选择的准确性

外交白皮书涉及的是国内外政府和民众都十分关注的重大或敏感事件或问题，向受众明确表明本国政府对该事件或问题的立场和态度，因而措辞必须清晰准确，翻译时更要注意措辞的准确传达。

"外延"（Denotation）和"内涵"（Connotation）是作者在选择措辞时需要考虑的两个方面，前者是指一个词在词典里的固有意义，而后者是指这个词所隐含的、引申的意义。比如同样是"家"，翻译成 house，强调的是包括房屋、屋内布局、家具设施等有形的外在，而译成 home 则更强调家的温馨，及带给人的安全感。因此，译者在翻译时要弄清楚一个词是否具有"内涵"，并且要尽可能地传达隐含意义。

> **原文** 斗转星移，兵团走过了不平凡的60年。

> **译文** The seasons change fast, and 60 <u>eventful</u> years have passed since the founding of the XPCC.

2014年是新疆生产建设兵团成立60周年，建设兵团发布了《新疆生产建设兵团的历史与发展》白皮书，全面介绍兵团的历史和发展状况，以助国际社会了解和认识兵团发挥什么样的作用、兵团是一个什么样的社会组织、兵团人是一个什么样的社会群体。60年来，新疆生产建设兵团白手起家，艰苦奋斗，广大兵团军垦职工栉风沐雨，扎根边疆，同当地各族人民一道，把亘古戈壁荒漠改造成生态绿洲。兵团为推动新疆发展、增进民族团结、维护社会稳定、巩固国家边防做出了不可磨灭的历史贡献。"不平凡"一般表示"杰出、卓越"之意，而在这句话中却有更深的隐含意义，摘自白皮书的末尾，总结兵团发展壮大之不易，强调兵团的发展经历过重重艰险，克服过重重困难。因此"不平凡"并未翻译成 outstanding，而是译成 eventful，体现出兵团取得如今傲人成就的不容易。

> **原文** 此次会议<u>通过</u>了《关于新疆维吾尔自治区筹备工作的报告》等文件。

> **译文** The meeting <u>approved</u> the Report on Preparatory Work for the Establishment of the Xinjiang Uygur Autonomous Region.

原文中"通过"一词，从字面上来看并无明显褒贬指涉。如果直接译作 pass，通指客观陈述一个事实和结果。但该例将其译为 approve，体现"赞成"之隐含意义，明显表达与会代表对这些文件支持和肯定的褒义意味。

> **原文** <u>加大</u>生态环境保护和建设<u>力度</u>，实现了经济发展与生态保护同步双赢。

> **译文** It has <u>devoted great efforts to</u> protecting and building its ecological system, carefully balancing the interests of economic growth and environmental protection.

在原文中，"加大……的力度"也无明显的褒贬指涉。如按照字典意义将其译为 strength，并不能表现新疆人民为保护环境所付出的努力。译者通过短语 devoted... efforts to，以及增加形容词 great，把其中蕴含的情感意味传达出来，表达了对新疆人民为环境保护所付出努力的肯定和赞许，显化了褒奖指涉。同样，词语中如果蕴含了贬义也应采用有效方式传达出来。

> **原文** 新中国成立前，新疆经济社会发展严重滞后，各族人民生活十分贫困，根本<u>无法享有</u>基本人权。

译文 Before the founding of the People's Republic of China, Xinjiang lagged far behind the rest of the country in economic and social development, and the ethnic peoples there lived in dire poverty and <u>were deprived of</u> basic human rights.

"无法享有"本身无明显的贬义，译者将"无法享有"译为"were deprived of"，表达出 1949 年以前由于新疆的经济和社会各方面的发展极其低下，新疆人民的基本人权受客观的外在条件所制约而"被剥夺了"，同时也能衬托出当时新疆经济社会发展滞后严重，以及各族人民生活的贫困程度。

另外，在措辞方面还要注意词语之间的上下义关系，上义词（superordinates）是对事物的概括性、抽象性说明，而下义词（hyponyms）是事物的具体表现形式或更为具体的说明。如果"动物"一词是上义词的话，那么猪、狗、牛、马等就是它的下义词。在翻译过程中为了使语言更精确、更明晰，有必要确定是否使用下义词。

原文 宗教文化遗产得到有效保护。目前，新疆有喀什艾提尕尔<u>清真寺</u>、昭苏<u>圣佑庙</u>、克孜尔<u>千佛洞</u>等 109 处宗教文化古迹被列入全国重点文物保护单位和自治区级文物保护单位。

译文 A total of 109 religious sites in Xinjiang, including Id Kah <u>Mosque</u> in Kashgar, Shengyou <u>Lamasery</u> in Zhaosu, and the Kizil Thousand-Buddha Caves have been designated as major cultural heritage sites under the protection of the autonomous region and the state.

宗教活动场所是寺观教堂和其他固定宗教活动处所，国内主要宗教活动场所包括佛教的寺、道教的观、天主教和基督教的教堂、伊斯兰教的清真寺以及祭祀祖先的庙等，如果宗教活动场所是上义词，那么寺、庙、观等就是它的下义词，翻译这些名称应当考虑其属于什么宗教。"艾提尕尔清真寺"是伊斯兰教的宗教活动场所，因此译为 Id Kah Mosque，而"昭苏圣佑庙"是藏传佛教的寺庙，因此译作 Shengyou Lamasery。另外，中国的庙通常译为 joss house；佛教的寺一般译为 temple，而 pagoda 特指佛教或印度教的寺，delubrum 是古代罗马的寺；church 是教堂的一般译法，而 cathedral 是大教堂，chapel 是小礼拜堂，basilica 是长方形会堂。译者应当尽可能根据不同宗教、不同用途、不同大小和形状找到确切的下义词才能准确传达意义。

原文 辉煌壮丽的人权<u>发展</u>历程

译文 A Splendid History of China's Human Rights <u>Protection</u>

上例源自的白皮书主题是关于中华人民共和国成立 70 多年来在人权事业上所取得的进步。我国奉行以人民为中心的人权理念，始终把生存权、发展权作为首要的基本人权，协调增进全体人民的各项权利，努力促进人的全面发展，不断提高人权保障水平。如果把"人权发展"译为 the development of human rights，并不能体现我国发展人权事业的侧重点和关注点，因为人权事业的发展有多个面向和可能，将"发展"理解为 development 过于笼统。我国在发展人权时始终强调对人权的保障，这是我国人权事业发展的主线，因此将"发展"一词译作"protection"更为具体，在这个语境下，protection 就是 development 的一个下义词。

3 形象语言的处理

有时为了将事实讲得更清楚、道理说得更明白、理由给得更充分，外交文书中也会使用一些形象生动的语言，这些形象性语言的翻译同样是翻译工作的难点。

> **原文** 2018 年召开全国教育大会，强调全社会要担负起青少年成长成才的责任，发挥家庭作为人生第一所学校、帮助<u>扣好人生第一粒扣子</u>的重要作用，坚持把立德树人作为家庭教育的根本任务，培养孩子的好思想、好品行、好习惯。

> **译文** In 2018, the National Education Conference was held, emphasizing the responsibility of the whole society for boosting the healthy growth of the young, and the important role of family, as the first school in life, in helping <u>fasten the first button of life</u>, persisting in the fundamental task of strengthening moral education and cultivating people in family education, and fostering children's good thinking, good conduct, and good habits.

2014 年 5 月 4 日，习近平主席在北京大学考察时对学子们说："青年的价值取向决定了未来整个社会的价值取向，而青年又处在价值观形成和确立的时期，抓好这一时期的价值观养成十分重要。这就像穿衣服扣扣子一样，如果第一粒扣子扣错了，剩余的扣子都会扣错。人生的扣子从一开始就要扣好。"扣好人生第一粒扣子就是指从人生最初的青少年时期就树立好正确的价值观，就像穿衣服扣扣子一样，第一粒扣子扣好了，才能保证衣服穿得整齐。这篇白皮书引用了这一形象比喻，强调家庭对青少年价值观形成的重要作用。这个形象比喻尽管源于中国，但是异域文化的读者也是可以理解的，因此译者采用了直译法，将其译为 fasten the first button，既保留了汉语的民族文化特色，又丰富了译入语的表达。

原文 中国的发展成就是辛辛苦苦干出来的。对于中国这样一个有着近14亿人口的大国，好日子等不来、要不来，唯有奋斗，别无他路。中国的发展，靠的是"8亿件衬衫换一架波音"的实干精神，几代人驰而不息、接续奋斗，付出别人难以想象的辛劳和汗水；靠的是"自己的担子自己扛"的担当精神，无论顺境还是逆境，不输出问题，不转嫁矛盾，不通过强买强卖、掠夺别国发展自己；靠的是"摸着石头过河"的探索精神，不走帝国主义、殖民主义老路，不照搬西方国家发展模式，而是结合中国实际、总结经验教训、借鉴人类文明，敢闯敢试，走出一条自己的路。

译文 China's successes have been achieved through hard work. A large country with a nearly 1.4 billion population, China cannot achieve prosperity by asking for assistance and waiting. The only option is hard work. China relied on the solid and unremitting efforts of generations of Chinese people, which is represented in the typical case of "800 million shirts in exchange for a Boeing airplane". China relied on fulfilling its own responsibility in good times and in adversity, without exporting or shifting problems elsewhere, and without seeking development by trading under coercion or exploiting other countries. China relied on a pioneering spirit, like crossing the river by feeling for stones, neither retracing the steps of imperialism and colonialism, nor copying the development model of Western countries, but blazing its own path with bold experiments, based on its own conditions, experience and lessons as well as the achievements of other civilizations.

此例中也有很多形象的说法，比如说国家的繁荣富强具体体现在让人民过上"好日子"；"8亿件衬衫换一架波音"是中国曾经有过的一段艰难历史，要用卖8亿件衬衫的利润才能买一架A380空客，体现了中国人的肯干、实干、吃苦耐劳的精神；"扛担子"是农业社会运送货物的传统方式，肩挑背驮在身上的不仅是负重也是责任，因此汉语中"扛担子"也常被隐喻为"负责任"，"自己的担子自己扛"是指中国人民不惧困难，勇于担当，不推诿或回避责任；"摸着石头过河"则是改革开放三条经验——"摸论"、"猫论"和"不争论"之一，是在勇敢实践中不断总结经验的一种形象说法。中国在改革之初对于如何改革并没有经验可循，所有的困难就像是一条横亘在改革者面前的不熟悉的河，改革者只能以身试水，摸索着河里的石头，靠石头的引导，安全稳妥地过河，他们既要敢于涉水，又要注意安全，这也是对待改革开放的态度，既要大胆解放思想，又要讲求稳妥安全。译者将比较具体的"好日子"一词译成比较概括抽象的 prosperity。prosperity 指一种繁荣、兴旺、获得好运或成功社会地位的状态。它往往包括财富，和其他独立于财富的因素，比如幸福、健康等。人们过上"好日子"也是 prosperity 的一种表现，译者用上义词来替代下义词，尽管失去了"好日子"一词的生动性，但却让原文意义更加完整地体现，从而达到了补偿作用。"8 亿件衬衫换一架波音"被译为 800 million shirts in exchange for a Boeing airplane，这样的直译浅显易懂，形象生动，更能唤起读者对中国人民艰苦奋斗史的回忆。英语国家文化主要是以海洋文明为基础，而汉语文化主要以农耕文明为基础，英文读者要理解"扛担子"之类在农耕文明中特有的比喻还是比较费力，因此译者将"自己的担子自己扛"意译为 fulfilling its own responsibility，减少了读者的阅读障碍；"摸着石头过河"是一种比较普遍的现象，译者采用直译的方法将其译为 crossing the river by feeling for stones 保留了原文的意象，并且在译文中加上本体 a pioneering spirit 和比喻词 like，从而将原文的隐喻变成译文中的明喻，更有益于读者的联想和理解。由此看来，在处理有文化特色的形象性语言时既要考虑读者的接受，在不增加读者阅读障碍的同时，也可以为译语增添一些来自异域的表达，起到丰富译语文化的作用。

五　中国关键词加油站

1 管辖权 *jurisdiction*

　　管辖权还是主权国家的基本权利之一。即国家对其领域内的一切人和物进行管辖的权利。除管辖权外，还有独立权、平等权和自卫权。独立权，即国家按照自己的意志处理内政处外交事务，而不受他国控制和干涉的权利。平等权，即一切国家在国际法上地位一律平等的权利。自卫权，即国家保卫自己生存和独立的权利。国家在享有基本权利的同时，也负有不侵犯别国、不干涉他国内政、外交以及和平解决国家之间争端的义务。管辖权是指国家对其领土内的一切人、物和所发生的事件，以及对在其领域外的本国人行使管辖的权利。一般来说，管辖权包括四个方面：属人管辖权。这是指各国对具有本国国籍的公民实行管辖的权利。属地管辖权。这是指国家对领域内的一切人（除享有外交豁免者外）、物和发生的事件具有的管辖权。

保护性管辖权。这是指国家对于外国人在该国领域外侵害该国的国家和公民的重大利益的犯罪行为有权行使管辖。普遍性管辖权。根据国际法，国家对于国际犯罪，无论犯罪人的国籍如何，也无论他在何处犯罪均有权实行管辖。

2 反恐维稳 fighting terrorism and maintaining social stability

中国《宪法》《国防法》《反恐怖主义法》等明确赋予中国武装力量依法防范和处置恐怖活动的职责，赋予中国人民武装警察部队担负国家安全保卫任务、维护社会秩序的职责，赋予中国人民解放军依法协助维护社会秩序的职责。近年来，中国武装力量积极构建反恐怖专业力量体系，成立了"猎鹰""雪豹"突击队等专业应急力量，不断提升应急处置能力，依法成功参与处置一系列恐怖袭击事件，稳妥应对一系列公共卫生和社会安全等突发事件，确保了国家安全、公共安全、环境安全和社会安全。

恐怖主义是全人类的公敌，没有任何国家能够独自应对，也没有任何国家可以独善其身。中国反对一切形式的恐怖主义。中国武装力量遵守《联合国宪章》和国际法准则，支持联合国安理会通过的一系列反恐决议，深化与国际和周边地区有关国家在反恐、执法方面的交流合作，积极参与上合组织、东盟、四国机制等区域组织框架内的双（多）边反恐联演联训，共同提升联合防范和应对恐怖主义威胁的能力，有效维护了国际和地区和平稳定。当今世界恐怖主义愈演愈烈，中国政府和武装力量愿同各方保持积极沟通，持续促进反恐合作，联手应对风险挑战，确保世界和地区的和平与发展。

3 和平发展道路 peaceful development

和平发展道路归结起来就是：既通过维护世界和平发展自己，又通过自身发展维护世界和平；在强调依靠自身力量和改革创新实现发展的同时，坚持对外开放，学习借鉴别国长处；顺应经济全球化发展潮流，寻求与各国互利共赢和共同发展；同国际社会一道努力，推动建设持久和平、共同繁荣的和谐世界。中国将坚定不移地走和平发展道路，同时也将推动各国共同坚持和平发展。中国将积极承担更多国际责任，同世界各国一道维护人类良知和国际公理，在世界和地区事务中主持公道、伸张正义。中国主张以和平方式解决国际争端，反对各种形式的霸权主义和强权政治，永远不称霸，永远不搞扩张。中国主张坚持共赢精神，在追求本国利益的同时兼顾别国利益，做到惠本国、利天下，推动走出一条合作共赢、良性互动的路子。中国改革开放 40 多年的历史已经证明，和平发展是中国基于自身国情、社会制度、文化传统作出的战略抉择，顺应时代潮流，符合中国根本利益，符合周边国家利益，符合世界各国利益。

4 海外利益攸关区 areas crucially related to China's overseas interests

海外利益攸关区是指与海外利益存在客观密切联系的区域。2015 年 5 月，中国发表《中国的军事战略》白皮书，提出"海外利益攸关区"概念。随着中国国家利益的拓展，维护海外利益安全已经成为军事战略高度关注的重要问题。在中国不断扩大全方位对外开放的过程中，中国海外能源资源、战略通道安全和海外机构、人员、资产安全问题日益凸显，开展海上护航、撤离海外公民、应急救援等海外行动和海外利益攸关区安全合作，成为中国军队维护国家利益和履行国际义务的重要方式。维护中国海外利益，是全球化时代保障国家可持续发展的需要，也有利于维护世界和地区安全稳定。中国的海外利益攸关区没有排他性和对抗性，不谋求划分势力范围和军事扩张。

5 中国特色大国外交 major-country diplomacy with distinctive Chinese characteristics

中国共产党是为中国人民谋幸福的政党，也是为人类进步事业而奋斗的政党。中国共产党始终把为人类作出新的更大的贡献作为自己的使命。2014 年 11 月，习近平在中央外事工作会议上指出，中国必须有自己的特色大国外交，这是中央首次明确提出中国特色大国外交，因此有人把 2014 年称为中国大国外交的元年。党的十九大报告强调，中国特色大国外交要推动构建新型国际关系，推动构建人类命运共同体。为此，中国将高举和平、发展、合作、共赢的旗帜，推动建设互相尊重、公平正义、合作共赢的新型国际关系；呼吁各国人民同心协力，构建人类命运共同体，建设持久和平、普遍安全、共同繁荣、开放包容、清洁美丽的世界；坚定奉行独立自主的和平外交政策，反对干涉别国内政，反对以强凌弱；中国绝不会以牺牲别国利益为代价来发展自己，也绝不放弃自己的正当权益，任何人不要幻想让中国吞下损害自身利益的苦果；奉行防御性的国防政策，中国发展不对任何国家构成威胁；积极发展全球伙伴关系，扩大同各国的利益交汇点；坚持对外开放的基本国策，坚持打开国门搞建设；秉持共商共建共享的全球治理观，倡导国际关系民主化；将继续发挥负责任大国作用，积极参与全球治理体系改革和建设，不断贡献中国智慧和力量。中国实施大国外交，根本一点就是不仅以中国观世界，也以世界观中国、以世界观世界，并在这种积极互动中展示具有鲜明中国特色的大国外交理念和外交实践。

6 国际传播能力建设 build up international communication capacity

在中国外文局成立70周年之际，中共中央总书记、国家主席、中央军委主席习近平发来贺信，希望外文局不断提升国际传播能力和水平，更好向世界介绍新时代的中国。习近平多次强调，要加强国际传播能力建设，精心构建对外话语体系，增强对外话语的创造力、感召力、公信力，讲好中国故事，传播好中国声音，阐释好中国特色。党的十八届三中全会通过的《中共中央关于全面深化改革若干重大问题的决定》也明确提出，要大力开展对外文化交流，加强国际传播能力和对外话语体系建设，推动中华文化走向世界。在党的新闻舆论工作座谈会上，习近平强调要遵循新闻传播规律，创新方法手段，建立对外传播话语体系，增强国际话语权。

7 新型亚洲安全观 new Asian security concept

2014年5月，习近平在上海举行的亚信峰会上，提出了共同安全、综合安全、合作安全、可持续安全的亚洲安全观。他建议，创新安全理念，搭建地区安全合作新架构，努力走出一条共建、共享、共赢的亚洲安全之路。共同安全，就是要尊重和保障每一个国家安全。综合安全，就是要统筹维护传统领域和非传统领域安全。合作安全，就是要通过对话合作，促进各国和本地区安全。可持续安全，就是要发展和安全并重以实现持久安全。

8 对非"真、实、亲、诚" building relations with Africa based on sincerity, real results, friendship, and good faith

2013年3月，习近平主席在达累斯萨拉姆发表演讲，总结中非友好关系发展历史经验，全面阐述了新时期中非共谋和平、同促发展的政策主张。第一，对待非洲朋友,讲一个"真"字,始终把发展同非洲国家的团结合作作为中国对外政策的重要基础。第二,开展对非合作,讲一个"实"字,只要是中方做出的承诺,就一定会不折不扣落到实处。第三,加强中非友好,讲一个"亲"字。中非人民有着天然的亲近感,要更加重视中非人文交流,积极推动青年交流,使中非友好事业后继有人。第四,解决合作中的问题,讲一个"诚"字,中方坦诚面对中非关系面临的新情况新问题,本着相互尊重、合作共赢的精神加以妥善解决。

9 中非全面战略合作伙伴关系 China-Africa comprehensive strategic and cooperative partnership

2015年12月5日,中国国家主席习近平在中非合作论坛约翰内斯堡峰会上,全面阐述了中国对非关系政策理念,提出把中非关系由"新型战略伙伴关系"提升为"全面战略合作伙伴关系"。它由五大支柱支撑,即政治上的平等互信,经济上的合作共赢,文明上的交流互鉴,安全上的守望相助,国际事务中的团结协作。为推进这一关系建设,习近平还同时提出了未来三年中方将同非方重点实施的"十大合作计划",涉及工业化、农业现代化、基础设施、金融、减贫惠民等领域,这为中非全面战略合作伙伴关系建设夯实了基础。中非全面战略合作伙伴关系的确立,彰显了中国将秉持"真、实、亲、诚"的对非政策理念和义利观,同非洲大陆携手迈向合作共赢、共同发展的新时代。

10 网络空间命运共同体 building a community with a shared future in cyberspace

互联网真正让世界变成了地球村,让国际社会越来越成为你中有我、我中有你的命运共同体。习近平总书记在历届世界互联网大会上,均阐释了"网络空间命运共同体"的理念和主张。他强调,网络空间是人类共同的活动空间,网络空间前途命运应由世界各国共同掌握。他提出了共建网络空间命运共同体的四项原则和五点主张。四项原则是:尊重网络主权,维护安全和平,促进开放合作,构建良好秩序。五点主张是:第一,加快全球网络基础设施建设,促进互联互通;第二,打造网上文化交流共享平台,促进交流互鉴;第三,推动网络经济创新发展,促进共同繁荣;第四,保障网络安全,促进有序发展;第五,构建互联网治理体系,促进公平正义。共建网络空间命运共同体,需要国际社会共同努力才能实现。

六 白皮书翻译练习

1. 翻译下列白皮书段落，注意专有名词的翻译。

1）中国历史上最早的几个王朝夏、商、周先后在中原地区兴起，与其周围的大小氏族、部落、部落联盟逐渐融合形成的族群统称为诸夏或华夏。经春秋至战国，华夏族群不断同王朝周边的氏族、部落、部落联盟交流融合，逐渐形成了齐、楚、燕、韩、赵、魏、秦等7个地区，并分别联系着东夷、南蛮、西戎、北狄等周边诸族。公元前221年，秦始皇建立第一个统一的封建王朝。公元前202年，汉高祖刘邦再次建立统一的封建王朝。

2）新疆自古以来就是多民族聚居地区。最早开发新疆地区的是先秦至秦汉时期生活在天山南北的塞人、月氏人、乌孙人、羌人、龟兹人、焉耆人、于阗人、疏勒人、莎车人、楼兰人、车师人，以及匈奴人、汉人等。

2. 翻译下列白皮书段落，注意画线部分的措辞。

1）从1840年到1949年，由于西方列强的一次次入侵，加之统治阶级的腐朽和社会制度的落后，中国<u>沦为</u>半殖民地半封建社会，战争频繁，社会动荡，经济凋敝，民不聊生，<u>坠入贫穷深渊</u>。

2）大量事实<u>表明</u>，宗教极端主义已成为危害国家统一和民族团结，破坏宗教和睦与社会和谐，影响新疆社会稳定和长治久安，危害各族人民生命财产安全的现实危险。

3）旧西藏与现代文明的距离，<u>十分遥远</u>。

4）加大对特定主体民事权利的保护，更好地保护<u>未成年人</u>的利益，将<u>老年人</u>纳入监护制度保护范围。

3. 翻译下列白皮书段落，注意画线部分的转换。

1）发布《关于加快推进失信被执行人信用监督、警示和惩戒机制建设的意见》，规定37项惩治<u>"老赖"</u>措施。

2）把南疆地区作为脱贫攻坚的<u>主战场</u>，加大财政扶贫资金投入力度，汇聚行业、社会、援疆等扶贫资源，大力推进就业扶贫"十大专项行动"，加快基础设施和基本公共服务建设步伐，贫困群众生产生活条件得到极大改善。

3）各国都应为维护地区和平稳定发挥作用。中国推动构建亚太安全架构，不是另起炉灶，不是推倒重来，而是对现有机制的完善和升级。
4）新疆各族人民在共同创建和发展中国统一多民族国家的历史过程中，形成了你中有我、我中有你的血肉联系。

第七章

外交条约翻译

一、外交条约的概念及文体特点

广义的外交条约是指由两个或两个以上国际法主体之间签订的、确定缔约各国权利和义务关系的任何协议，它可以有不同的名称；狭义的外交条约则指以条约为名称的、有关政治、经济、军事、文化、法律等重要问题的、有效期较长的国际协议。任何国际法主体与非国际法主体间，或非国际法主体相互间缔结的协议不能被视为条约。条约是受国际法支配的协议，条约确定的国际法主体之间的权利和义务关系应符合国际法的原则和规则，否则不能生效；条约的缔结、生效、无效、解释、保留、修订和暂停施行受国际条约法的调整。条约是具有法律约束力的协议，并且通常是书面形式的协议。条约一般具有时间性，如果有效期期满不再续签，该条约即会失效。由两个国家签订的条约称"双边条约"；三个或三个以上国家签订的条约称"多边条约"。广义的外交条约包括狭义的外交条约在内，另外还有公约、协定、换文、联合宣言、宪章、谅解备忘录等其他形式。

外交条约主要用以明确签约各方的权利和义务，具有一定法律约束力，因此也属于法律文书。法律文书是一个国家意志和规范的承载体，体现了国家的政治、文化和法治思想，用语言作为呈现工具，法律文书具有与其他文本不同的特征。首先，从词汇层面来看，法律文书的措辞要规范、准确、严谨、简明、具体，词汇体现法律特征，符合法律语域的要求，常用法律术语和行话、套话，具有一定的专业性；其次，从句子层面来看，长句较多，修饰成分繁杂，大量使用状语，多用被动和名词化结构，为避免造成混乱和误解，句中少用或不用代词；另外，从篇章结构的层面来看，法律文本在一定程度上程式化，故而语篇层次分明，逻辑清晰，周密有序，既利于清楚准确地表达规范和要求，又能更好地体现法律的权威性。

二　外交条约汉英对照举隅

范例一：条约

中华人民共和国和加拿大关于刑事司法协助的条约
Treaty Between the People's Republic of China and Canada on Mutual Legal Assistance in Criminal Matter

中华人民共和国和加拿大（以下简称"双方"），在相互尊重主权和平等互利的基础上，为加强两国在刑事司法协助领域的密切合作，决定缔结本条约。

为此目的，双方议定下列各条：

第一章　总则
第一条　刑事司法协助

一、双方应根据本条约的规定，相互提供刑事司法协助。

二、司法协助系指被请求方为在请求方进行的刑事调查取证或诉讼所提供的任何协助，无论该协助是由法院或其他机关寻求或提供。

The People's Republic of China and Canada (thereinafter referred to as "the Parties") desiring to strengthen their close cooperation in the field of mutual legal assistance in criminal matters on the basis of mutual respect for sovereignty and equality and mutual benefit, have hereby resolved to conclude this Treaty.

To this end the Parties have agreed as follows:

CHAPTER I GENERAL PROVISIONS
ARTICLE 1 MUTUAL LEGAL ASSISTANCE IN CRIMINAL MATTERS

1. The Parties shall, in accordance with this Treaty, grant each other mutual legal assistance in criminal matters.

2. Mutual legal assistance shall be any assistance given by the Requested Party in respect of investigations or proceedings in the Requesting Party in a criminal matter, irrespective of whether the assistance is sought or to be provided by a court or some other authority.

三、第一款所述"刑事",在中华人民共和国方面系指全国人民代表大会及其常务委员会制定和颁布的法律所规定的与犯罪有关的调查取证或诉讼;在加拿大方面系指联邦议会法律所规定的与犯罪有关的调查取证或诉讼。

第二条 司法协助的范围

协助应包括:

(一)刑事诉讼文书的送达;

(二)调查取证和获取有关人员的陈述;

(三)搜查和扣押;

(四)获取和提供鉴定人鉴定;

(五)移交物证;

(六)提供犯罪记录和法庭记录;

(七)提供书证;

(八)准许或协助包括在押人员在内的有关人员赴请求方作证或协助调查取证;

(九)涉及赃款赃物和归还被害人财物的措施。

第三条 协助的途径

一、除本条约另有规定外,双方的法院和其他机关应

3. Criminal matters for the purpose of paragraph 1 mean, for the People's Republic of China, investigations or proceedings relating to any offence created by the laws enacted and issued by the National People's Congress and its Standing Committee; and for Canada, investigations or proceedings relating to any offence created by a law of Parliament.

ARTICLE 2 SCOPE OF MUTUAL LEGAL ASSISTANCE

Assistance shall include:

a) Service of documents for proceedings in criminal matters;

b) Taking of evidence and obtaining of statements of persons;

c) Search and seizure;

d) Obtaining and providing expert evaluations;

e) Transfer of material evidence;

f) Provision of criminal records, and court records;

g) Provision of documentary evidence;

h) Authorizing or assisting persons, including detained persons, to travel to the Requesting Party to give evidence or assist investigations; and

i) Measures related to the proceeds of crime and the restoration of property to victims.

ARTICLE 3 CHANNELS OF COMMUNICATIONS FOR LEGAL ASSISTANCE

1. Unless otherwise stipulated in this Treaty, the courts and other authorities of the Parties

通过各自的中央机关相互请求和提供司法协助。

二、前款所述"中央机关",在中华人民共和国方面系指其司法部,在加拿大方面系指其司法部长或司法部长指定的官员。

第四条 司法协助适用的法律

一、被请求方应按照其本国法律提供协助。

二、在被请求方法律未予禁止的范围内,应按请求方要求的方式执行请求。

第五条 语言

协助请求书应用请求方的文字书写,请求书及其附件应附有被请求方官方文字的译文。

第六条 司法协助的费用

一、被请求方应支付提供司法协助的费用,但下列费用应由请求方负担:

(一)根据一项协助请求赴请求方的有关人员的旅费、膳食费和住宿费以及应向其支付的任何补助费。这些费用应

shall, through their respective Central Authorities, request and render each other mutual legal assistance.

2. Central Authorities for the purpose of preceding paragraph mean, for the People's Republic of China, the Ministry of Justice; and for Canada, the Minister of Justice or an official designated by the Minister of Justice.

ARTICLE 4 LAWS APPLICABLE IN LEGAL ASSISTANCE

1. The Requested Party shall provide assistance in accordance with its national law.

2. Insofar as it is not prohibited by the law of the Requested Party, requests shall be executed in the manner requested by the Requesting Party.

ARTICLE 5 LANGUAGE

Letters of request for assistance shall be written in the language of the Requesting Party. Letters of request and their annexes shall be accompanied by a translation into an official language of the Requested Party.

ARTICLE 6 EXPENSES FOR LEGAL ASSISTANCE

1. The Requested Party shall pay the costs of providing legal assistance, except for the following expenses which shall be borne by the Requesting Party:

a) the travel, board and lodging expenses of persons travelling to the Requesting Party pursuant to a request for assistance as well as any allowances payable to that person. These shall be

按请求方的标准和规定支付；

（二）在请求方或被请求方的鉴定人的费用和酬金。

二、请求方应在请求中或所附文件中详细说明应付费用和酬金，若应当事人或鉴定人要求，请求方应预付这些费用和酬金。

三、如果执行请求明显需要一项巨大开支，双方应协商确定能够提供被请求的协助的费用和条件。

第七条 司法协助的拒绝

一、如有下列情况，被请求方可以拒绝协助：

（一）被请求方认为执行请求将损害其主权、安全、公共秩序或其他基本公共利益，或者认为案件在被请求方审理可能更为合适；

（二）按照被请求方的法律，请求书中提及的嫌疑犯、被告人或罪犯的行为在被请求方不构成犯罪；

（三）被请求方有充分的依据相信提供协助将便利对请求书所涉及的当事人基于种

paid according to the standards or regulations of the Requesting Party; and

b) the expenses and fees of experts either in the Requested or Requesting Party.

2. The Requesting Party shall specify in the request or accompanying document the expenses and fees payable and shall pay the expenses and fees in advance if so requested by the person or expert.

3. If it becomes apparent that the execution of the request requires expenses of an extraordinary nature, the Parties shall consult to determine the terms and conditions under which the requested assistance can be provided.

ARTICLE 7 REFUSAL OF LEGAL ASSISTANCE

1. Assistance may be refused by the Requested Party if:

a) the Requested Party considers that the execution of the request would impair its sovereignty, security, public order or other essential public interest, or the case may be more properly prosecuted by the Requested Party;

b) in accordance with the law of the Requested Party, the conduct of the suspect, defendant or convicted person referred to in the letter of request does not constitute an offence in the Requested Party; or

c) there are substantial grounds leading the Requested Party to believe that compliance would facilitate the prosecution or punishment of the

族、宗教、国籍或政治见解原因进行诉讼或处罚。

二、由于第一款所述原因或因为国内法律予以禁止而不能执行请求时,被请求方应迅速将请求和所附文件退回请求方,并应说明此项决定的理由。

三、在拒绝一项协助请求或暂缓提供此项协助前,被请求方应考虑是否可以根据它认为是必要的附加条件同意提供协助。如果请求方接受附加条件的协助,则应遵守这些条件。

第八条 认证

除第十六条规定的情况外,根据本条约转递的任何文件及其译文,无须任何形式的认证。

第二章 协助的请求

第九条 请求的内容

一、所有协助的请求均应包括以下内容:

(一)请求所涉及的进行调查取证或诉讼的主管机关的名称;

(二)对于调查取证或诉讼的说明,包括有关事实和法律的概述;

(三)提出请求的目的,

person to whom the request refers on account of race, religion, nationality or political opinions.

2. Where a request cannot be executed for the reasons in paragraph 1 or because execution is prohibited by domestic law, the Requested Party shall promptly return the request and accompanying documentation to the Requesting Party and shall give reasons for the decision.

3. Before refusing to grant a request for assistance or before postponing the grant of such assistance, the Requested Party shall consider whether assistance may be granted subject to such conditions as it deems necessary. If the Requesting Party accepts assistance subject to there conditions, it shall comply with them.

ARTICLE 8 AUTHENTICATION

Any documents or translations transmitted pursuant to this Treaty shall not require any form of authentication, subject to Article 16.

CHAPTER II REQUESTS FOR ASSISTANCE
ARTICLE 9 CONTENTS OF REQUESTS

1. In all cases requests for assistance shall include:

a) the name of the competent authority conducting the investigation or proceedings to which the request relates;

b) a description of the investigation or proceedings, including a summary of the relevant facts and laws;

c) the purpose for which the request is made

以及所寻求协助的性质;

（四）是否有保密的需要，以及需要保密的理由;

（五）执行请求的时间限制。

二、协助的请求还应包括以下情况：

（一）如有可能，作为调查取证或诉讼对象的人员的身份、国籍和所在地;

（二）如有必要，对请求方希望予以遵守的特定程序或要求的详细说明及其理由;

（三）如果请求调查取证或者搜查和扣押，表明有根据相信在被请求方管辖范围内可能发现证据的陈述;

（四）如果请求向个人调查取证，是否需要其宣誓或不经宣誓而提供正式证词的陈述，以及对所寻求的证据或证言的说明;

（五）如遇转借证据的情况，保管证据的人员，证据将移送的地点，进行检验和归还证据的时间;

（六）如遇在押人员作证的情况，在移交期间实施拘押的人员的情况，移交在押人员

and the nature of the assistance sought;

d) the need, if any, for confidentiality and the reasons therefore; and

e) any time limit within which compliance with the request is desired.

2. Requests for assistance shall also contain the following information:

a) where possible, the identity, nationality and location of the person or persons who are the subject of the investigation or proceedings;

b) where necessary, details of any particular procedure or requirement that the Requesting Party wishes to be followed and the reasons therefore;

c) in the case of requests for the taking of evidence or search and seizure, a statement indicating the basis for belief that evidence may be found in the jurisdiction of the Requested Party;

d) in the case of requests to take evidence from a person, a statement as to whether sworn or affirmed statements are required, and a description of the subject matter of the evidence or statement sought;

e) in the case of lending of exhibits, the person or class of persons who will have custody of the exhibit, the place to which the exhibit is to be removed, any tests to be conducted and the date by which the exhibit will be returned; and

f) in the case of making detained persons available, the person or class of persons who will have custody during the transfer, the place to

地点和交还该人的时间。

三、如果被请求方认为请求中提供的材料不足以使该项请求得以执行，可以要求提供补充材料。

四、请求应以书面方式提出。在紧急情况下或在被请求方允许的其他情况下，请求也可以口头方式提出，但在此后应迅速以书面方式确认。

第十条 延期

如果执行请求将妨碍被请求方正在进行的调查取证或诉讼，被请求方可以暂缓提供协助，但应迅速将此通知请求方。

第十一条 通知执行结果

一、被请求方应通过本条约第三条规定的途径，将执行请求的结果以书面方式通知请求方。适当时，通知应附有送达证明或已获得的证据。

二、送达证明应包括日期、地点和送达方法的说明，并应由送达文件的机关和收件人签署。如果收件人拒绝签署，送达证明中应对此加以说明。

which the detained person is to be transferred and the date of that person's return.

3. If the Requested Party considers that the information contained in the request is not sufficient to enable the request to be dealt with, that Party may request that additional details be furnished.

4. A request shall be made in writing. In urgent circumstances or where otherwise permitted by the Requested Party, a request may be made orally but shall be confirmed in writing promptly thereafter.

ARTICLE 10 POSTPONEMENT

Assistance may be postponed by the Requested Party if execution of the request would interfere with an ongoing investigation or prosecution in the Requested Party, however it shall promptly notify this to the Requesting Party.

ARTICLE 11 NOTIFICATION OF THE RESULTS OF EXECUTION

1. The Requested Party, shall through the channels stipulated in Article 3 of this Treaty, notify the Requesting Party in written form of the results of the execution of the request. As appropriate, notification shall be accompanied by any proof of service of evidence obtained.

2. Proof of service shall contain the date, place and a description of the method of service. It should be signed by the authority who served the document and by the addressee. If the addressee refuses to sign, the proof of service should include

第十二条 在被请求方进行的协助

一、被请求方应当根据请求，将其执行协助请求的时间和地点通知请求方。

二、在被请求方法律不予禁止的范围内，被请求方应准许请求方与调查取证或诉讼有关的司法人员或其他人员在被请求方的主管机关根据一项请求进行调查取证或提供其他协助时到场，并按照被请求方同意的方式提问和进行逐字记录。

第十三条 在押人员作证

一、一方应根据另一方的请求将已在其境内被拘禁的人移交到请求方到场作证，但须经该人同意且有双方中央机关已就移交条件事先达成的书面协议。

二、根据被请求方的要求，请求方应对移交到其境内的上述人员继续予以拘禁，并在作证完毕或双方商定的期限内将其交还被请求方。

a statement to this effect.

ARTICLE 12 ASSISTANCE IN THE REQUESTED PARTY

1. The Requested Party shall, upon request, inform the Requesting Party of the time and place of execution of the request for assistance.

2. To the extent not prohibited by the law of the Requested Party, the Requested Party shall permit the judicial personnel or other persons concerned in the investigation or proceeding in the Requesting Party to be present when the competent authorities of the Requested Party carry out investigations or provide other assistance pursuant to a request and to pose questions and make a verbatim transcript in a manner agreed to by the Requested Party.

ARTICLE 13 TESTIMONY BY THE DETAINED PERSON

1. For the purpose of testimony by personal appearance, a person in custody in the territory of one Party shall, at the request of the other Party, be transferred to the Requesting Party, provided the person consents and there is prior written agreement by the Central Authorities on the conditions of the transfer.

2. In accordance with the request of the Requested Party, the Requesting Party shall keep the person transferred to its territory in custody and shall return that person to the Requested Party at the conclusion of the testimony or within the time limit agreed to by both parties.

三、请求方接到被请求方有关无须对上述人员继续予以拘禁的通知时,应恢复该人的自由,并按照第十四条和第十五条有关提供协助或证据的人员的规定,给予其应有的待遇。

第十四条 在请求方境内作证或协助调查

一、请求方可以邀请被请求方境内的人员到请求方境内作证或协助调查。

二、被请求方应向被邀请人转交上述请求,并通知请求方该人是否同意接受此项请求。

第十五条 证人和鉴定人的保护

一、请求方对于到其境内作证的证人或进行鉴定的鉴定人,不得因其入境前的任何犯罪而追究其刑事责任、逮捕、拘留,或以任何其他方式剥夺或限制其人身自由,也不应强迫该人在与请求无关的任何诉讼中作证。

二、如果证人或鉴定人在

3. Where the Requesting Party receives notice from the Requested Party that the transferred person is no longer required to be held in custody, that person shall be set at liberty and treated as a person giving assistance or evidence as provided for in Article 14 and Article 15.

ARTICLE 14 GIVING EVIDENCE OR ASSISTING INVESTIGATIONS IN THE REQUESTING PAPTY

1. The Requesting Party may invite a person in the territory of the Requested Party to appear in the territory of the Requesting Party to testify or to assist an investigation.

2. The Requested Party shall transmit the said request to that person and notify the Requesting Party as to whether the person agrees to comply with the request.

ARTICLE 15 PROTECTION OF WITNESSES AND EXPERTS

1. A witness or expert appearing in the Requesting Party to give evidence or expert evaluation shall not be subjected to investigation of criminal responsibilities, arrest, to detention or deprivation or limit of personal liberty in any other form by the Requesting Party for any offence committed before entry into its territory nor shall that person be obliged to give evidence in any proceeding other than the proceedings to which the request relates.

2. A witness or expert shall forfeit the

接到请求方关于其不必继续停留的通知之日起十五天后仍未离境，或者离境后又自愿返回，则丧失第一款给予的保护。但是，证人或鉴定人因本人无法控制的原因而未离开请求方领土的时间不应包括在内。

三、双方均不应对未按照请求或传唤到请求方境内的人进行威胁或予以惩罚。

四、主管机关请求被请求方的证人前来作证明，应保证向证人充分说明其对法庭所负的责任和义务，以保证该证人避免因蔑视法庭或类似的行为而被起诉。

五、本条不应妨碍第十三条第二款规定的交还已经被移交的在押人员的义务。

第十六条 文件和物品的转递

一、当协助的请求涉及转递文件和记录时，被请求方可以转递经证明无误的真实副本，除非请求方明示要求原件。

protection granted in paragraph 1 if that person has not left the territory of the Requesting Party after fifteen days from the date of notification by the Requesting Party that person's presence is no longer required or, having left that territory has voluntarily returned. But this period of time shall not include the time during which the witness or expert is unable to leave the territory of the Requesting Party for reasons beyond that person's control.

3. Neither of the Parties shall threaten or impose any sanctions against a person who fails to appear in the Requesting Party in response to a request or summons.

4. The competent authority which seeks the appearance of a witness from the Requested Party for the purpose of testimony, shall ensure that the witness is properly instructed regarding responsibilities and obligations to the court so as to ensure that the witness is not subjected to contempt or similar proceedings.

5. This Article shall not affect the obligation to return a person transferred in custody, as provided in Article 13(2).

ARTICLE 16 TRANSMISSION OF DOCUMENTS AND OBJECTS

1. When the request for assistance concerns the transmission of records and documents, the Requested Party may transmit certified true copies thereof, unless the Requesting Party expressly requests the originals.

二、转递给请求方的记录或文件的原件和物品，应根据被请求方的要求尽快予以返还。

三、在被请求方法律不予禁止的范围内，转递文件、物品和记录应符合请求方要求的方式或附有其要求的证明，以使它们可根据请求方的法律得以接受。

第十七条 赃款赃物

一、一方可以根据请求，尽力确定因发生在另一方境内的犯罪而产生的赃款赃物是否在其境内，并将调查结果通知该另一方。为此，请求方应向被请求方提供据以确认赃款赃物在被请求方境内的情况和资料。

二、被请求方一旦发现前款所述赃款赃物，则应采取其法律所允许的措施对赃款赃物予以冻结、扣押或没收。

三、在法律允许的范围内，被请求方可以根据请求方的请求将上述赃款赃物移交给请求方。但此项移交不得侵害与这些财物有关的第三者的权利。

2. The original records or documents and the objects transmitted to the Requesting Party shall be returned to the Requested Party as soon as possible, upon the latter's request.

3. Insofar as not prohibited by the law of the Requested Party, documents, objects and records shall be transmitted in a form or accompanied by such certification as may be requested by the Requesting Party in order to make them admissible according to the law of the Requesting Party.

ARTICLE 17 PROCEEDS OF CRIME

1. One Party may, upon request, endeavour to ascertain whether any proceeds of a crime committed in the territory of the other Party are located within its jurisdiction and shall notify the other Party of the results of its inquiries. The Requesting Party shall provide the Requested Party with data and information which constitute the basis of its belief that such proceeds may be located in this jurisdiction.

2. Where, pursuant to paragraph 1 of this Article, the suspected proceeds of crime are found, the Requested Party shall take such measures as are permitted by its law to freeze, seize and confiscate such proceeds.

3. To the extent permitted by its law, the Requested Party may, at the request of the Requesting Party, transfer to the latter the above-mentioned proceeds of crime, but such transfer shall not infringe upon the rights of a third party

四、如果上述赃款赃物对被请求方境内其他未决刑事案件的审理是必不可少的，被请求方得暂缓移交。

五、双方应在各自法律允许的范围内，在向被害人进行补偿的有关诉讼中相互协助。

第十八条　外交和领事官员送达文书和调查取证

一方可以通过其派驻在另一方的外交或领事官员向在该另一方境内的本国国民送达文书和调查取证，但不得违反驻在国法律，并不得采取任何强制措施。

第十九条　刑事诉讼结果的通报

一方应根据请求向另一方通报其对该另一方国民做出的刑事判决和裁定，并提供判决书和裁定书的副本。

第二十条　犯罪记录的提供

一方应根据请求，向另一方提供正在该另一方境内被追究刑事责任的人在前一方的犯罪记录和法院对其进行审判的有关情况。

to such proceeds.

4. If the above-mentioned proceeds of crime are indispensable to other pending criminal proceedings in the territory of the Requested Party, the Requested Party may delay such transfer.

5. The Parties shall assist each other, to the extent permitted by their respective laws, in proceedings related to restitution to the victims of crime.

ARTICLE 18 SERVICE OF DOCUMENTS AND TAKING OF EVIDENCE BY DIPLOMATIC AND CONSULAR OFFICIALS

Either Party may serve documents on and take evidence from its nationals in the territory of the other Party through its diplomatic or consular officials therein, provided that the laws of the other Party will not be violated and no compulsory measures of any kind will be taken.

ARTICLE 19 NOTIFICATION OF RESULTS OF PROCEEDINGS IN CRIMINAL MATTERS

One Party shall, upon request, inform the other Party of judgments and decisions in criminal matters against nationals of the other Party, and provide copies of the judgments and decisions.

ARTICLE 20 SUPPLY OF CRIMINAL RECORDS

One Party shall, upon request, provide the other Party with criminal records and information concerning its court proceedings against the person being investigated in a criminal matter in the territory of the other Party.

第二十一条 保密和使用的限制

一、被请求方在与请求方协商后，可以要求对其所提供的情报、证据或者这些情报、证据的来源予以保密，或者仅在它所确定的条件和情况下予以公开或使用。

二、被请求方应根据请求，对一项请求及其内容、辅助文件和按照请求所采取的行动予以保密，但为执行该请求所必需时则不受此限制。

三、请求方在未事先得到被请求方同意时，不应超出请求书中所说明的目的公开或使用所提供的情报或证据。

第三章 最后条款

第二十二条 争议的解决

本条约执行中产生的任何争议均应通过外交途径解决。

第二十三条 其他协助

一、本条约不应损害双方根据其他条约、协定或在其他方面承担的义务，也不妨碍双方根据其他条约、协定或在其他方面相互提供或继续提供协助。

二、本条约适用于条约生

ARTICLE 21 CONFIDENTIALITY AND LIMITATION OF USE

1. The Requested Party may require, after consultation with the Requesting Party, that information or evidence furnished or the source of such information or evidence be kept confidential or be disclosed or used only subject to such terms and conditions as it may specify.

2. The Requested Party shall, to the extent requested, keep confidential a request, its contents, supporting documents and any action taken pursuant to the request except to the extent necessary to execute it.

3. The Requesting Party shall not disclose or use information or evidence furnished for purposes other than those stated in the request without the prior consent of the Requested Party.

CHAPTER III FINAL PROVISIONS

ARTICLE 22 SETTLEMENT OF DISPUTES

Any difficulties arising from the implementation of this Treaty shall be settled through the diplomatic channel.

ARTICLE 23 OTHER ASSISTANCE

1. This Treaty shall not derogate from obligations subsisting between the Parties whether pursuant to other treaties, arrangements or otherwise, or prevent the Parties providing or continuing to provide assistance to each other pursuant to other treaties, arrangements or otherwise.

2. This Treaty shall apply to any requests

效后提出的任何请求,即使该请求所涉及的行为或不行为发生在条约生效之前。

第二十四条 生效

本条约应自双方通过外交途径相互通知已经完成各自的法律手续之日起第二个月的第一天开始生效。

第二十五条 终止

本条约自任何一方通过外交途径书面提出终止之日起六个月后失效。否则,本条约应持续有效。

下列签署人经各自政府正式授权在本条约上签字,以昭信守。

本条约于一九九四年七月二十九日在北京签订,一式两份;每份均用中文、英文和法文写成,三种文本同等作准。

中华人民共和国代表钱其琛(签字)加拿大代表安德烈·乌莱特(签字)

presented after its entry into force even if the relevant acts or omissions occurred before that date.

ARTICLE 24 ENTRY INTO FORCE

This Treaty shall enter into force on the first day of the second month after the date on which the Parties have notified each other through the diplomatic channel that their legal procedures have been complied with.

ARTICLE 25 TERMINATION

This Treaty shall remain in force until the expiry of six months after the date when either Party has given written notice of termination through the diplomatic channel. Otherwise, the present Treaty shall remain valid.

IN WITNESS WHEREOF, the undersigned, being duly authorized thereto by their respective Governments, have signed this Treaty.

DONE at Beijing on this 29 day of July. One thousand nine hundred and ninety four in two copies, in the Chinese, English and French languages, each version being equally authentic.

For the government of the People's Republic of China Qian Qichen(signature)

For the government of Canada Andrea Houlette (signature)

范例二:备忘录

> **中华人民共和国政府和菲律宾共和国政府关于油气开发合作的谅解备忘录**
> Memorandum of Understanding on Cooperation on Oil and Gas Development Between the Government of the People's Republic of China and the Government of the Republic of the Philippines

一、基础。

忆及《联合国宪章》,1982年《联合国海洋法公约》和2002年《南海各方行为宣言》,认识到中华人民共和国政府和菲律宾共和国政府通过积极对话和务实合作在探索海上合作的机遇和方式上取得实质进展和有意义的收获,并为地区和平、稳定和发展做出重要贡献。

二、基本原则。

本着"相互尊重、公平互利、灵活务实、协商一致"的原则,经过平等友好协商,双方决定根据有关国际法加快谈判相关安排(下称合作安排),为双方在有关海域的油气勘探

I. Context.

Recalling the Charter of the United Nations, the 1982 United Nations Convention on the Law of the Sea (UNCLOS) and the 2002 Declaration on the Conduct of Parties in the South China Sea, and acknowledging that through positive dialogue and practical cooperation, the government of the People's Republic of China and the government of the Republic of the Philippines (hereinafter referred to as "the two governments") have made substantial progress and meaningful gains in exploring opportunities and means to cooperate with each other in maritime activities, which has made significant contributions to peace, stability and development in the region.

II. Basic Principle.

In accordance with the principles of "mutual respect, fairness and mutual benefit, flexibility and pragmatism and consensus", through equal and friendly consultation, the two governments have decided to negotiate on an accelerated basis arrangements to facilitate oil and gas exploration

和开采提供便利。

三、工作机制。

（一）双方将设立政府间联合指导委员会（下称委员会）和企业间工作组（下称工作组）。委员会由双方外交部担任共同主席，由双方能源部门担任共同副主席，双方相关部门参与。委员会由双方提名相同人数的成员组成。工作组由经双方授权的企业代表组成。

（二）委员会负责谈判、达成合作安排及其适用的海域（下称合作区域），并决定需建立的工作组数量及具体位置（下称工作区块）。工作组负责谈判、达成适用于相关工作区块的企业间技术和商业安排。

（三）中方授权中国海洋

and exploitation in relevant maritime areas consistent with applicable rules of international law (hereinafter referred to as "the cooperation arrangements").

Ⅲ. Working Mechanism.

(1) The two governments will establish an Inter-Governmental Joint Steering Committee (hereinafter referred to as "Committee") and one or more Inter-Entrepreneurial Working Group (hereinafter referred to as "Working Group"). The Committee will be co-chaired by the Foreign Ministries, and co-vice chaired by the Energy Ministries, with the participation of relevant agencies of the two governments, and will comprise an equal number of members nominated by the two governments. Each Working Group will consist of representatives from enterprises authorized by the two governments.

(2) The Committee will be responsible for negotiating and agreeing the cooperation arrangements and the maritime areas to which they will apply (hereinafter referred to as the "cooperation area"),and deciding the number of Working Groups to be established and for which part of the cooperation area each Working Group is established (hereinafter referred to as its "working area"). Each Working Group will negotiate and agree on inter-entrepreneurial technical and commercial arrangements that will apply in the relevant working area.

(3) China authorizes China National Offshore

石油集团有限公司作为中方参与企业。菲方将授权在适用本协议的工作区块内与菲律宾有服务合同的一家或多家企业，若特定工作区块无此类企业则授权菲律宾国家石油勘探公司作为菲方参与企业。

（四）双方将在本备忘录签订后12个月内致力于就合作安排达成一致。委员会和工作组将定期接触，以推进相关工作。

四、有关立场。

本谅解备忘录以及双方或双方企业根据该备忘录进行的所有讨论、谈判和活动都不影响双方各自法律立场。本谅解备忘录不产生任何国际法或国内法上的权利和义务。

五、信息性质。

双方以及根据本谅解备忘录授权参与的企业所共享的任何信息应予保密，除非双方另有规定。

Oil Corporation as the Chinese enterprise for each Working Group. The Philippines will authorize the enterprise(s) that has/have entered into a service contract with the Philippines with respect to the applicable working area or, if there is no such enterprise for a particular working area, the Philippine National Oil Company—Exploration Corporation (PNOC-EC), as the Philippine enterprise(s) for the relevant Working Group.

(4) The two governments will endeavour to agree on the cooperation arrangements within twelve (12) months of this Memorandum of Understanding. The Committee and each Working Group will meet regularly to discharge their respective functions.

Ⅳ. Relevant Position.

This Memorandum of Understanding, and all discussions, negotiations and activities of the two governments or their authorized enterprises under or pursuant to this Memorandum of Understanding, will be without prejudice to the respective legal positions of both governments. This Memorandum of Understanding does not create rights or obligations under international or domestic law.

V. Nature of Information.

Any information shared by the two governments or their authorized enterprises under or pursuant to this Memorandum of Understanding will be kept confidential, unless the two governments decide otherwise.

六、其他事项。

任何与本谅解备忘录有关的其他事项可提交委员会或工作组商定。

本谅解备忘录于二〇一八年十一月二十日在马尼拉签署，一式两份，每份均用中文和英文写成，两种文本同等作准。

中华人民共和国政府代表

王毅（签名）

菲律宾共和国政府代表

Teodoro Locsin（签名）

VI. Other Matters.

Any other matters relating to this Memorandum of Understanding may be referred jointly by the two governments to the Committee or a Working Group for consultation and agreement.

Done in Manila on the 20th November, 2018, in duplicated in the Chinese and English languages, both texts being equally authentic.

For the government of the People's Republic of China

Wang Yi (signature)

For the government of the Republic of the Philippines

Teodoro Locsin (signature)

三、外交条约的翻译原则与难点

外交条约是一种法律文本，法律的主要作用在于调节法律主体的关系、规范法律主体的行为。这种调节和规范作用主要通过法律条文实现，因此法律文本的语言与一般的文本语言相比有独特鲜明的特征，无论在用词、句法还是篇章结构方面都体现了法律制定者的意愿或意志。译者在翻译外交条约时首先要考虑其作为法律文本的语言特征，在此基础上尽可能做到忠实与精确，既要忠实于条约制定者的意愿和意志，更要精确地把该意愿或意志表达出来，不但要忠实于原文的内容，还要尽可能保留原文的表达方式。法律文本一般采用直接、简洁、清楚的语言表述其规范和要求，这样能让读者立刻了解文本内容、不产生歧义，杜绝费解或误解现象的发生。考虑到外交条约的阅读对象不但包括懂法律的专业人士，也有普通的、不懂法律的读者，译者在翻译外交条约时也应确保语言通顺易懂，扫除读者的阅读障碍。最后，译者翻译外交条约时还需再现原文风格。从行文风格来看，法律文本一般不讲求语言的生动形象，而是以冷静客观、理性权威作为主要特征，并且也忌讳语言的变化多样。译者应当剥离情感，保持客观理性，体现法律文本的客观性和权威性，并且在翻译专业术语时力求保持上下文的统一。

外交条约翻译的难点与其特点相关。外交条约是一种法律条文，涉及非常多的法律专业知识，因此从事外交条约翻译的译者应当具备相应的法律知识储备，不但需要了解相关的术语内容和行业知识，还要具备在特定语境中灵活运用知识、精准把握术语内涵的能力。语言的精确性和专业性是翻译外交条约时译者不得不面对的两个难点。

四 外交条约的英译技巧

1 外交条约的概念、内涵的理解及翻译

上文中选取的第一个例子《中华人民共和国和加拿大关于刑事司法协助的条约》是外交条约中法律效力最强的类型。条约内容是两国关于刑事司法方面的协议，因此从文体上来看特别讲求严谨准确。第二个例子《中华人民共和国政府和菲律宾共和国政府关于油气开发合作的谅解备忘录》是外交条约中受法律约束最弱、甚至没有法律约束力的协议文书。主要内容是两国关于未来油气开发合作初步框架的协商，因此在遵循法律语言规范要求方面并不是很严格。

正如前文所言，广义的外交条约不但包括条约，还涵盖了公约、协定、换文、联合宣言、宪章、谅解备忘录等多种形式。英语中也有 agreement、bond、bargain、compact、contract、convention、covenant、entente、pact、settlement、treaty、understanding 等词，用以表达"协议、契约、合同"等意义。在翻译具体的法律术语时必须从细微处着手，深入理解其内涵，从而选择恰当的词汇，外交条约标题的翻译尤其如此。比如从《中华人民共和国和加拿大关于刑事司法协助的条约》标题可见，该协议文书属于狭义的外交条约。"条约"一词在中文中定义为"国家和国家签订的有关政治、军事、经济或文化等方面的权利和义务的文书"[1]，与"条约"最契合的英文翻译是 treaty，因为从法律层面来看，treaty 是指 A compact made between two or more independent nations with a view to the public welfare. A treaty is an agreement in written form between nation-states (or international agencies, such

---

[1] 中国社会科学院语言研究所词典编辑室.2008.现代汉语词典（第7版）.北京：商务印书馆，1299.

as the United Nations, that have been given treaty-making capacity by the states that created them) that is intended to establish a relationship governed by International Law. It may be contained in a single instrument or in two or more related instruments such as an exchange of diplomatic notes. 对比可见，"条约"是"国家与国家签订的"，treaty 是 made between two or more independent nations；"条约"是"文书"，treaty 是 in written form。因此，这个文书标题被译作 Treaty Between the People's Republic of China and Canada on Mutual Legal Assistance in Criminal Matter。第二个例子的文本属于"谅解备忘录"。"谅解备忘录"一词是由英语中的名词短语 Memorandum of Understanding（有时也写作 Memo of Understanding，简写为 MOU）直译而来。因此，《中华人民共和国政府和菲律宾共和国政府关于油气开发合作的谅解备忘录》可以直接回译成 Memorandum of Understanding on Cooperation on Oil and Gas Development Between the Government of the People's Republic of China and the Government of the Republic of the Philippines。译者一定要厘清所译文书是外交条约中的哪种类型，掌握定义内涵，才能正确翻译条约文书的标题，这是外交条约翻译的首要任务。

  公约一般是多边条约，通常指三个以上的国际法主体为解决政治、经济、文化、技术等重大国际问题举行国际会议，最后缔结的多方面条约。公约通常为开放性的，非缔约主体可以在公约生效前或生效后的任何时候加入，有的公约由专门召集的国际会议制定。"公约"译成英语常用 convention，比如《联合国海洋法公约》译作 United Nations Convention on the Law of the Sea，《维也纳外交关系公约》译作 Vienna Convention on Diplomatic Relations。"协定"是指国际法主体为解决专门或临时性问题而签订的契约性条约，主要包括文化交流协定、贸易协定、停战协定等。协定的时效性一般较短，协定缔结的程序比较简便，除必须经过一定部门批准外，一般签字后即可生效。"协定"译成英语一般用 agreement，比如《关税与贸易总协定》译作 General Agreement on Tariffs and Trade，《中华人民共和国政府和毛里求斯共和国政府关于互免签证的协定》译作 Agreement on Mutual Visa Exemption Between the Government of the People's Republic of China and the Government of the Republic of Mauritius。宪章是指国际法主体间关于某一重要国际组织的基本文件，具有国际条约的性质。一般规定该国际组织的宗旨、原则、组织机构、职权范围、议事程序以及成员国的权利义务等，属于多边条约的一种。"宪章"译成英语一般用 charter，比如《联合国宪章》译作 Charter of the United Nations，《世界卫生组织宪章》译作 The Charter of the World Health Organization。

2 外交条约的体例特点及英译

外交条约都有相应的体例。翻译时应当注意各种条约文书的体例特征，尽量保持原文的结构、程式及体例安排，遵循法律文书的体例要求。

首先，从结构布局来看，第一个例子的体例包括"章""条""款"和"项"。一方面，译者必须明白"章""条""款""项"之间的层级关系，专有名词不能跨级越界使用，比如"章"译作 chapter，而"条"译作 article，两者的层次关系明确，"条"在"章"之下，因此 article 也在 chapter 之下，不能因为译名不同而出现层级混乱。"款"和"项"在原文中本身就没有用专名表示，而是采用不同的数字形式加以体现。比如，原文第六条司法协助的费用中一共有三款，每款用中文数字"一、二、三"标明，第一款包含了两项，用带括号的中文数字"（一）、（二）"表示。在译文中，译者也采用了相应的数字或符号表示，用阿拉伯数字"1. 2. 3."替代表示"款"的中文数字"一、二、三"，而表示"项"、带括号的中文数字"（一）、（二）"在翻译时用带半括号的小写英文字母"a), b)"来表示。据此，读者可以确定表示方法，明确全文的体例关系。另一方面，整个条约文书中的体例要有连贯性，确保每个层级之间的一致性，Chapter I 之后是 Chapter II 而不是 Chapter 2；Article 1 之后是 Article 2，而不是 Article II。也就是说，如"章"的层级上使用罗马数字表示顺序，不能中途变换为拉丁数字，反之亦然。除此在外，大小写也需在同一个层级上保持一致。比如，译者在翻译"章""条"及其标题时使用的都是大写字母，那么通篇文书的翻译都应一致。最后，译文条款数目应与原文一致。比如，原文有三章，译文也应有三章；原文的某一章有二十条，译文也应当有二十条；某一款有十项，译文同样应有十项。不能因为其中某两项有意义重复而自作主张合并，或者某一项内容比较多而拆成多项。因此，在翻译外交条约时不但要保留原文的体例结构布局，而且要保持不同体例形式的前后一致以及同一体例的始终相同。

其次，从内容来看，外交条约文书一般包括说明条约的缔结、生效、适用、解释、无效、终止和暂停施行等内容，但具体到每一个外交文书时又各不相同。比如第一个范例就几乎涵盖了上述所有内容，介绍了开展刑事司法协助的缔结主体，生效的条件，协助的范围，协助的途径，条约实施时适用的法律，采用的语言，具体情形的解释，产生争议的解决方法，条约生效和终止的前提和时间期限等。而第二个范例则更为简明，整个谅解备忘录只包括了合作的前提和基础，合作的原则，合作的机制以及法律效力等。作为译者，不但需要了解外交条约文书的一般内容，还应透彻掌握条约每一个款项的具体内容和内涵，在此基础上完成文本的翻译工作。

3 外交条约的文体特点及英译

1）外交条约的措辞特征及英译

外交条约文本属于法律文献，常用到法律专有术语，且在行文措辞上不带感情色彩。用词比较正式、严谨，喜欢用一些所谓的大词，比如不用 tell 而用 inform，不用 ask 而用 inquire，不用 after 而用 sequent，不用 given 而用 accorded，不用 begin 或 start 而用 institute 或 commence，不用 stop 而用 cease，不用 next to 而用 contiguous to，不用 hide 而用 conceal，不用 Minnesota corporation 而用 corporation organized and existing under Minnesota Laws 等等，不一而足[1]。

> **原文** 一方应根据另一方的请求将已在其境内被拘禁的人移交到请求方到场作证，但须经该人同意且有双方中央机关已就移交条件事先达成的书面协议。

> **译文** <u>For the purpose of</u> testimony by personal appearance, a person in custody in the territory of one Party shall, at the request of the other Party, be transferred to the Requesting Party, <u>provided</u> the person consents and there is <u>prior</u> written agreement by the Central Authorities on the conditions of the transfer.

在此例中，For the purpose of、provided、prior 相较于 for、if 和 before 来说是大词，使用这些词让译文显得庄重正式，书面意味浓厚。

在法律文本中经常出现法律语域中的专有术语，往往涉及特定的法律概念，翻译时要尽可能体现法律语言的专业性，尽可能找到与之对应的准确词汇，而不是随便找一个意思相近的词代替。译文中尽量使用专业词汇，以使译文更专业、更权威、更可信。比如"被告"一词，英语中就有几个词表示这个意思，译者需弄清是民事、行政案件中的被告，还是刑事案件中的被告，前者是 defendant，而后者是 the accused；同样是裁决书，仲裁出具的是 award，而陪审团出具的是 verdict；同样是判决，民事或行政案件的判决是 judgement，终审判决是 determination，而刑事判决是 sentence。

> **原文** 本条约自任何一方通过外交途径书面提出<u>终止</u>之日起六个月后<u>失效</u>。否则，本条约应持续<u>有效</u>。

---

1 李长栓. 2004. 非文学翻译理论与实践. 北京：中国对外翻译出版公司，第189页.

> **译文** This Treaty shall remain in force until the <u>expiry</u> of six months after the date when either Party has given written notice of <u>termination</u> through the diplomatic channel. Otherwise, the present Treaty shall remain <u>valid</u>.

这句话里的 expiry、termination 和 valid 分别表示法律上的"终了，(期)满了"，"终止"和"有效"的意思，并没有翻译成更为常见的 cease、end 或者 effective。

> **原文** 如遇<u>在押人员</u>作证的情况，在移交期间<u>实施拘押</u>的人员的情况，移交在押人的地点和交还该人的时间。

> **译文** In the case of making <u>detained persons</u> available, the person or class of persons who will have <u>custody</u> during the transfer, the place to which the detained person is to be transferred and the date of that person's return.

> **原文** 双方均不应对未按照请求或<u>传唤</u>到请求方境内的人进行威胁或予以<u>惩罚</u>。

> **译文** Neither of the Parties shall threaten or impose any <u>sanctions</u> against a person who fails to appear in the Requesting Party in response to a request or <u>summons</u>.

从上面两个例子的原文来看，"在押人员""实施拘押""传唤""惩罚"等词语明显提示这是一篇法律文本，因此译文要体现法律语域的特征就必须使用专业术语，它们分别被译作 detained persons、have custody、summons 和 sanctions。这些措辞反映了文本的法律特征，尤其是 custody 这个词，由于词意过于专业，极少在普通文本中使用。

同时，还有一些常见词汇，用于法律语域时，常被赋予特别的意义。翻译这些词汇时，不但要掌握其常见的基本意义，更要了解其在法律文本中的特有意义。比如 deed 在一般文本中表示"行为"，但是在法律文书中表示"文据、契约、证书"；satisfaction 不但可以表"满意"，还可以表示法律意义上的"清偿、补偿"；prejudice 不仅仅是"偏见"，还能表达"损害、侵害"之意。

> **原文** 如遇转借<u>证据</u>的情况，<u>保管证据</u>的人员，证据将移送的地点，进行检验和归还证据的时间。

> **译文** In the case of lending of <u>exhibits</u>, the person or class of persons who will <u>have custody of the exhibit</u>, the place to which the exhibit is to be removed, any tests to be conducted and the date by which the exhibit will be returned.

exhibit 一般作动词用，表示"展示、展览、陈列"，但也可作名词，表示"展览（品）、陈列（品）"之意。当这个常见词用在法律语域，所表达的意思就和常见意义不同了。在法律领域中的 exhibit 一般表达两个意思：一是展示证据，指审判期间向法院、仲裁员等提交的、作为证据的文件或物品（包括照片），比如向证人出示的以及证人在作证过程中提到的文件或物品；二是在提出申请或进行辩护时附于诉状、声明、口供或其他文件的证据材料。原文的证据一词，之所以没有翻译成常见的 evidence，是因为 evidence 的概念相对而言比较宽泛，而这里的证据是指要向法庭提交的证据材料，因此使用 exhibit 一词更为准确。

原文 本条约适用于条约生效后提出的任何请求，即使该请求所涉及的行为或不行为发生在条约生效之前。

译文 This Treaty shall apply to any requests presented after its entry into force even if the relevant acts or omissions occurred before that date.

omissions 常见的意思是"省略、遗漏、缺漏"，但此处不指常见意义，而是表示个人或公众有义务，或法律要求其采取行动却未执行应有行动的状态，指引发诉讼的玩忽职守或不当行为。在此意义上，omission 是 act 的反义词。如果不认真查阅字典和资料，就无法获知此意义。

原文 被请求方一旦发现前款所述赃款赃物，则应采取其法律所允许的措施对赃款赃物予以冻结、扣押或没收。

译文 Where, pursuant to Paragraph 1 of this Article, the suspected proceeds of crime are found, the Requested Party shall take such measures as are permitted by its law to freeze, seize and confiscate such proceeds.

proceeds 最常见的意思是"收益、销售额、结果"，但是在法律语境，它指通过犯罪行为获得的现金或实物收益，这个词就引申出赃款、赃物的意思。同样 freeze, seize 和 confiscate 由于处在法律语域，也被赋予专业的法律意义。另外 pursuant to 相当于 in accordance with，是一个非常正式的法律用语。

通常而言，"之乎者也""兹""系"等为古汉语常用词汇，但在现代汉语中使用较少。然而，这些词汇在中文外交条约文书中频频出现，一方面能让文本更为简洁，同时也使文本更显庄重正式。翻译此类古汉语词汇时，应当尽量避免使用过于口语化的词汇，多使用与法律相关的套语和习语。

原文 前款所述"中央机关",在中华人民共和国方面系指其司法部,在加拿大方面系指其司法部长或司法部长指定的官员。

译文 Central Authorities <u>for the purpose of</u> preceding paragraph <u>mean</u>, for the People's Republic of China, the Ministry of Justice; and for Canada, the Minister of Justice or an official designated by the Minister of Justice.

在这个例子中,"所"和"系"是古代汉语中的常用词汇,此处的"所"应当和"为"配合使用,表示被动,比如"先即制人,后则为人所制"[1],因此这里的完整表达应是"为前款所述",即指"中央机关",这一概念在前文已经被提及过,接下来就是给这个概念下定义。"前款所述"对"中央机关"一词起修饰限定作用。译文采用 for the purpose of 表达"关乎,涉及"之意,而未采用更为常见的同义短语 in regards to 来表达类似意义,从而使译文更为书面化。此处的"系"字在古代汉语里意为"是",是个判断词,相当于英语系动词 be,因此可译成 are,但译文中却使用了 mean 代替 are,用来下定义,书面性更强,同时增添了文章的庄重性。与此相似的是,在英语的法律平行文本中,经常使用古英语或中古英语。这些古体词在现代英语文本中同样少见,但在法律英语中这些词的使用会让文本更显权威性,其中使用频率较高的是用 here、there 或者 where 加介词构成的副词,比如 hereafter、herein、hereunder、hereby、hereinafter、hereinbefore、hereunto、thereto、thereunto、therewith、thereby、whereby、wherein、whereas、wheresoever、whereof。此外,值得注意的是,法律文本几乎不使用如 very、rather 等带有主观情绪或起加强作用的副词。

原文 中华人民共和国和加拿大(以下简称"双方"),在相互尊重主权和平等互利的基础上,为加强两国在刑事司法协助领域的密切合作,决定缔结本条约。

译文 The People's Republic of China and Canada (<u>thereinafter</u> referred to as "the Parties") desiring to strengthen their close cooperation in the field of mutual legal assistance in criminal matters on the basis of mutual respect for sovereignty and equality and mutual benefit, have <u>hereby</u> resolved to conclude this Treaty.

---

1 《古代汉语词典》编写组. 2012. 古代汉语词典. 北京:商务印书馆,第1505页。

Thereinafter 表 from this point on in that document 之意，而 hereby 表示 by means of or as a result of this 之意。如果在非法律文本中这两个副词可以省略，但是在法律文本中，添加这些词能让陈述更加精确。用了 thereinafter 一词则能精确说明用 the Parties 来替代缔约的双方是从此时此刻才开始生效，在此之前，文本出现的 the Parties 并不表示缔约双方；hereby 则提示缔约双方，或者读者，缔结本条约需要一定的基础和前提条件，正是在相互尊重主权、平等互利以及双方有密切合作意愿的前提下，才能够缔结此条约。hereby 一词经常会被误用，比如"证书／兹证明＿＿ 参加了 2008 年第 29 届奥林匹克运动会翻译服务"这句话被译作 Certificate/ It is hereby to certify that ＿＿ took part in the translation and interpretation services for the Games of the XXIX Olympiad. 李长栓指出这个译文有很多错误，其中最严重的问题有二：一是"兹证明"这个短语的翻译，应当译作 This is to certify that... 或者 This certifies that...，其次就是 hereby 的使用存在问题。hereby 此处表示 by this means，即"据此"，一般主语是人，比如可以说 I hereby certify that...，但因这里开具证明的是一个翻译公司，所以不能用人（I）作为主语，出现这种错误正是由于译者将两种说法混杂在一起[1]，因此，译者在使用这些古体词的时候一定要小心谨慎，不能错用。另外，在进行外交条约等法律文书的英译时，也要注意在英语法律平行文本中存在大量使用拉丁语等外来语汇的现象。de facto 表 factual 或 in fact 之意；in re 表 in the matter of 之意；inter alia 相当于 among other things，在诉状中经常使用，表示提及的某个法规仅是与诉讼事实相关的、法规的一部分，而不是整个法规；alibi 则是被指控或涉嫌犯罪的人使用的借口，拉丁语中表示"在另一个地方"，指最终的不在场证明；bona fide 表 in good faith，honest，指行事时无欺诈之意愿；quasi 作为法律术语，表示一个主题具有与另一个主题相同的某些特征，但是它们之间存在内在的和本质的差异；per se 表 itself，指以其本身的性质而不参考其关系。ad hoc 表 for this special purpose，比如 an attorney ad hoc，或者 a guardian or curator ad hoc 就是专为特定目的而任命的、通常代表委托人、监护人或子女参加进行该特定任命的诉讼。这些拉丁词汇增加了文本的书面性、学术性，使得文本更具权威性，译者要了解这些拉丁语的意义，并且在汉英翻译时尝试运用。

外交条约翻译要注重精确，为了避免模棱两可、含混不清，翻译时不提倡用词的多样化，而要遵守法律文本前后一致的原则，也就是相同的意思在同一个文书中不提倡使用不同的表达方式，而是不忌重复，可以反复使用上文出现过的同一个表

---

1 李长栓. 2009. 非文学翻译. 北京：外语教学与研究出版社，253.

达，这样有利于减少产生歧义的可能性。

原文 如有下列情况，被请求方可以拒绝协助：（一）被请求方认为执行请求将损害其主权、安全、公共秩序或其他基本公共利益，或者认为案件在被请求方审理可能更为合适；（二）按照被请求方的法律，请求书中提及的嫌疑犯、被告人或罪犯的行为在被请求方不构成犯罪；（三）被请求方有充分的依据相信提供协助将便利对请求书所涉及的当事人基于种族、宗教、国籍或政治见解原因进行诉讼或处罚。

译文 Assistance may be refused by the Requested Party if: a) the Requested Party considers that the execution of the request would impair its sovereignty, security, public order or other essential public interest, or the case may be more properly prosecuted by the Requested Party; b) in accordance with the law of the Requested Party, the conduct of the suspect, defendant or convicted person referred to in the letter of request does not constitute an offence in the Requested Party; or c) there are substantial grounds leading the Requested Party to believe that compliance would facilitate the prosecution or punishment of the person to whom the request refers on account of race, religion, nationality or political opinions.

原文中的名词词组"被请求方"，被译作 the Requested Party。"被请求方"在原文中出现了六次，而 the Requested Party 在译文中也出现了六次，考虑到英汉语之间的差别，就会意识到这里的数字对应存在不小问题。汉语的语篇衔接手段之一是用词汇重复达到衔接目的，可以说汉语篇章中不忌词汇的反复出现，因此上文中名词词组"被请求方"反复出现在汉语中习以为常。相对而言，英语中更多使用代词、指示词或者是指示性副词等指称手段，或者用替代手段达到衔接目的，指称和替代手段一方面能起到衔接语篇的作用，另一方面也避免了词语的重复出现，使得行文更为简洁、精练。但这种英汉差异似乎在法律文本中并不存在，英语法律文本中也像汉语文本一样不忌重复，译文没有使用更简短的代词 it 来替代 the Requested Party，而任由其在译文中重复出现，目的在于让译文的意思更明确，避免产生误解和歧义，维护法律的公平公正，因此不忌重复也成为英文法律文本的特点之一，译者应当对这一现象有所了解。

2）外交条约的句法特征及英译

从句子层面来看，一方面法律文书需要简洁、明确、高效地传达法律指令，祈使句和陈述句使用更为常见，此时以句子短小精炼为宜；另一方面，在阐述一些复杂的法律问题或现象时，又应当全面周到，可以使用长句子，结构不忌复杂。因此，对法律文书句法和结构的认真分析是理解原文的基础，也是正确翻译的前提。

首先，法律文书中涉及强力规定、法律术语的定义，以及权威行为的规定、宣告、发布等问题时，常常使用简单陈述句以确立权威。通常会用"……规定""……是……""……颁布""……认定""实施……"等。英语中常用一些表示判断的句式如…be/have(has) the meaning of /mean(s)/refer(s) to…。

> **原文** 本谅解备忘录以及双方或双方企业根据该备忘录进行的所有讨论、谈判和活动都不影响双方各自法律立场。本谅解备忘录不产生任何国际法或国内法上的权利和义务。

> **译文** This Memorandum of Understanding, and all discussions, negotiations and activities of the two governments or their authorized enterprises under or pursuant to this Memorandum of Understanding, will be without prejudice to the respective legal positions of both governments. This Memorandum of Understanding does not create rights or obligations under international or domestic law.

此例涉及强力规定，说明该谅解备忘录的性质，不是论证性的阐述，原文的表述不容反驳和质疑，两个句子使用的都是简单陈述句，译文再现了客观规定，表现出法律文本的理性、客观。

其次，法律文本常用于发布禁止（或命令）、确定义务、明确责任，因而祈使句使用频繁。祈使句通常都是不带主语的，但是在法律文本中使用的祈使句都要带主语，以明确命令、义务或责任的主体。通常而言，祈使句谓语动词会用动词原形，但在法律文本中的祈使句却常用 shall，may 和 must 三个道义性情态动词，特别是 shall 的使用在法律文本中最为常见。比如，在第一篇译文中，shall 出现了 59 次，may 出现了 17 次，但未使用 must。shall 的主语如果是第一人称，常常用来表示将来，但当主语为第二或第三人称时，却有责任、权利和义务的意味。

> **原文** 请求方<u>应</u>在请求中或所附文件中详细说明应付费用和酬金，若应当事人或鉴定人要求，请求方<u>应</u>预付这些费用和酬金。

> **译文** The Requesting Party <u>shall</u> specify in the request or accompanying document the expenses and fees payable and <u>shall</u> pay the expenses and fees in advance

if so requested by the person or expert.

原文 协助请求书<u>应</u>用请求方的文字书写，请求书及其附件<u>应</u>附有被请求方官方文字的译文。

译文 Letters of request for assistance <u>shall be written</u> in the language of the Requesting Party. Letters of request and their annexes <u>shall be accompanied</u> by a translation into an official language of the Requested Party.

上文第一个例子中，原文表达的是请求方有详细说明应付费用和酬金的义务，并在当事人或鉴定的要求下，有预付费用的责任，因此是对主体的一种责任和义务要求。当汉语中出现了"（必）须……""应（当）……""要"等明确主体责任或义务的句式就可以使用 shall 加动词来表达相应的道义内涵。另外，这种责任和义务也可以像第二个例子中那样，用 shall 加被动语态来表达。

原文 除第十六条规定的情况外，根据本条约转递的任何文件及其译文，<u>无须</u>任何形式的认证。

译文 Any documents or translations transmitted pursuant to this Treaty <u>shall not</u> require any form of authentication, subject to Article 16.

原文 请求方对于到其境内作证的证人或进行鉴定的鉴定人，<u>不得</u>因其入境前的任何犯罪而追究其刑事责任、逮捕、拘留，或以任何其他方式剥夺或限制其人身自由，也<u>不应</u>强迫该人在与请求无关的任何诉讼中作证。

译文 A witness or expert appearing in the Requesting Party to give evidence or expert evaluation <u>shall not</u> be subjected to investigation of criminal responsibilities, arrest, to detention or deprivation or limit of personal liberty in any other form by the Requesting Party for any offence committed before entry into its territory <u>nor shall</u> that person be obliged to give evidence in any proceeding other than the proceedings to which the request relates.

shall 后面加上 not 的否定形式可以用来表达一种责任的免除，比如上文第一个例子中所说的"无须任何形式的认证"，就是对主体责任的免除，译文正是借助 shall not 表达相应的意思。除此之外，shall 的否定形式还能像在第二个例子里那样用来表示"不得""不允许""不应"等禁止含义。

此外，为了使条款表述准确、严谨规范，条约制定者还会大量使用并列结构。并列结构一方面能最大限度地穷尽所有可能性，使条款的适用范围更具体，更确凿，另一方面也让条款更具弹性和包容性。

原文	如果执行请求明显需要一项巨大开支，双方应协商确定能够提供被请求的协助的费用和<u>条件</u>。
译文	If it becomes apparent that the execution of the request requires expenses of an extraordinary nature, the Parties shall consult to determine the <u>terms and conditions</u> under which the requested assistance can be provided.
原文	如果请求向个人调查取证，是否需要其<u>宣誓</u>或不经宣誓而提供正式证词的陈述，以及对所寻求的证据或证言的说明；
译文	In the case of requests to take evidence from a person, a statement as to whether <u>sworn or affirmed</u> statements are required, and a description of the subject matter of the evidence or statement sought;
原文	一方应根据请求向另一方通报其对该另一方国民做出的刑事<u>判决和裁定</u>，并提供判决书和裁定书的副本。
译文	One Party shall, upon request, inform the other Party of <u>judgments and decisions</u> in criminal matters against nationals of the other Party, and provide copies of the <u>judgments and decisions.</u>
原文	在请求方或被请求方的鉴定人的<u>费用和酬金</u>。
译文	The <u>expenses and fees</u> of experts either in the Requested or Requesting Party.

在上文例子中，and 或者 or 连接的两个词语意思相近或相似，比如第一个例子里的 terms 和 conditions 都指请求执行协助的前提和条件；第二个例子中的 sworn 和 affirmed 涵盖了证人确定其所供证词是否真实的所有方式，不管是一般的断言还是庄重的发誓；第三个例子中的 judgments 和 decisions 囊括了一方对另一方国民做出的任何司法裁决；而第四个例子中的 expenses 和 fees 则将参与司法协助人员的一切费用，无论是差旅、膳食、住宿或者是补助等花费都包含在内。制定条约时并不能做到完全缜密细致、面面俱到，这些包含近义词的并列结构能让条款的包容度和弹性

更大，涵盖的范围更广，更具适应性。但是，如果 and 连接的词语不是近义词，则有尽可能穷尽所有条件和情形的意味。

> **原文** 如有可能，作为调查取证或诉讼对象的人员的身份、国籍和所在地；

> **译文** Where possible, the identity, nationality and location of the person or persons who are the subject of the investigation or proceedings;

这个款项明确了请求协助提供的、被调查人的资料仅局限于其身份、国籍和所在地，除此三项资料，被调查人的其他信息被请求方不用、甚至可拒绝披露。由此看来，正是由于 and 连接的 identity，nationality，location 非同义词，才具有这种排他的意味。另外，在这个例子里，原文中被调查人的数目未被明确，因此即使被请求方只提供其中一个被调查人的资料也履行了其法律义务。然而，在译文中，被请求方无法用一个被调查人的资料来敷衍请求方，因为译文中的连词 or 连接了 person 及其复数形式 persons，使得被请求方提供资料的范围增大，要提供与案件相关的所有被调查人的资料。除了在词汇层面，and 和 or 也可用于连接短语、句子和段落。

> **原文** 在拒绝一项协助请求<u>或</u>暂缓提供此项协助前，被请求方应考虑是否可以根据它认为是必要的附加条件同意提供协助。

> **译文** Before refusing to grant a request for assistance <u>or</u> before postponing the grant of such assistance, the Requested Party shall consider whether assistance may be granted subject to such conditions as it deems necessary.

上文用 or 连接两个分词短语用作时间状语，明确了被请求方需要考虑是否提供协助条件的两种情形，具有排他性，暗含除此两种情形，其他情形可不予考虑之意。另外，如果在某条款的下面包括多个项，需要用 and 或 or 连接最后两项，比如本章范例译文中的第二条中有九项，第八项与第九项之间就用了 and 连接：

> **译文** h) Authorizing or assisting persons, including detained persons, to travel to the Requesting Party to give evidence or assist investigations; <u>and</u>
>
> i) Measures related to the proceeds of crime and the restoration of property to victims.

而第七条第一款中有三项，第二项和第三项之间就用了 or 连接，具体译文如下：

译文 b) in accordance with the law of the requested Party, the conduct of the suspect, defendant or convicted person referred to in the letter of request does not constitute an offence in the Requested Party; or

c) there are substantial grounds leading the Requested Party to believe that compliance would facilitate the prosecution or punishment of the person to whom the request refers on account of race, religion, nationality or political opinions.

法律文本，特别是英语的法律文本，大量使用被动结构，有意隐藏或弱化施事者，强调某个结果或事实的存在，让文本显得更为理性客观。

原文 如有下列情况，被请求方可以拒绝协助：

译文 Assistance may be refused by the Requested Party if:

原文的主语是"被请求方"，是实施"拒绝"这一动作的施事者，译成英语时使用了被动结构，强调协助遭拒绝这一事实，而故意弱化"拒绝"行为的发出者"被请求方"这一施事者。

汉语中也会使用被动：一种是隐性的被动，也就是从句子结构来看并没有采用表示被动的词汇，但句子包含被动含义；另外一种就是带有如"被""由""叫""让"等显性被动词的被动句。译者应据语义选择适当的语态。

原文 如遇转借证据的情况，保管证据的人员，证据将移送的地点，进行检验和归还证据的时间；

译文 In the case of lending of exhibits, the person or class of persons who will have custody of the exhibit, the place to which the exhibit is to be removed, any tests to be conducted and the date by which the exhibit will be returned;

这个例子的原文没有被动词，但是包含了被动意义，是上文所谓的隐性被动句，"证据将移送的地点，进行检验和归还证据的时间"，这句话包含了"证据被移送，被检验和被移交"的意思，由于移送、检验或移交由谁完成不重要，所以施事者可以不出现，强调的是最后的结果，即证据要被移送，被检验和被移交，并确定这些动作完成的地点和时间。

原文 由于第一款所述原因或因为国内法律予以禁止而不能执行请求时，被请求方应迅速将请求在被请求方法律不予禁止的范围内，转递文件、物品和记录应符合请求方要求的方式或附有其要求的证明，以使它们可根据请求方的法律得以接受。

译文 Insofar as not prohibited by the law of the Requested Party, documents, objects and records shall be transmitted in a form or accompanied by such certification as may be requested by the Requesting Party in order to make them admissible according to the law of the Requesting Party.

这个例子的原文就是显性的被动句，原文包括"予以""不予"等明显的被动词，此时可以译成相应的被动语态。而"不能执行请求"表示的是"请求不能（被）执行"之意，也是一种被动结构。"使 A（某物或某物）得以 B（某种行为及其结果）"表示某个施事者对 A 施加了 B 的行为，因此有 A 被动接受了施事者 B 行为的意思，也是一种被动。这里尽管使用的是 make them admissible 的结构，但是宾语和形容词之间有逻辑上的主谓关系，也就是 they are admitted。另外"被请求方"这个名词词组包含了"被"字，所以也用了表被动含义的过去分词 requested 来修饰中心名词 party。

名词化结构就是将形容词、副词尤其是动词等非名词的词类转化成名词。在法律文本中使用名词化结构能让行文更为严密清晰，也让条文更加准确和更具包容性，和被动结构一样，能够起到隐藏、弱化、模糊施事者的作用，扩大法律的适用范围。

原文 主管机关请求被请求方的证人前来作证明，应保证向证人充分说明其对法庭所负的责任和义务，以保证该证人避免因藐视法庭或类似的行为而被起诉。

译文 The competent authority which seeks <u>the appearance of a witness</u> from the Requested Party <u>for the purpose of testimony</u>, shall ensure that the witness is properly instructed regarding responsibilities and obligations to the court so as to ensure that the witness is not subjected to contempt or similar <u>proceedings</u>.

原文表达了三层意思：一是主管机关请证人作证；二是主管机关要向证人说明证人所承担的责任和义务；三是主管机关向证人说明其所负责任的原因在于让其不犯错，从而免于起诉。译文弱化了前来、证明、所负（担）、藐视、起诉等动词的动作意味，而将这些动词处理为名词化结构，让它们在句子中充当除谓语之外的其他成分，从而使得句子的逻辑关系清晰明白，减少产生歧义的可能性，同时名词化结构的使用，也让译文显得更严谨正式。

五 中国关键词加油站

1 涉外民事诉讼 *foreign-related civil litigation*

涉外民事诉讼是指具有涉外因素的民事诉讼。所谓的涉外因素体现在三个方面：争议法律关系主体的一方或双方是外国人、无国籍人、外国企业或组织；导致当事人之间设立、变更、终止法律关系的法律事实发生在国外；双方当事人之间争执的标的物在国外。涉外民事诉讼涉及国家主权；期间较长；审理时存在适用法律的选择问题；人民法院审理涉外民事案件，有时需要外国法院协助。涉外民事诉讼的一般原则是人民法院审理涉外民事案件的基本准则，也是涉外民事案件当事人和有关诉讼参与人必须遵循的基本依据。适用《民事诉讼法》的原则。由于涉外民事案件具有涉外因素，人民法院审理时必须坚持国家主权原则。国家主权原则突出体现在以下几个方面：必须坚持我国法院对涉外民事案件的司法管辖权；当事人进行诉讼时，必须使用中国通用的语言、文字；凡委托律师代理出庭诉讼的，必须委托中华人民共和国律师；外国法院或其他机关请求我国执行其生效裁判时，我国人民法院必须全面审查。司法豁免原则指国家根据本国法律或参加、缔结的国际条约对住在本国的外国和国际组织的代表和机构赋予的免受司法管辖的权利。适用我国缔结或参加的国际条约原则。

2 涉外刑事诉讼 *foreign criminal proceeding*

涉外刑事诉讼是指我国公安机关、国家安全机关、人民检察院、人民法院和监狱在处理具有涉外因素的刑事案件时所适用的一种特别刑事诉讼。涉外刑事诉讼的主权原则即追究外国人犯罪适用中国法律的原则，是涉外刑事诉讼程序的首要原则。信守国际条约原则即公安司法机关处理涉外刑事案件时，在适用我国刑事诉讼法的同时，还须兼顾我国缔结或参加的国际条约，根据条约的规定履行相应的义务。诉讼权利同等原则，指外国人在我国参与刑事诉讼，依法享有与我国公民同等的诉讼权利，承担同等的诉讼义务。这既是国际法和国际惯例上的"国民待遇"原则在涉外刑事诉讼中的体现，也是作为社会主义国家的我国长期坚持的独立自主外交政策和"和平共处"五项原则的相应贯彻。使用我国通用语言和文字进行诉讼的原则是各国立法通行做法，也是独立行使国家司法主权的重要体现，因而也是我国涉外刑事诉讼的指导原则。依据这一原则，在我国涉外刑事诉讼中全部诉讼活动的进行和司法文书的制作，都必须使用我国通用的语言、文字。外国诉讼参与人向我国司法机关递交诉讼文书、外国司法机关请求我国给予司法协助应当附有中文译本。为方便外国人参与诉讼，利于查明案情，切实维护其诉讼权利和实体权益，应根据外国诉讼参与人的要求为其提供翻译。指定或委托中国律师参加诉讼原则。律师制度是一国司法制度的重要组成部分，并且只应在本国领域内适用，不应延伸到国外。一个主权国家也不允许外国司法制度在其领域内干涉它的司法事务，这也是主权原则的重要体现。所以一国的律师通常只能在其本国内执行律师职务。涉外刑事诉讼中的程序包括立案侦查、起诉、审判和执行。

3 海牙认证 apostiile

海牙认证是指由国家政府机构统一出具的（一般为最高人民法院），对原认证的签发人（通常是当地公证处或国际公证人）进行的二级认证，并在认证书上加盖印章或标签，这个过程就叫作加签（海牙认证）。海牙认证不是对所需认证文件内容的认证，是对原认证的签发人（公证处或国际公证人）的二次认证，认证该公证处或国际公证人是否有资质出具原认证文件。加签之前要先对认证文件做国际公证，再到最高人民法院做加签，整个过程叫作海牙认证或加签。比如中国国内生产眼镜、鞋、文具、服饰的企业因拓展海外市场，销售到俄罗斯、土耳其、委内瑞拉、阿根廷、美国等国家时，国内的有些文件（例如营业执照、税务证、生产许可证、自由销售证明、完税证明、ISO证书、产品的检测报告、授权书、公司注册资料、商标注册证、CE认证证书等文件、出口商登记表海牙认证）需要携带出国外使用时，需要办理海牙认证（也叫海牙办签）。

4 网络外交 cyber diplomacy

网络外交是指在信息时代条件下，国际行为体为了维护和发展自己的利益，利用互联网技术和网络平台而开展的对外交往、对外宣传和外交参与等活动。网络外交以维护和发展国际行为体自身的政治、经济、军事和文化诸方面利益为目的，主要包括国际行为体之间通过网络而开展的外事交往、对外传播及政治参与等。

5 金融外交 financial diplomacy

金融外交是指一国中央政府及其所属具体执行部门,围绕金融事务,针对其他国家政府、国际组织以及跨国公司等国际行为体所展开的官方交往活动,其目的是实现在金融事务上的国际合作和有效治理,或者通过影响国际金融关系来实现其他目标。这种官方交往活动的内容主要包括金融信息的传递、金融政策的协调、金融事务的谈判以及金融协议的签署等,其具体形式主要体现为跨国访问和国际会议。金融外交主要围绕两个方面的核心事务展开:一是政府间的跨国资金信贷、短期的流动性供给;二是货币的国际使用和汇率的跨国协商。它们通常分别由财政部和中央银行直接负责,所以随着金融外交的大规模兴起,财政部和中央银行开始成为一国政府对外交往活动的重要执行者,金融外交也因此可以被简单理解为一国财政部和中央银行所从事的外交活动。由于货币是金融的核心,狭义的金融外交因此又被称为货币外交(monetary diplomacy)。

6 媒体外交 media diplomacy

媒体外交是指利用新闻媒介来阐述和推进外交政策的方式或新闻媒介积极参与并发挥影响的外交方式,或指政府运用新闻、出版、无线电广播、电视、电影、录像带以及新兴的电子通信手段,宣传对外政策。简言之,媒体外交是媒体进行或参与的外交,也可专指在政府控制下媒体参与并完成的外交。各国政府之间的外交活动通过媒体的新闻传播最终得以完成。媒体外交发端于一国政府,终端是另一国政府,或者多国政府甚至整个国际社会。媒体外交的理论基于媒体对政治家、政府以及对跨国的和国家的政治精英的影响这一相对比较新的设想。1965 年,美国塔夫茨大学弗莱彻法律与外交学院院长埃德蒙·葛里昂(Edmund Gullion)首次提出了"公共外交"的概念,自此以后这个概念进入了官方和学术的话语体系中,并且被付诸国际关系和外交事务的具体实践中,逐渐发展成为一个与传统外交不同的理论和实践范式。在当时的冷战语境下,公共外交最为直接和典型的表征便是国际广播,葛里昂将其称之为"外交的新武器"。因此,"媒体外交"从一开始便成为"公共外交"的核心与主体。

7 智库外交 the diplomacy of think-tanks

智库外交,大致包括两层含义:一是以智库为主体、智库之间的国际交流;二是以外国智库为对象与目标的国际交流，包括由本国政府官员到外国重要智库进行专题演讲，向外国智库派出访问学者等。智库外交主要有三种形式：1. 知识外交（Knowledgeable Diplomacy）：在知识外交中，智库扮演了"思想掮客"和"幕僚"的角色，主要任务是为外交系统提供思想、理念知识和政策等方面的咨询和建议，不直接参与任何具体履行外交使命的外交实践。比如美国人柯庆生在离开国务院后继续被聘请为美国国务院的亚太政策顾问、中国很多研究机构的专家参加外交部的政策咨询会等，都是知识为外交服务的活动。2. 二轨外交（Track Two Diplomacy）：二轨外交是非官方或半官方人士（包括学者、退休官员、公共人物和社会积极分子等）参与外交对话，目的在于寻找冲突解决和信任创建的机会。在二轨外交中，智库开始接受外交使命，参与官方外交对话，或者得到官方授意以公开的、非官方论坛的形式探索实现外交目的的途径。按照参与程度不同还有二轨外交和 1.5 轨外交的差异。比如被称为东亚二轨领头羊的东亚思想库网络、"9·11"后亚太地区新出现的英国国际战略研究所（IISS）发起、在新加坡政府支持下举办的香格里拉对话会中的智库参与等，都是二轨外交或 1.5 轨外交的典型案例。3. 公民外交（Citizen Diplomacy）：公民外交是普通公民无意中或者精心设计作为国家代表参与的科技交流、文化交流、教育交流以及体育交流等国际交流，进而为两国外交关系创造机会之窗，特别是当两国官方交流渠道不可靠或者不畅通的时候，公民外交就是理想的外交工具，它可以补充官方外交甚至突破官方外交的限制。冷战期间的物理学家罗伯特·W. 富勒（Robert W. Fuller）在 20 世纪七八十年代对苏联的访问就对缓和美苏冷战起到了十分重要的作用。在公民外交中，智库所扮演的角色更加自主，对外交的参与仅仅是"呼应者"的角色。随着全球化和信息革命的发展，智库网络化趋势加快，智库的此种公民外交影响力必将稳步上升。

8 能源外交 energy diplomacy

能源外交是指一国政府、企业及个人围绕能源战略目标而进行的一系列对外行动，包括制定对外能源战略和政策，以及具体的对外交往活动。从能源外交的主体看，政府（包括国家领导人以及外交、经贸、能源等政府机构）承担了主要角色，其中外交部门通常是能源外交的先锋。企业、非政府组织以及个人也是能源外交的重要参与者，官商结合是能源外交的典型特点。从能源外交的客体看，它涉及的范围很广，既包括政府间的重要访问及各种合作协议，也包括贸易、投资、勘探与开发、技术合作、交通运输（如通道外交）等内容；既有双边合作，也有多边合作（如欧佩克、国际能源机构等）。

9 科技外交 science diplomacy

科技外交是指以主权国家的元首（政府首脑）、外交机构、科技部门、专门机构（如中国科学院、国家自然科学基金委员会）和企业等为主体，以促进科技进步、经济和社会的可持续发展为宗旨，以互惠互利、共同发展为原则而开展与世界其他国家或地区以及国际组织等之间的谈判、访问、参加国际会议、建立研究机构等多边或双边的科技合作与交流。进行科技外交活动的主体不仅包括政府，还包括非政府机构、学术界、企业等。由于主体多样化，科技外交形式灵活，会议、谈判、访问等都是科技外交可以采取的形式。官方与民间渠道互为补充的特点使科技外交具有"以官促民""以民掩官"的优势。科技外交具有促进科技进步、创造经济与社会效益、维护国家安全与利益、改善国际关系的多重目的。值得注意的是，以科技外交改善国际关系方面的国内研究不多。而在实践中，以美国为首的发达国家十分重视这一点，在美国，"科学外交"被认为是"支持推动美国与其他国家——有时是一些与美国没有任何其他外交关系的国家，进行科学交流、科学合作与研究的做法"。科技外交既可以推动国家之间的合作与交流（国际科技合作、交流和技术援助），也可以是一国对他国施压的工具（技术出口管制、军售禁令、技术贸易壁垒、技术遏制性并购）。科技外交包含了合作也包含了冲突。

10 全球治理观 concept of global governance

当今世界正处于大发展大变革大调整时期，和平与发展仍然是时代主题。同时，世界面临的不稳定性不确定性突出，世界经济增长动能不足，贫富分化日益严重，地区热点问题此起彼伏，恐怖主义、网络安全、重大传染性疾病、气候变化等非传统安全威胁持续蔓延，人类面临许多共同挑战。在这样的时代背景下，党的十九大报告提出了中国的全球治理观，即秉持共商共建共享的全球治理观，倡导国际关系民主化，坚持国家不分大小、强弱、贫富一律平等，支持联合国发挥积极作用，支持扩大发展中国家在国际事务中的代表性和发言权。这一新型全球治理观意味着全球治理的主体是构成国际体系的世界各国，而不是世界的某一个部分和某一类国家；意味着要遵循更具包容性的治理原则和更具开放性的治理方式；意味着以构建人类命运共同体为目标。

六　外交条约翻译练习

1. 请将下列法律词汇译成英文。

1）法律渊源　　　2）制定法　　　3）判例法　　　4）普通法
5）特别法　　　　6）固有法　　　7）继受法　　　8）实体法
9）程序法　　　　10）原则法　　　11）例外法　　　12）习惯法
13）自然法　　　　14）罗马法　　　15）私法　　　　16）公法
17）普通法　　　　18）大陆法　　　19）义务性规范　20）命令性规范
21）民法基本原则　22）平等原则　　23）自愿原则　　24）公平原则
25）等价有偿原则　26）诚实信用原则　27）行为　　　28）不作为
29）合法行为　　　30）违法行为

2. 翻译下列句子，注意法律文书的句法特征。

——技术安全上，各国应不断提升人工智能技术的安全性、可靠性和可控性，增强对人工智能技术的安全评估和管控能力，确保有关武器系统永远处于人类控制之下，保障人类可随时中止其运行。人工智能数据的安全必须得到保证，应限制人工智能数据的军事化使用。

——研发操作上，各国应加强对人工智能研发活动的自我约束，在综合考虑作战环境和武器特点的基础上，在武器全生命周期实施必要的人机交互。各国应始终坚持人类是最终责任主体，建立人工智能问责机制，对操作人员进行必要的培训。

——风险管控上，各国应加强对人工智能军事应用的监管，特别是实施分级、分类管理，避免使用可能产生严重消极后果的不成熟技术。各国应加强对人工智能潜在风险的研判，包括采取必要措施，降低人工智能军事应用的扩散风险。

3. 翻译下列条文，注意格式，适当运用被动结构、名词化结构和连词 and 和 or。

第七条
引渡请求及所需文件

一、请求方应当提交引渡请求书。引渡请求书应当包括：

（一）请求机关的名称；

（二）被请求引渡人的姓名、年龄、性别、国籍、身份证件的号码、职业、可能的所在地点，所掌握的有关该人外表的描述及其照片和指纹，以及其他有助于确定和查找该人的信息；

（三）犯罪事实的简要说明，包括犯罪事件、地点、行为和结果的说明；

（四）有关定罪和对该犯罪可判处刑罚的法律条文，以及有关追诉或者执行刑罚的时效的法律条文。

二、旨在对犯罪嫌疑人或者被告人进行刑事诉讼的引渡请求应当附有请求方主管机关签发的逮捕证或者其他与逮捕证具有同等效力的文件的副本。

三、旨在对被请求印度人执行刑罚的引渡请求应当附有可执行的判决书的副本和关于已经执行刑期的说明。

四、被请求方根据本条第一款、第二款和第三款提交的引渡请求书和其他相关文件应当由请求方主管机关正式签署或者盖章，并且应当附有被请求方文字的译文。